D1719844

# ZEITGESCHICHTE

zeitgeschichte
51. Jg., Heft 1 (2024)

# *Lebensborn* Maternity Home *Wienerwald*, 1938–1945

Edited by
Barbara Stelzl-Marx and Lukas Schretter

V&R unipress

Vienna University Press

# Contents

Lukas Schretter / Barbara Stelzl-Marx

# Editorial

## I.   Introduction

In 1904, Jewish pulmonologists Hugo Kraus and Arthur Baer opened the *Wienerwald* lung sanatorium in Feichtenbach. After the so-called *Anschluss* of Austria with the German Reich in 1938, the *SS* seized the building and set up the *Heim Ostmark* (from 1942: *Heim Wienerwald*). It served *Lebensborn* as a maternity home designed to boost the birth rate of "Aryan" children. After 1945, the building was used in quick succession by the *Wiener Jugendhilfswerk* (Vienna Youth Welfare Office), the *Österreichischer Gewerkschaftsbund* (Austrian Trade Union Federation) as a recreational home and the *Wiener Gebietskrankenkasse* (Vienna Regional Health Insurance Fund), which used it as a rehabilitation centre until 2002. Since then, the building has been consigned to decay.

Since the 1990s the building and its history have been the subject of investigations that differed widely in focus. Ethnographer and local historian Hiltraud Ast wrote a conspectus of the history from 1904 to 1994.[1] Martina Pippal taught a course at the Department of Art History at the University of Vienna in 2007, which tackled the house and its grounds from the perspective of architectural history. Two theses, written at the Vienna University of Technology in 1983 and 2022, focused on the architectural design of the building.[2] Bertl Mütter wrote a piece of music evocative of the history of the building.[3] Studies on Franz Kafka, a patient in the *Wienerwald* lung Sanatorium a few weeks before his death in 1924, and on Austria's Federal Chancellor Ignaz Seipel (1922–1924 and 1926–1929),

---

1 Hiltraud Ast, *Feichtenbach. Eine Tallandschaft im Niederösterreichischen Schneeberggebiet* (Wien: Brüder Hollinek, 1994), 61–77.
2 Daniel Trimmel, "Ein Dialog über Zeit. Der Entwurf einer Umbaustrategie," unpublished thesis, Vienna University of Technology, 2022; Renate Wechdorn, "Sanatorium Wienerwald," unpublished thesis, Vienna University of Technology, 1983.
3 Bertl Mütter, *Born. Rondo. Für Toypiano mit innerer Stimme.* https://muetter.at/komposition /born/ (20 October 2023).

who died there in 1932 of sepsis from a bullet that had lodged in his lungs since an assassination attempt in 1924, also touch on the history of the building.[4]

Günther Knotzinger wrote an extensively researched study on the history of *Lebensborn* in Feichtenbach, which has been awaiting publication since 2001.[5] The PhD thesis by Elisabeth Märker on *Lebensborn* after the *Anschluss* of Austria with the German Reich is based on her research in Polish and Austrian archives and on written and oral reports by contemporary witnesses.[6] In addition, several historical and artistic diploma, bachelor and master theses have been written on the history of *Lebensborn*.[7] Sandro Rupprecht has collected and published material on the history of *Lebensborn* in Feichtenbach.[8] In addition to these studies, autobiographical contributions by Astrid Eggers, Elke Sauer, and Brigitte Rambeck and a novel by Eleonore Rodler are important ports of call for studying the *Heim Wienerwald*.[9] There are TV documentaries and reports by directors such as Beate Thalberg, the duo Robert Altenburger and Andreas Nowak, and Christoph

---

4  Rudolf Blüml, *Ignaz Seipel. Mensch, Christ, Priester in seinem Tagebuch* (Wien: Hilfswerk für Schulsiedlungen 1933), 266–68.

5  Günther Knotzinger, *"Das SS-Heim 'Wienerwald' und die Geschichte des Hauses von 1904 bis zur Gegenwart,"* unpublished manuscript, Feichtenbach, 2001. At the time of publication of this editorial, Knotzinger's manuscript is available through Adelgunde Knotzinger, Feichtenbach. For an overview of the history of the *Wienerwald* home based on Knotzinger's research results, see Anton Blaha, "Das Heim 'Wienerwald' in Feichtenbach," 14–15, <http://stolpersteine-wiene rneustadt.at/wp-content/uploads/2016/04/2015-10-Feichtenbach.pdf>(20 October 2023).

6  Elisabeth Andrea Märker, "Rassisch wertvoll. Die positive Eugenik: Ihre Handhabung am Beispiel des Lebensbornvereins im 'Heim Alpenland' und 'Heim Wienerwald,'" unpublished PhD thesis, University of Innsbruck, 1999.

7  See, among others, Katja Aumayr, "Der Lebensborn e.V. zwischen Mythos und Realität. Ideologie, Organisation und Nachwirkungen," unpublished thesis, Johannes Kepler University Linz, 2021; Corinna Fürstaller, "Lebensbornheime in Österreich," unpublished thesis, University of Graz, 2010; Sandro Rupprecht, "Aktion Lebensborn – Die 'Züchtung' von 'Herrenmenschen' in Feichtenbach," unpublished thesis, University of Education Baden, 2014; Reinhard Seifert, "Der 'Lebensborn' e.V.: Eine Zuchtanstalt? Himmlers 'Rassenpolitik' und seine Pläne für ein 'germanisches Reich'. Der 'Lebensborn' im niederösterreichischen Pernitz – Heim Wienerwald," unpublished thesis, University of Vienna, 2003; Marlene Wanzenböck, "Zu einer Vergangenheit kommen. Third-Generation-Postmemory. Der Video-Essay als Mediator von Erinnerung," unpublished thesis, Academy of Fine Arts Vienna, 2018.

8  Sandro Rupprecht, "Aktion Lebensborn – Die Züchtung von Herrenmenschen in Feichtenbach," in *Wie es bei uns in Niederösterreich war 1938–1945. Spurensuche im Nationalsozialismus. Materialien zur Zeitgeschichte*, edited by Franz Vonwald and Margarethe Kainig-Huber (Berndorf: Kral, 2015).

9  Astrid Eggers, "Ich war die Marionette meiner Mutter," in *Verschwiegene Opfer der SS. Lebensborn-Kinder erzählen ihr Leben*, edited by Astrid Eggers and Elke Sauer (Leipzig: Engelsdorfer, 2015), 134–50; Brigitta Rambeck, "Ich war ein Schubladenkind," in *Born of War – Vom Krieg geboren: Europas verleugnete Kinder*, edited by Gisela Heidenreich (Berlin: Ch. Links, 2017), 155–61; Eleonore Rodler, *Feichtenbach. Eine Faction* (Wien – Klosterneuburg: EDITION VA bEnE, 2009); Elke Sauer, "Der Lebensborn – eine Lebenslüge," in *Verschwiegene Opfer der SS. Lebensborn-Kinder erzählen ihr Leben*, edited by Astrid Eggers and Elke Sauer (Leipzig: Engelsdorfer, 2015), 151–64.

Bendas.[10] The family history of a woman born in the *Heim Wienerwald* – her mother was a guard at the *Ravensbrück* concentration camp – is told by Gesa Knolle and Birthe Templin in the documentary *Was bleibt* (What Remains) and by Simone Bader and Jo Schmeiser in the documentary *Liebe Geschichte* (Love History).[11] Since the 2000s, especially since 2020 and not least in connection with the research done at the *Ludwig Boltzmann Institut für Kriegsfolgenforschung* (Ludwig Boltzmann Institute for Research on Consequences of War, BIK) conducted in cooperation with the Institute of History of the University of Graz, statements on *Lebensborn* have appeared in Austrian print media, on television, and radio.[12] In the official remembrance of the Second World War, the building in Feichtenbach has hardly featured at all so far. The pulmonologists who were expropriated by the Gestapo in 1938 have received little attention in commemorative media such as school textbooks, museums, and street names. A memorial for the doctors was erected in front of the building in 1994. Established in 2017, Lower Austria's *Haus der Geschichte* (House of History, HGNOE) in Sankt Pölten has a showcase dedicated to the history of the building.[13]

This volume presents research conducted at the BIK in collaboration with the University of Graz on the *Heim Wienerwald* in the period between 1938 and 1945. The research was funded by the Jubilee Fund of the Austrian National Bank, the Province of Lower Austria, the Future Fund of the Republic of Austria, and the Open Innovation in Science Center of the Ludwig Boltzmann Society. Our thanks go to these funding bodies for their financial support. We would like to express our gratitude to the archives and institutions that have given us access to valuable

---

10  *Geheimsache Lebensborn.* Film. Austria. Directed by Beate Thalberg. 42 min., Vienna, ORF 2003 (CultFilm); *Lebensborn – die vergessenen Opfer.* Directed by Robert Altenburger and Andreas Novak. 53 min., Vienna, Menschen und Mächte, ORF 2019; *Kinder für das Vaterland: Das Schicksal der Lebensborn-Kinder.* Directed by Christoph Bendas, News Magazine Thema, Vienna ORF2, 5 December 2016. *Die "Auserwählten" – das Schicksal der Lebensborn-Kinder.* Directed by Christoph Bendas. 11 min., Vienna News Magazine Thema, ORF2, 21 April 2021.

11  *Was bleibt.* Directed by Gesa Knolle and Birtha Templin. Silvia Loinjak production, 57 minutes, 2008; *Liebe Geschichte.* Directed by Simone Bader and Jo Schmeiser, Klub Zwei production, 98 minutes, 2010.

12  See, for example, Judith Brandner, "Lebensborn im Wienerwald," *gehÖrt,* Mai 2004, 10–11; Judith Brandner, "Lebensborn im Wienerwald – ein Lungensanatorium als Gebäranstalt für arisches Leben," *Ö1 Hörbilder,* 15 May 2004; Judith Brandner, "Menschenzucht – Der Lebensborn e.V. als Instrument nationalsozialistischer Rassenpolitik," *Ö1 Dimensionen,* 31 August 2004; Barbara Schleicher, "Es steht ein Haus in Österreich," *Spectrum, Die Presse,* 9 December, 2002; Barbara Schleicher, "'Herrenmenschen' und arische Frauen. Das SS-Lebensbornheim Wienerwald," *morgen. Kulturzeitschrift aus Niederösterreich 3,* 2003, 28–30; Christoph Bendas, "Die Auserwählten," *Profil,* 6 August 2018, 48–53; Cornelia Grobner, "Das NS-Entbindungsheim im Wienerwald," *Die Presse,* 9 May 2020; Christian Hütterer, "Ein Zauberberg in Ruinen," *Wiener Zeitung,* 31 January 2021.

13  See *Haus der Geschichte,* ed. Niederösterreichische Museum Betriebsgesellschaft, Heidrun Wenzel (St. Pölten: Niederösterreichische Museum Betriebs GmbH, 2022).

sources, in particular the *Marktgemeinde* Pernitz, the Arolsen Archives, the *Niederösterreichisches Landesarchiv* (Lower Austrian Provincial Archives), the *Wiener Stadt- und Landesarchiv* (Municipal and Provincial Archives of Vienna), the *Bundesarchiv* (German Federal Archives) in Berlin, and the *Sammlung Frauennachlässe* (Collection of Women's Personal Papers) at the University of Vienna. Our thanks go to those born in the *Heim Wienerwald* who shared documents and personal or family memories. Furthermore, our thanks go to the relatives of those born in this *Lebensborn* facility, the people living in the vicinity of the building, and to researchers and students of the history of the building driven by an interest in contemporary history, who have shared their knowledge with the project team. Last, not least, we would like to thank Otmar Binder and Katy Burgess-Fladerer for the translations and/or the copy-editing of the papers in this volume.

## II.    Breeding Farms or Welfare Institutions: Rumors about *Lebensborn*

Few organisations of the National Socialist regime are the subject of as many legends as *Lebensborn*. The myth that *Lebensborn* facilities were places for blond and blue-eyed men to impregnate blue-eyed blondes still persists today. This perception was deepened by the German movie *Lebensborn. Liebe auf Staats-befehl* (*Lebensborn*. Love at the behest of the State) from 1961,[14] which is based on a novel by post-war best-selling Will Berthold.[15]

Other popular novels and movies elaborated on this image of *Lebensborn*, such as the 1965 novel *Die Schande* (The Disgrace) by Benno Voelkner and the movie *Lebensborn – Gestohlene Liebe* (Lebensborn – Stolen Love) from 2000.[16] A book and a documentary by French journalists Marc Hillel and Clarissa Henry from 1975, while claiming to stick to facts, nevertheless maintain that *Lebensborn* maternity homes were "breeding farms" designed for the optimization of pro-creation.[17] In the recent past, two productions stand out that, deliberately or by accident, promote this image. The BBC series *World On Fire* aims to depict the effects the first year of the war, 1939, had on Europeans. One storyline in the

---

14  *Lebensborn. Liebe auf Staatsbefehl.* Film. Germany. Directed by Werner Klinger, 1961, 84 min.
15  Will Berthold, *Lebensborn: Roman aus Deutschlands dunkelster Zeit* (München: Kindler, 1958). At the same time, first stories with a fictionalised narrative about *Lebensborn* were published by Berthold in the German magazine "Revue".
16  *Lebensborn – Gestohlene Liebe* (orig. *Pramen života* [Spring of Life]). Film. CZ. Directed by Milnan Cieslar, 2000, 107 min; Benno Voelkner, *Die Schande* (Rostock: Hirnstorff, 1965).
17  Marc Hillel and Clarissa Henry, *Lebensborn e.V. im Namen der Rasse* (Wien – Hamburg: Zsolnay, 1975).

second series, first broadcast in 2023, follows a 16-year-old girl, Marga, who signs up for *Lebensborn* and conceives a child with an *SS* man in a *Lebensborn* home.[18] The fourth series of *Das Boot*, produced in Germany with Austrian participation, was aired in 2023. In it, underage girls and women are even forced into *Lebensborn* homes to be made pregnant by *SS* men and to give birth there to the children thus conceived.[19]

However, such myths attached to *Lebensborn* had been around even before the 1960s. Already in the Third Reich, popular misgiving about the *Lebensborn* homes was widespread. There were rumours that the association paired up selected women and men in a coercive breeding programme. The *Lebensborn* leadership was aware of claims that "in Lebensborn, SS men made themselves available to women who wished to have a child." It should be obvious that such rumours "are malicious gossip and only serve the purpose of damaging the reputation of the SS,"[20] according to *SS-Oberführer* Gregor Ebner. Ebner served as *Lebensborn*'s head of healthcare from 1937 to 1945, as an executive board member of *Lebensborn* from 1938 to March 1942, and concurrently as the director of the first *Lebensborn* maternity home, *Hochland*, which opened in Steinhöring near Munich in 1936. Incidentally, Ebner said, "we feel that it is not the worst fruit that wasps nibble on and therefore pursue with all the greater enthusiasm and fanatical idealism this admirably beautiful work, which is, of course, beyond the comprehension of whimps and moralizers."[21]

Throughout its existence, *Lebensborn* offered the services of its maternity homes only to women who were already pregnant. Requests such as that of an *SS-Unterführer* were refused, who asked for a woman who would carry his child; his wife, whom he did not want to divorce, was infertile. While *Lebensborn* per se was not involved in match-making or artificial fertilisation, it did propagate such initiatives and, with its maternity homes, it incentivised a population policy that openly disregarded bourgeois and Christian notions of morality.[22]

The myth of *Lebensborn* homes as facilities for coercive breeding is often countered by the narrative that it was primarily a charitable organisation. In fact, Himmler and the *Lebensborn* leadership had justified founding the association in 1935 by arguing that unmarried "Aryan" mothers were to be protected from

---

18  *World on Fire.* Directed by Drew Casson, Barney Cokeliss, and Meenu Gaur (Series 2). Written by Peter Bowker, Matt Jones, and Rachel Bennette. BBC One, 2023.

19  *Das Boot.* Directed by Andreas Prochaska, Matthias Glasner, and Rick Ostermann (Staffel 4). Written by Toy Saint and Johannes W. Betz. Sky Deutschland, 2023.

20  *Ebner an Gefreiten Rudolf Müller,* 13 July 1943, Arolsen Archives (hereinafter: AA), 4.1.0/ 8210200, Ref. 82448953.

21  Ibid, Ref. 82448954.

22  Lilienthal, *Der "Lebensborn e.V." Ein Instrument nationalsozialistischer Rassenpolitik.* 2n. ed (Frankfurt am Main: Fischer, 2008), 147–59.

discrimination and defamation. To this end, *Lebensborn* offered them the possibility of anonymous childbirth in its maternity homes and sought to provide high-quality care around pregnancy and birth.

Even the Allied judges at the Nuremberg trials acquitted *Lebensborn* of the charge of involvement in National Socialist crimes. Instead, they emphasised *Lebensborn*'s charitable purpose: "It is quite clear from the evidence that the *Lebensborn* Society, which existed long prior to the war, was a welfare institution, and primarily a maternity home" and "that of the numerous organizations operating in Germany who were connected with foreign children brought into Germany, *Lebensborn* was the one organization which did everything in its power to provide for the children and protect the legal interests of the children placed in its care."[23] Since then, numerous studies have shown that *Lebensborn*'s primary goal was to prevent unmarried pregnant women classified as "Aryan" from having an – illegal – abortion, and at the same time to encourage *SS* men to beget children without regard to any existing marriage. As historian Georg Lilienthal put it in his mid-1980s landmark study, *Lebensborn* homes such as the *Heim Wienerwald* were neither an institution for coercive breeding nor a charitable institution. They were solely tasked with implementing the National Socialist regime's racial policy.[24]

---

23 Quoted in Lilienthal, *Der "Lebensborn e.V."*, 9.
24 Lilienthal, *Der "Lebensborn e.V."* Further studies on the history of *Lebensborn* include, among others, chapters in the following volumes: Angelika Baumann and Andreas Heusler, *Der Lebensborn in München. Kinder für den "Führer"* (München: Schiermeier 2013); Gisela Heidenreich, *Born of War – Vom Krieg geboren. Europas verleugnete Kinder* (Berlin: Ch. Links, 2017). Monographs published on *Lebensborn* include Thomas Bryant, *Himmlers Kinder. Zur Geschichte der SS-Organisation "Lebensborn e.V." 1935–1945* (Wiesbaden: Marix, 2011); Caterine Clay and Michael Leapman, *Herrenmenschen. Das Lebensborn-Experiment der Nazis* (München: Heyne, 1997); Volker Koop, *"Dem Führer ein Kind schenken." Die SS-Organisation Lebensborn e.V.* (Köln – Wien – Weimar: Böhlau, 2007); Dorothee Neumaier, *Das Lebensbornheim "Schwarzwald" in Nordrach* (Marburg: Tectum, 2017); Rudolf Oswald, *Den Opfern verpflichtet. Katholische Jugendfürsorge, Caritas und die SS-Organisation "Lebensborn" nach 1945* (München: Sankt Michaelsbund, 2020); Dorothee Schmitz-Köster, *"Deutsche Mutter, bist du bereit…" Der Lebensborn und seine Kinder.* 2nd ed. (Berlin: Aufbau, 2011); Dorothee Schmitz-Köster, *Kind L 364. Eine Lebensborn-Familiengeschichte* (Berlin: Rowohlt, 2007); Dorothee Schmitz-Köster and Tristan Vankann, *Lebenslang Lebensborn. Die Wunschkinder der SS und was aus ihnen wurde* (München – Zürich: Piper, 2012); Dorothee Schmitz-Köster, *Unbrauchbare Väter. Über Muster-Männer, Seitenspringer und flüchtende Erzeuger im Lebensborn* (Göttingen: Wallstein, 2022).

## III. *Lebensborn* Maternity Homes and the "Germanisation" of Children From the Occupied Territories

"Racial hygiene" was one of the central elements of National Socialist ideology. It was based on eugenic, social Darwinist, racist population policy ideas that had been discussed internationally since the end of the 19th century. After the National Socialists came to power in Germany, however, the radicalism of the propaganda and the strict implementation of "racial hygiene" policies differed considerably from other countries and from Germany before 1933.

One of the most important steps on the path from exclusion to the murder of minorities classified as "racially undesirable," "inferior," or "unworthy of life" was the *Gesetz zur Verhütung erbkranken Nachwuchses* (Law for the Prevention of Genetically Diseased Offspring) of 1933, which legalised forced sterilisations.[25] Between January 1934, when the law came into force, and the outbreak of war in 1939, more than 300,000 people were sterilised on the basis of this law.[26] Another measure of the National Socialist regime affected Jews and other "non-Aryans" such as Sinti and Roma. The *Gesetz zum Schutz des deutschen Blutes und der deutschen Ehre* (Law for the Protection of German Blood and German Honour) criminalised marriages and sexual relations between Jews and "Aryans". On 18 October 1935, the *Gesetz zum Schutz der Erbgesundheit des deutschen Volkes* (Law for the Protection of the Hereditary Health of the German People) was passed, which effectively excluded "inferiors" and "foreigners" from the *Volksgemeinschaft*. The *Nürnberger Gesetze* of 1935 paved the way for the persecution of Jews that would eventually lead to the Holocaust.[27] After the *Anschluss*, the *Gesetz zur Verhütung erbkranken Nachwuchses* came into force in annexed Austria in early 1940, much later than other anti-natalist laws, such as the *Nürnberger Gesetze* (from May 1938) or the *Gesetz über die Vereinheitlichung des*

---

25 Arthur Gütt, Ernst Rüdin, and Falk Ruttke, *Gesetz zur Verhütung erbkranken Nachwuchses* (München: Lehmann, 1934).

26 See, for example, Gisela Bock, *Zwangssterilisation im Nationalsozialismus. Studien zur Rassenpolitik und Frauenpolitik (Schriften des Zentralinstituts für Sozialwissenschaftliche Forschung der Freien Universität Berlin 48).* (Münster: Monsenstein und Vannerdat, 2010); Gisela Bock, "Nazi Sterilization and Reproductive Policies," in *Deadly Medicine: Creating the Master Race* (Washington: US Holocaust Memorial Museum, 2004), 61–88; Stefanie Westermann, *Verschwiegenes Leid: Der Umgang mit den NS-Zwangssteriliationen in der Bundesrepublik Deutschland* (Köln: Böhlau, 2010).

27 See, for example, Cornelia Essner, *Die "Nürnberger Gesetze" oder die Verwaltung des Rassenwahns 1933–1945* (Paderborn: Ferdinand Schöningh, 2002); *Die Nürnberger Gesetze – 80 Jahre danach. Vorgeschichte, Entstehung, Auswirkungen,* edited by Magnus Brechtken, Hans-Christian Jasch, and Christoph Kreutzmüller (Göttingen: Wallstein, 2017); David Cesarani, *Final Solution: The Fate of the Jews 1933–49* (New York: Macmillan, 2016).

*Gesundheitswesens* (from December 1938).[28] The 1939 *Euthanasie* decree allowed the "mercy killing" (*Gnadentod*) of patients who were classified as "incurably ill". This marked the beginning of the systematic mass murder of thousands of children and later also of physically or mentally disabled adults.[29]

In contrast to its anti-natalist measures, the National Socialist race and population policy provided for the promotion of children classified as "hereditarily healthy" for, among other things, military service and use as labourers at the so-called *Heimatfront. Lebensborn* was one of these pro-natalist measures, alongside material benefits and the public honouring of families with families with many children, such as the bestowal of the *Mutterkreuz* (Mother's Cross), and the celebration of Mother's Day. *Lebensborn* sought to downplay the notion of "illegitimacy" by making the living conditions of unwed "Aryan" mothers essentially comparable to those of married "Aryan" mothers, thus increasing the birth rate among the "Aryan" population. From 1936 onwards, the association operated several maternity homes in the German Reich – one of them was the *Heim Wienerwald* in Feichtenbach, which opened after *Anschluss* in 1938.

A *Lebensborn* brochure contains the following information on who should be admitted to its maternity homes: "The *Lebensborn* homes were created for women and members of the SS and the German police, as well as for single and unmarried mothers in general who need special protection." It goes on to say that "the precondition for admission to the home is proof of health, hereditary health, and Aryan ancestry up to and including the grandparents, which it is incumbent upon the father and mother of the child to be born to provide."[30] It was important to *Lebensborn* to emphasise that its institutions were not recreational homes after pregnancy and birth. Indeed, SS leaders in Vienna seem to have assumed that they were, as a 1941 letter from Ebner to the *Lebensborn*'s home admissions department indicates: "In our experience, women in need of recovery do not fit into the Lebensborn homes either, since in all cases they have been known to demand certain privileges and extra care."[31] *Lebensborn* admitted to its maternity homes only unmarried pregnant women who met the racist criteria that also applied in the SS and the pregnant wives of SS and police members. After birth, *Lebensborn* took care of only those children it credited with a positive development – and only those mothers whose mindset passed muster with the SS.

---

28 Claudia Spring, *Zwischen Krieg und Euthanasie. Zwangssterilisationen in Wien 1940–1945* (Wien: Böhlau, 2009), 51–74.
29 See, for example, Ernst Klee, *"Euthanasie" im NS-Staat. Die "Vernichtung lebensunwerten Lebens"* (Frankfurt: Fischer, 2010); Michael Burleigh, *Death and Deliverance. "Euthanasia" in Germany, 1900–1945* (Cambridge: Cambridge University Press, 1994); Götz Aly, *Die Belasteten. "Euthanasie" 1939–1945. Eine Gesellschaftsgeschichte* (Frankfurt am Main: Fischer, 2013).
30 *Lebensborn-Broschüre*, n.d. (prior to 1941), 9. BIK, collection of Helga S., Vienna.
31 *Aufnahme von Frau M. geb. S.*, 8 March 1941, AA, 4.1.0/8211100, Ref. 82451230.

As the Second World War wore on, the role of *Lebensborn* as a hub of the National Socialist regime's population policy became more and more pronounced. More maternity and children's homes were established, especially in Norway. In doing so, *Lebensborn* wanted to draw illegitimate children of SS and of military and civilian members of the German occupying forces into its sphere of influence. A number of mothers gave their children up for adoption to the *Lebensborn*, although they were not always informed that the children would be taken to the German Reich.[32] Anni-Frid Synni Lyngstad, singer of the band ABBA, is one of the best known personalities to have been born in a *Lebensborn* home. After the war, having given birth to a child fathered by a member of the German occupying forces heaped public-opinion opprobrium on Norwegian women. Lyngstad grew up with her grandmother in Sweden, partly to escape the hostility that would have been meted out to her in her home country. In 2018, in a national reckoning with the past, the Norwegian government officially apologised to the women in question and their descendants for the stigmatisation and ostracism they had been subjected to.[33]

From 1942, in addition to setting up new maternity homes in the occupied territories, *Lebensborn* turned to a second field of activity, the "germanisation" policy. Choosing Eastern Europe as its chief battleground, the association searched for children who could be passed off as "Aryan". Thousands of these

---

32  See, for example, Kjersti Ericsson and Eva Simonsen, "Life Stories of Norwegian War Children," in *Children of World War II: The Hidden Enemy Legacy*, edited by Kjersti Ericsson and Eva Simonsen (New York: Berg Publishers, 2005), 93–113; Caroline Nilsen, "Romance, Marriage, and the Lebensborn Program: Gendering German Expectations and Reality in Occupied Norway", in *German-Occupied Europe in the Second World War*, edited by Raffael Scheck, Julia Torrie, and Fabian Théofilakis (London and New York: Routledge, 2019), 181–94; Caroline Nilsen, "Breeding Hate. The Norwegian Lebensborn Children," unpublished PhD Thesis, University of Houston, 2013; Kåre Olsen, *Krigens barn: Die norske krigsbarna og deres mødre.* (Oslo: Forum Aschehoug, 1998); Kåre Olsen, *Vater: Deutscher. Das Schicksal der norwegischen Lebensbornkinder und ihrer Mütter von 1940 bis heute* (Frankfurt am Main: Campus, 2002); Kåre Olsen, "Under the care of Lebensborn: Norwegian War Children and their Mothers," in *Children of World War II: The Hidden Enemy Legacy,* edited by Kjersti Ericsson and Eva Simonsen (New York: Berg Publishers, 2005), 15–35; Sarah Rehberg, Die deutsche Besatzung in Norwegen und das Schicksal der "Kriegskinder," in *Born of War. Vom Krieg geboren. Europas verleugnete Kinder*, edited by Gisela Heidenreich (Berlin: Links, 2017), 173–90.

33  In Norway, the story of *Lebensborn* became known especially through a book by Veslemøy Kjendsli. It is about *Lebensborn* child Turid, the daughter of a German father and a Norwegian mother, who was born in a *Lebensborn* maternity home in Norway, given up for adoption, taken to Germany and returned to Norway after the war, where she lived in a home until she grew up with Norwegian adoptive parents. See Veslemøy Kjendsli, *Skammens Barn* (Oslo: Metope, 1986). The Norwegian *Lebensborn* children who grew up in the GDR and spent their adult lives there have been little researched to date. In the 1960s, the Stasi used the identities of some of them for espionage. Klaus Neumann, conference report "*Lebensborn*"-*Kinder in der DDR. Erinnerungen im Spannungsfeld zweier Diktaturen* in H-Soz-Kult, 15 June 2011, www.h sozkult.de/conferencereport/id/fdkn-122311 (20 October 2023).

children were deported after a racial biological screening. Their true identity was kept secret.[34] A second *Lebensborn* home, *Alpenland* near Gmunden, was to provide a temporary home for those children who in the end would be placed with selected childless foster parents to round off their "germanisation". After the war, the search for the biological families of these children often led nowhere; decades later, these former *Lebensborn* children often described the return to their home countries as difficult and painful.[35]

Both people born in *Lebensborn* maternity homes in the German Reich and the occupied territories and those who were abducted by *Lebensborn* have been sharing their experiences with a wider public for years now. In addition to autobiographies, a number of novels featuring *Lebensborn* have been published in German-speaking countries.[36] Particularly noteworthy is the much acclaimed autobiography *Das endlose Jahr* (The Endless Year) by Gisela Heidenreich, who was born to a German mother in the *Lebensborn* home in Klekken in Norway in 1943.[37] Alois Hotschnig's novel *Der Silberfuchs meiner Mutter* (My Mother's Silver Fox) interweaves life and family stories with aspects of the *Lebensborn* organisation. Protagonist Heinz Fritz was born in Vorarlberg in 1942 as the son of a *Wehrmacht* soldier and a Norwegian woman, whom *Lebensborn* had enabled to travel from Kirkenes to Hohenems.[38] A radically different approach is adopted by *My Child Lebensborn*, a computer game designed by a Norwegian studio that casts players as adoptive parents of a *Lebensborn* child in post-war Norway.[39] In Germany, the *Lebensspuren* association is an umbrella organisation of people

---

34　See also Verena Buser, "'Mass Detective Operation' im befreiten Deutschland: UNRRA und die Suche nach den eingedeutschten Kindern nach dem Zweiten Weltkrieg," in *HISTORIE* 8, 2016, 347–60; Isabel Heinemann, "'Bis zum letzten Tropfen guten Blutes.' The Kidnapping of 'Racially Valuable' Children as Another Aspect of Nazi Racial Policy in the Occupied East," in *Genocide and Settler Society. Frontier Violence and Stolen Indigenous Children in Australian History*, edited by Dirk Moses (Oxford and New York: Berghahn, 2004), 244–66; Isabel Heinemann, "Fundament der Volksgemeinschaft. Familientrennungen und -gründungen in der nationalsozialistischen In- und Exklusionspolitik," in *Familientrennungen im nationalsozialistischen Krieg. Erfahrungen und Praktiken in Deutschland und im besetzten Europa 1939-1945*, edited by Wiebke Lisner, Johannes Hürter, Cornelia Rau, and Lu Seegers (Göttingen: Wallstein, 2022), 57–80; Dorothee Schmitz-Köster, *Raubkind. Von der SS nach Deutschland verschleppt* (Freiburg im Breisgau: Herder, 2018).

35　Ines Hopfer, *Geraubte Kindheit. Die gewaltsame Eindeutschung von polnischen Kindern in der NS-Zeit* (Wien – Köln – Weimar: Böhlau, 2010).

36　Most recent publications include: Ulrike Draesner, *Die Verwandelten* (München: Penguin, 2023); Dirk Kaesler, *Lügen und Scham. Deutsche Leben* (Berlin: Vergangenheitsverlag, 2023); Gudrun Eussner, *Heime für Himmlers Väter. Eine Lebensbornkind fordert Auskunft* (Uhingen: Gerhard Hess, 2023).

37　Gisela Heidenreich, *Das endlose Jahr. Die langsame Entdeckung der eigenen Biografie – ein Lebensbornschicksal* (München: Scherz, 2002).

38　Alois Hotschnig, *Der Silberfuchs meiner Mutter* (Köln: Kiepenheuer & Witsch, 2021).

39　https://mychildlebensborn.com/ (20 October 2023).

who were born in *Lebensborn* maternity homes or abducted by *Lebensborn*. It supports families in their efforts to come to terms with the past.[40] In Austria, the BIK organised a first exchange and networking meeting of people born in the *Heim Wienerwald* in the HGNÖ in Sankt Pölten and a visit to their birthplace in September 2022.[41]

## IV.  Research on the *Heim Wienerwald*: Source Material and Analytical Approach

The articles in this volume pull together current BIK research findings on the history of the *Heim Wienerwald*. Focusing on the *Heim Wienerwald* in the broader context of *Lebensborn* maternity homes, they present the results of quantitative and qualitative analyses of the available data on the veil of secrecy surrounding childbirth in the *Heim Wienerwald*, home admissions, and the racial assessment of mother and child. Secondly, the volume deals with everyday life in the *Heim Wienerwald* and the extent to which the stay of pregnant women and mothers in maternity homes was regulated. Sources related to daily routines and regulations provide insights both into the organisational structure of the home and the ideological goals of *Lebensborn*. Thirdly, the volume gives an insight into the experiences and everyday life of the home staff, especially the nurses. Fourthly, the volume concerns itself with children who did not meet the SS selection criteria. While *Lebensborn* wanted to promote "hereditarily healthy" offspring, the ambivalence of pro- and antinatalist measures in National Socialist racial policy is reflected in the biographies of those children of the *Heim Wienerwald* who were murdered in the context of National Socialist child "euthanasia".[42]

A central source for researching the history of the *Heim Wienerwald* was provided by the civil records at the registry office Pernitz II, which were sifted through in situ, having been made available to BIK researchers for anonymised evaluation.[43]

---

40  https://lebensspuren-deutschland.eu/ (20 October 2023).

41  Hans Bogenreiter and Lukas Schretter, *Vor 85 Jahren: Lebensborn-Heim Wienerwald*, <www.museumnoe.at/de/das-museum/blog/vor-85-jahren-lebensborn-heim-wienerwald> (20 October 2023).

42  Preliminary results were presented and discussed at a workshop organised by the BIK in January 2022. Nadjeschda Stoffers, conference report "*Lebensborn. Nationalsozialistische Geburtenpolitik, Entbindungsheime und die "Eindeutschung" von Kindern aus den besetzten Gebieten*," in H-Soz-Kult, 29 March 2022, <www.hsozkult.de/conferencereport/id/fdkn-127 926> (20 October 2023).

43  BIK Project *Lebensborn-Heim Wienerwald, 1938–1945. Tabu und Projektion*, funded by the Jubilee Fund of the Austrian National Bank (18270) and the Province of Lower Austria.

The registry office Pernitz II goes back to *Lebensborn* intentions to guarantee women anonymity in pregnancy and birth if they so desired. In the *Heim Wienerwald*, as in the other *Lebensborn* maternity homes, there was a separate registry office in addition to the local one. The *Heim Wienerwald* registry office bore the Roman numeral II after the name of the municipality where the home was situated. The purpose of this registry office was for *Lebensborn* mothers to be exempt from having to inform their home municipality of their whereabouts. The tasks of the *Lebensborn* registry offices included registering the birth of a child without reporting it to the home registry office of its mother or father. This ensured that relatives and the social environment did not learn of the child's existence.[44]

For the analysis of the files of the registry office Pernitz II, the BIK has created its own database, which, among other things, allows access to information on the number of children born in the *Heim Wienerwald* and the places of residence of their mothers at the time of impregnation. The database also provides information on the age structure of the women who gave birth in the home, and the mothers' and children's length of stay in the home.[45]

The files of the registry office Pernitz II, together with the files from Ebner's sphere of activity preserved in the Arolsen Archives, form a solid base for research into the history of the *Heim Wienerwald*. The *Lebensborn* holdings in the Arolsen Archives contain files from the *Lebensborn* central administration, the *Lebensborn* Main Department G, and the head of the *Lebensborn* maternity home in Steinhöring. They deal with the care of mothers and children in the homes, medical statistics, correspondence with and about *Lebensborn* staff, building and property management, and private correspondence. The files thus not only provide information about conditions in the *Heim Wienerwald*, but also allow the history of the *Heim Wienerwald* to be placed in relation to other *Lebensborn* facilities.

The Arolsen Archives also have in their keeping the material collected by Dorothee Schmitz-Köster, which in these pages is referred to as "Bestand Dorothee Schmitz-Köster". She has been researching and publishing on *Lebensborn* since the 1990s and has gathered countless documents and interviews, some of which relate to the history of the *Heim Wienerwald*.

Relevant source material was found in the *Bundesarchiv* in Berlin, for example, from Heinrich Himmler's personal staff. Similarly relevant are individual case files from the marriage department of the *Rasse- und Siedlungshauptamt SS* (Race and Settlement Main Office; *RuSHA*), which provide information about the private living conditions of *SS* members and their brides, wives, and children. From 1 January 1932, all *SS* members had to obtain a marriage permit and, later, a

---

44  Lilienthal, *Der "Lebensborn e.V."*, 79–89; Schmitz-Köster, *"Deutsche Mutter,"* 193–96.
45  BIK database, *Lebensborn-Heim Wienerwald*. We would like to thank Felix Hafner, Mariana Kienzl, Theresa Reinalter, and Richard Wallenstorfer for their support in reviewing the files.

permit to become engaged, with a view to "the selection and preservation of racially and hereditarily good blood."[46] The documents typically to be submitted by those wishing to marry included a *RuSHA* questionnaire, an *SS* hereditary health questionnaire, an *SS* investigation form, an *Ahnenpass* (proof of ancestry, pedigree) and an affidavit listing assets and liabilities. In those cases where the father was an *SS* man, the holdings thus provide some information about the parents of children in the *Heim Wienerwald*.

In addition, files on the *Heim Wienerwald* can be found in the *Niederösterreichisches Landesarchiv*. Another remarkable store of archival material is the *Sammlung Frauennachlässe* at the University of Vienna, the recipient of the bequest of former student nurse and infant nurse in the *Heim Wienerwald*, Marianne Leitner.

Soon after the BIK started researching the *Heim Wienerwald*, it obtained data from the archives on hundreds of children who were born there. However, the project team decided not to indiscriminately locate and contact the former *Lebensborn* children known to them from the archives – after all, it had to be taken in consideration that some of them are not aware to this day that they were born in a *Lebensborn* facility. Being confronted by a research team with this aspect of family history for the first time via an interview request, with the potentially attendant consequences of bringing to light family secrets or repressed memories, could have had incalculable personal or familial repercussions. Instead, a decision was made to only trace and contact individuals born in the *Heim Wienerwald,* who had already gone public with their stories through autobiographical publications of one sort or another. A few interview partners were referred to the BIK through so-called snowball sampling, a sampling technique where currently enrolled research participants informally help to recruit other participants. In addition, calls for participation published in Austrian media proved successful at the end of 2020 and led to a great deal of written correspondence and oral interviews.

While not every contact with someone born in the *Heim Wienerwald* resulted in an interview, the BIK did conduct a total of 34 interviews.[47] In addition, the BIK conducted interviews with family members of former *Lebensborn* children, one

---

46 *SS-Befehl-A-Nr. 65*, 31 December 1931 *(Verlobungs- und Heiratsbefehl)*, quoted in Gudrun Schwarz, *Eine Frau an seiner Seite. Ehefrauen in der "SS-Sippengemeinschaft"* (Hamburg: Hamburger Edition, 1997), 24–25.

47 BIK, Project *Geboren im Lebensborn-Heim Wienerwald. Sammlung, Dokumentation und Aufbereitung lebensgeschichtlicher Interviews*, funded by the Future Fund of the Republic of Austria, P21–4314. Lukas Schretter and Nadjeschda Stoffers, "Ambivalent but Not Indifferent: Interview Narratives of Lebensborn Children from the Wienerwald Maternity Home, 1938–1945," in *Childhood during War and Genocide: Agency, Survival, and Representation*, edited by Joanna Beate Michlic, Yuliya von Saal, and Anna Ullrich (Göttingen: Wallstein, 2024), 283–96. (European Holocaust Studies 5).

interview with a woman who gave birth in the *Heim Wienerwald*, a former student nurse of the *Lebensborn* maternity home, one interview with a former employee of the *Wienerwald* lung sanatorium before 1938, and one with the daughter of a former employee of the *Lebensborn* home within the framework of the research projects.

Since those born in the *Heim Wienerwald* inevitably have no memories of *Lebensborn* themselves, the focus is on how they make sense of the past and what meaning they attach to *Lebensborn* in their family and life history. The interviewees spent only the first days, weeks or, in a few cases, the first years of their lives in the *Heim Wienerwald*; therefore, in the stories they tell about the home, different layers of individual experience and interpretation overlap with ideas and stories that were passed on in their families.[48] The project included the painstaking study of photo albums in the possession of some of the interviewees and of letters, postcards, and other documents, with a view to extracting information pertaining to the *Heim Wienerwald* from them. To this day, some of the families of those born there and the people living near the former home are loath to talk about *Lebensborn* and the history of the *Heim Wienerwald*. It is therefore all the more welcome that the BIK studies on *Lebensborn* have found a sequel since 2023 in the form of a project to disseminate the research findings.[49] Moreover, a participatory research project coopts people born in the *Heim Wienerwald*, their families, and people from the vicinity into the process of historical research. Workshops and field trips serve to propagate the skills that are the historian's stock in trade with which to tackle historical and biographical sources. These so-called co-researchers will also be involved in the presentation of the project results. The participatory research project is thus intended to encourage people to engage with family history, explore the history of the *Heim Wienerwald*, and promote civic engagement.[50]

---

48  One of the most well-known works on family memory and family history concerning the National Socialist period is by Welzer et al. The authors analyse family discussions in order to understand what "normal Germans" remember about the past. See Harald Welzer, Sabine Moller, and Karoline Tschuggnall, *"Opa war kein Nazi." Nationalsozialismus und Holocaust im Familiengedächtnis* (Frankfurt am Main: Fischer, 2014). See also, among others: Margit Reiter, *Die Generation danach. Der Nationalsozialismus im Familiengedächtnis* (Wien: StudienVerlag, 2006); Gabriele Rosenthal (ed.), *Der Holocaust im Leben von drei Generationen. Familien von Überlebenden und von Nazi-Tätern* (Gießen: Psychosozial, 1997); Harald Welzer, Robert Montau, and Christine Plaß, *"Was wir für böse Menschen sind!" Der Nationalsozialismus im Gespräch zwischen den Generationen* (Tübingen: Edition discord, 1997).

49  BIK, Project *Lebensborn-Heim. Wienerwald. Umstrittenes Erbe, gemeinsame Verantwortung*, funded by the Province of Lower Austria.

50  BIK, Project *MEMORY LAB. Partizipative Forschung zum Lebensborn-Heim Wienerwald, 1938–1945*, funded by the Open Innovation in Science Center of the Ludwig Boltzmann Society.

# Articles

Lukas Schretter / Martin Sauerbrey-Almasy / Barbara Stelzl-Marx

# National Socialist Population Policy, Racial Hygiene, and *Lebensborn:* Pregnancy and Childbirth in the *Heim Wienerwald,* 1938–1945

## I.   Introduction

Charlotte H., born in 1924, gave birth to her first son, Wolfgang, in March 1944 in the *Heim Wienerwald*, a maternity home run by the *Schutzstaffel (SS) Lebensborn* association. She had met the child's father, Richard S., a year earlier at a dance in Tulln, near Vienna. Richard S. was an on-board aviation mechanic with the *Sturzkampfgeschwader,* stationed at the Langenlebarn air base, which had been built in 1939.

In 2021, at the age of 97, Charlotte H. reminisced to an interviewer on her pregnancy and on what it was like for her to give birth at the *Heim Wienerwald*. Having mentioned her socialist background, she recounted how her godmother and Richard S. nevertheless got her admitted to *Lebensborn* towards the end of her pregnancy. She arrived at the *Heim Wienerwald* four weeks before her child was due. It was only when she went into labour that it was discovered that the child presented in the brow position, which she felt the medical staff proved insufficiently qualified to handle. However, her six-week stay after delivery lived up to her expectations: during air raids, mothers sought shelter in the basement of the home with their newborns, who were kept in a separate nursery. She also came into contact with children older than her son, some of whom, Charlotte H. suspected, were the offspring of the home's staff. She spent sociable hours at lecture evenings, in needlework classes, and in sing-alongs of folk songs such as *Auf de schwäbsche Eisebahne* and *Heidenröslein*. After her release, Charlotte H. was taken in by her mother. She never saw Richard S., the child's father, again. She later learned from his sister that he had been killed on the Western Front in the same year, 1944, some time after she had given birth to their son.[1]

---

1   Charlotte H., interviewed by Sabine Nachbaur, 19 August 2021, interview in the possession of the Ludwig Boltzman Institute for Research on Consequences of War (BIK). The interview was not recorded. This summary of Charlotte H.'s experiences in the *Heim Wienerwald* is based on a report of the interview, released by Charlotte H. and available at the BIK. – The genesis of this

Charlotte H. and the father of the child were classified by *Lebensborn* as "Aryan," and Charlotte H. was therefore allowed to give birth in the *Heim Wienerwald*. *Lebensborn* sought to ensure that "Aryan" unwed women would choose not to have an abortion if they faced social stigma or even ostracism from their own families. Instead, they were encouraged to foster "Aryan" life and contribute to a future "racially pure" nation by being offered discreet childbirth. According to its 1938 statutes, the mission of *Lebensborn* included "supporting racially and hereditarily valuable large families" through financial aid, "providing accommodation [...] for racially and hereditarily valuable expectant mothers who, after a careful screening of their own family and the family of the genitor can be expected to give birth to equally valuable children," "caring for these children," and "caring for the mothers of these children."[2] Despite its emphasis on racial aspects, *Lebensborn* and the *Heim Wienerwald* might appear to have been an additional benefit for *SS* families, combined on the part of the *SS* with a charitable gesture towards unwed mothers. In reality, *Lebensborn* was an integral component of the National Socialist racial and population policy.

With Charlotte H.'s story as a point of departure, this article first situates the history of the *Heim Wienerwald* in the context of National Socialist population policy, racial hygiene, and *Lebensborn*. Case studies explain the measures taken by *Lebensborn* to keep pregnancy and childbirth secret, the admission of women to *Lebensborn*, and the assessment of the "racial suitability" of mother and child by *Lebensborn*.

The article builds on Georg Lilienthal's landmark study on *Lebensborn*, which establishes both its function in various phases of the Third Reich and its place in National Socialist racial policy, and Dorothee Schmitz-Köster's social history studies on *Lebensborn*.[3] Studies on the *Heim Wienerwald* include those by Hiltraud Ast, Günther Knotzinger, and Elisabeth Märker.[4] The article is based on a

---

article was funded by the Jubilee Fund of the Austrian National Bank, the Future Fund of the Republic of Austria, and the Province of Lower Austria. Associated research was conducted at BIK in collaboration with the Institute of History of the University of Graz.

2  *Lebensborn e.V. in München*, brochure, Miesbach, 8. Provincial Archives of Lower Austria (NÖLA), Office of the Lower Austrian Provincial Government, Provincial Office I/2, number 33/1975, see also *Ziele des "Lebensborn" e.V.*, Arolsen Archives (hereinafter AA), 4.1.0/8209800, Ref. 82448155. The authors thank Otmar Binder for translations of German-language quotations of documents and interviews and for copy-editing the English version of this article.

3  See, for example, Georg Lilienthal, *Der "Lebensborn e.V." Ein Instrument nationalsozialistischer Rassenpolitik*. 2nd ed. (Frankfurt/Main: Fischer, 2003); Dorothee Schmitz-Köster, *"Deutsche Mutter, bist du bereit..." Der Lebensborn und seine Kinder*, 2nd ed. (Berlin: Aufbau, 2011). For more information on volumes and monographs as well as unpublished works on *Lebensborn* and the *Heim Wienerwald* in particular see the editorial in this volume.

4  Hiltraud Ast, *Feichtenbach. Eine Tallandschaft im Niederösterreichischen Schneeberggebiet* (Wien: Brüder Hollinek, 1994), 61–77; Günther Knotzinger, *Das SS-Heim 'Wienerwald' und die Geschichte des Hauses von 1904 bis zur Gegenwart*, unpublished manuscript, Feichtenbach,

database-driven and anonymised analysis of 946 surviving files of the registry office Pernitz II, including the so-called *Reichsführer SS Fragebögen* (*Reichsführer SS* Questionnaires), of which 346 drafts have been preserved in the Pernitz municipal office. In addition, the article refers to documents from the sphere of activity of Gregor Ebner, who served as *Lebensborn*'s head of health care from 1937 to 1945, and as a member of the *Lebensborn* board from 1938 to March 1942. Concurrently, he was the director of the first *Lebensborn* maternity home, *Heim Hochland*, which opened in Steinhöring near Munich on 15 August 1936. These documents are accessible in the Arolsen Archives.

In the preparation of this article, mothers and fathers of children born in the *Heim Wienerwald* could no longer be interviewed, with the sole exception of Charlotte H.. The oldest woman known from written records to have given birth in the *Heim Wienerwald* was born in 1899 and was admitted to *Lebensborn* on 3 February 1939.[5] The youngest was born in 1925 and was admitted on 23 January 1941.[6] The analysis of these documents was therefore supplemented by information from biographical interviews with former *Lebensborn* children who had spent the first days, weeks or months of their lives in the *Heim Wienerwald*. Being a *Lebensborn* "child" is an indication of parental involvement in National Socialist racial and population policies. The interviews, conducted between 2021 and 2023, therefore not only provide an insight into what the "children" were told about their parents' applications to *Lebensborn* and their mothers' stay in the home, but also shed light on the significance – if any – of being born in the *Heim Wienerwald* for their own family and life stories.[7]

## II.  National Socialist Racial Policy, *Lebensborn*, and the *Heim Wienerwald*

The *SS* association *Lebensborn* was founded in December 1935 in the context of National Socialist racial policy. In addition to the *Heim Wienerwald*, which opened in 1938 and where Charlotte H. gave birth to her child in 1944, *Lebensborn*

---

2001; Elisabeth Andrea Märker, "Rassisch wertvoll. Die positive Eugenik: Ihre Handhabung am Beispiel des Lebensbornvereins im 'Heim Alpenland' und 'Heim Wienerwald'," unpublished PhD thesis, University of Innsbruck, 1999.

5  Franziska M., 51/1939, registry office Pernitz II.

6  Bernd T., 48/1941, registry office Pernitz II; list of residents, registry office Pernitz II.

7  For information on the interview project and the interview methodology, see Lukas Schretter and Nadjeschda Stoffers, "Ambivalent but Not Indifferent: Interview Narratives of *Lebensborn* Children from the Wienerwald Maternity Home, 1938–1945, in *Childhood during War and Genocide: Agency, Survival, and Representation*, edited by Joanna Beate Michlic, Yuliya von Saal, and Anna Ullrich (Göttingen: Wallstein, 2024), 283–96. (European Holocaust Studies 5).

established more than twenty maternity and children's homes in the Third Reich and in occupied Europe. The *Heim Wienerwald* was the only *Lebensborn* maternity home in the territory of present-day Austria.

*Lebensborn*, which aimed at creating and raising an "elite" of "Aryan" children, was one of the regime's measures to reverse the decline in the birth rate after World War I and to increase the "Nordic" or "Germanic" population.

No sooner had the National Socialist regime seized power in Germany in 1933 than it began to promote its racial ideas about family, gender, and sexuality through posters, exhibitions, and writings. The intent was translated into action through various pro-natalist welfare policies that favoured "Aryan" families. For example, the regime encouraged marriage of "Aryan" couples through income tax benefits, child support, and marriage loans, which were included in the *Gesetz zur Verhinderung der Arbeitslosigkeit* (Law for the Reduction of Unemployment) of 1 June 1933.[8] Material benefits were supported by rituals and rhetoric, such as the public honouring of families with many children, the bestowal of the *Mutterkreuz* (Mother's Cross), and the celebration of Mother's Day, which the regime used for propaganda purposes.[9] At the same time, the regime controlled access to abortion and contraception in line with its policy of racial hygiene. The reintroduction of the 1871 abortion ban was supposed to deny "hereditarily healthy" women access to terminating their pregnancies; from 1943, performing an illegal abortion was punishable by death.[10] In addition, in 1938 the marriage law was reformed and a new divorce law was introduced that made divorce easier: premature infertility became a ground for divorce, as did the refusal of either partner to have a child.[11] However, pro-natalist measures in National Socialist racial policy, such as the total ban on abortion and the promotion of families and births among the "racially

---

8 Detlev Humann, *"Arbeitsschlacht." Arbeitsbeschaffung und Propaganda in der NS-Zeit 1933–1939* (Göttingen: Wallstein, 2011), 118–35. (Moderne Zeit. Neue Forschungen zur Gesellschafts- und Kulturgeschichte des 19. und 20. Jahrhunderts XXIII).

9 Irmgard Weyrather, *Mutterkreuz und Muttertag. Der Kult um die "deutsche Mutter" im Nationalsozialismus* (Frankfurt/Main: Fischer, 1993).

10 Atina Grossmann, *Reforming Sex. The German Movement of Birth Control and Abortion Reform, 1920–1950* (New York – Oxford: Oxford University Press, 1995), 136–65.

11 Annemone Christians, "Familien vor Gericht. Zur nationalsozialistischen Scheidungspraxis im Krieg," in *Familientrennungen im nationalsozialistischen Krieg. Erfahrungen und Praktiken in Deutschland und im besetzten Europa 1939–1945*, edited by Wiebke Lisner, Johannes Hürter, Cornelia Rauh, and Lu Seegers (Göttingen: Wallstein, 2022), 147–73; Annemone Christians, "The Vulnerable Dwelling. Local Privacy before the Courts," in *Private Life and Privacy in Nazi Germany*, edited by Elizabeth Harvey, Johannes Hürter, Maiken Umbach, and Andreas Wirsching (Cambridge: Cambridge University Press, 2019), 182–205; Gabriele Czarnowski, "'Der Wert der Ehe für die Volksgemeinschaft.' Frauen und Männer in der nationalsozialistischen Ehepolitik," in *Zwischen Karriere und Verfolgung. Handlungsräume von Frauen im nationalsozialistischen Deutschland*, edited by Kirsten Heinsohn, Barbara Vogel, and Ulrike Weckel (Frankfurt/Main – New York: Campus, 1997), 78–95, here 84–90. (Geschichte und Geschlechter 20).

pure," were subordinated to anti-natalist measures. These included forced sterilisation of the eugenically and racially "unfit," the forced abortion on women deemed "inferior," and clinical negligence, as well as marriage bans, the forced dissolution of marriages, and the denial of financial benefits to prevent women and men categorised as "hereditarily ill" from becoming parents.[12] *Lebensborn* – originally designed by the SS to encourage women deemed "racially valuabe" by providing them with a series of private maternity homes in which to give birth, financial support and adoption services – was founded the same year the Nuremberg Laws outlawed intermarriage between so-called "ethnic" Germans and Jews. National Socialist pro-natalism for "desirable" births and its anti-natalism for "undesirable" ones were thus tightly connected; efforts to control the composition of the population went as far as "euthanasia" and genocide.

The regime's politics of reproduction were gendered, as studies on women, gender relations, and sexuality in the Third Reich have shown since the 1980s.[13] Still, "race" always took priority over gender, and the status of men and women depended on their assigned racial classifications. Anti-natalist measures also applied for those classified a priori as "Aryans," whose "inappropiate" sexual behaviour earned them the label of "asocial."[14]

---

12 Gisela Bock, *Zwangssterilisation im Nationalsozialismus. Studien zur Rassenpolitik und Frauenpolitik,* 2nd. ed (Münster: Monsenstein und Vannerdat, 2010), 195–336; Gisela Bock, "Frauen und Geschlechterbeziehungen in der nationalsozialistischen Rassenpolitik," in *Nach Osten. Verdeckte Spuren nationalsozialistischer Verbrechen,* edited by Theresa Wobbe (Frankfurt/Main: Neue Kritik, 1992), 99–133, here 117–20.

13 Scholarly research focusing on the gender relations in the Third Reich includes, for example, Renata Bridenthal, Atina Grossmann, and Marion A. Kaplan (eds.), *When Biology Became Destiny. Women in Weimar and Nazi Germany* (New York: Monthly Review Pr., 1984); Gabriele Czarnowksi, *Das kontrollierte Paar. Ehe- und Sozialpolitik im Nationalsozialismus* (Weinheim: Deutscher Studien Verlag, 1991); Elizabeth Harvey, *Women and the Nazi East: Agents and Witnesses of Germanization* (New Haven: Yale University Press, 2003); Elizabeth Heineman, *What Difference Does a Husband Make? Women and Marital Status in Nazi and Postwar Germany* (Berkley – Los Angeles – London: University of California Press, 1999), 17–74; Dagmar Herzog (ed.), *Sexuality and German Fascism* (New York – Oxford: Berghahn, 2005); Claudia Koonz, *Mothers in the Fatherland. Women, the Family and Nazi Politics* (New York: St. Martin's Press, 1987); Dagmar Reese, *Growing Up Female in Nazi Germany* (Ann Arbor: University of Michigan Press, 2006).

14 In 1983, Gisela Bock argued that the National Socialist imposition on ethnically or socially "inferior" women not to have children might be labelled "sexist racism," since their procreation was prohibited not only because of their "genes" and "race," but also because of their actual or perceived deviation as women from the social or ethnic norms for "superior" women. Accordingly, the imposition on ethnically or socially "superior" women to have children they may not have wanted might be labelled "racist sexism," since their procreation was encouraged not only because they were women, but because they were women of a certain ethnicity or social status declared to be "superior." See Gisela Bock, "Racism and Sexism in Nazi Germany: Motherhood, Compulsory Sterilization, and the State," *Women and Violence* 8 (1983) 3: 420. While Gisela Bock used her studies of the regime's sterilisation policy to draw attention to the importance of the category of "race" in all areas of National Socialism,

Since the ideal "Aryan" family in the Third Reich consisted of a man in the role of breadwinner and a woman in the role of housewife and mother, producing as many children as possible, the regime's sexual politics constituted a definitive and violent response against progressivism and tolerance in the Weimar Republic. At the same time, however, as Dagmar Herzog argues, for the majority of the population – predominantly heterosexual and non-disabled non-Jews – National Socialism was not experienced as entirely sexually repressive, but rather brought a redefinition, extension, and intensification of already existing liberalising tendencies.[15]

As an example of the complex connection between "race" and gender in the Third Reich, *Lebensborn* sought to downplay the notion of "illegitimacy" by making the living conditions of unwed "Aryan" mothers essentially comparable to those of married "Aryan" mothers, for example by providing financial support. On a wider scale, the regime also had plans to reform the law of "illegitimacy," which would give legal privileges to "Aryan" women and their "illegitimate" children. These reform plans were met with criticism from the churches and the *Wehrmacht*, who saw them as a threat to the status of marriage, but were

---

emphasising that forced sterilisation and forced abortion were the preconditions for birth-promoting measures such as marriage loans and tax benefits for the "Aryan" population, the US historian Claudia Koonz argued that housewives and mothers in particular became facilitators of racial persecution, above all through their "emotional labour" in the family. The so-called *Historikerinnenstreit* (an allusion to the *Historikerstreit*) in the late 1980s/early 1990s whether German women had become "perpetrators" in the "men's state" of the Third Reich or whether they mostly had been "victims" in the gender hierarchy of National Socialism was followed by studies, which set aside the perpetrator-victim dichotomy and examined the *Handlungsräume* (spheres of action) of women in the *Volksgemeinschaft*. On this debate see, for example, Susanne Lanwerd and Irene Stoehr, "Frauen- und Geschlechterforschung zum Nationalsozialismus seit den 1970er Jahren. Forschungsstand, Veränderungen, Perspektiven," in *Frauen- und Geschlechtergeschichte des Nationalsozialismus*, edited by Johanna Gehmacher and Gabriella Hauch (Innsbruck – Wien – Bozen: StudienVerlag, 2007), 22–68, here 23–28; Christina Herkommer, *Frauen im Nationalsozialismus – Opfer oder Täterinnen? Eine Kontroverse der Frauenforschung im Spiegel feministischer Theoriebildung und der allgemeinen historischen Aufarbeitung der NS-Vergangenheit* (München: Martin Meidenbauer, 2005); Adelheid Saldern, "Victims or Perpetrators? Controversies about the Role of Women in the Nazi State," in *Nazism and German Society, 1933–1945*, edited by Davic Crew (London: Routledge, 1994), 141–65. For the debate in Austria, see Johanna Gehmacher, "Kein Historikerinnenstreit... Fragen einer frauen- und geschlechtergeschichtlichen Erforschung des Nationalsozialismus in Österreich," *Zeitgeschichte* 22 (1995) 3/4: 109–23. At the same time, research on National Socialism increasingly included gender-historical perspectives and has also shown how "ordinary men" became involved in crimes and how ideas of masculinity and comradeship shaped their actions. See, for example, Christopher Browning, *Ordinary Men: Reserve Battalion 101 and the Final Solution in Poland* (New York: Harper Collins, 1992); Thomas Kühne, *Kameradschaft. Die Soldaten des nationalsozialistischen Krieges und das 20. Jahrhundert* (Göttingen: Vandenhoeck and Ruprecht, 2006).

15 Dagmar Herzog, *Sex after Fascism. Memory and Morality in Twentieth-Century Germany* (Princeton University Press: Princeton and Oxford, 2005), 15–16.

not concerned about their racial implications. Despite extensive debate and preparation, and the conviction of leading party members that the reform would be essential, it was not implemented. Nevertheless, during the war years, the distinction between "legitimate" and "illegitimate" children of "Aryan" parents was further eroded in terms of family benefits such as child support.[16]

When Himmler established *Lebensborn* in 1935 as a home for married and unwed pregnant women who could prove the racial acceptability of their offspring-to-be, he did so under pressure. With the establishment of the *Hilfswerk Mutter und Kind* (Mother and Child Relief Agency) on 28 February 1934, the Third Reich's umbrella social welfare organisation, the *Nationalsozialistische Volkswohlfahrt* (National Socialist People's Welfare, *NSV*), took an active role in the care of pregnant women and mothers. It was intended to coordinate welfare measures and to provide help for "hereditarily valuable" families in the form of financial support, health promotion, and childcare, while at the same time enabling unwed women to work by setting up infant and maternity homes. As a result, Himmler feared that the *SS* might lose its pre-eminent position in aiding unwed mothers of "Aryan" descent and as a protagonist in National Socialist population and racial policies.[17] The competition between the *NSV* and *Lebensborn* developed into rivalry at the latest during the war, and the *NSV*, an important financial sponsor of *Lebensborn*, stopped its payments in 1940.[18]

From the outset, *Lebensborn* was institutionally integrated into the *Rasse- und Siedlungshauptamt SS* (*SS* Race and Settlement Main Office, *RuSHA*), which had its head office in Berlin.[19] In August 1936, the association opened its first own maternity home, *Heim Hochland*, which served as a model for all *Lebensborn* maternity homes until the end of the war.[20] In June 1937, *Lebensborn* opened

16  Sybille Buske, *Fräulein Mutter und ihr Bastard. Eine Geschichte der Unehelichkeit in Deutschland 1900–1970* (Göttingen: Wallstein, 2014), 147–294. (Moderne Zeit V).

17  Lilienthal, *Der "Lebensborn e.V."*, 42. For more information on the NSV, see Wolf Gruner, *Öffentliche Wohlfahrt und Judenverfolgung: Wechselwirkungen lokaler und zentraler Politik im NS-Staat (1933–1942)* (München: Oldenbourg, 2009), 29–31; Daniel Hadwiger, *Nationale Solidarität und ihre Grenzen: Die deutsche "Nationalsozialistische Volkswohlfahrt" und der französische "Secours national" im Zweiten Weltkrieg* (Stuttgart: Steiner, 2021). (Schriftenreihe des Deutsch-Französischen Historikerkomitees 18); Herwart Vorländer, "NS-Volkswohlfahrt und Winterhilfswerk des deutschen Volkes," *Vierteljahrshefte für Zeitgeschichte* 34 (1986) 3: 341–80; Florian Wimmer, "Das 'Hilfswerk Mutter und Kind' der NSV," in *Kinder für den "Führer". Der Lebensborn in München*, edited by Angelika Baumann and Andreas Heusler (München: Franz Schiermeier, 2013), 49–50.

18  Lilienthal, *Der "Lebensborn e.V."*, 124–30.

19  Isabel Heinemann, *"Rasse, Siedlung, Deutsches Blut." Das Rasse- und Siedlungshauptamt der SS und die rassenpolitische Neuordnung Europas* (Göttingen: Wallstein, 2003), 101–12.

20  Anna Bräsel, "Das Lebensborn-Heim Hochland in Steinhöring," in *Kinder für den "Führer"*, 96–108.

*Heim Harz* in Wernigerode,[21] and in September 1937 *Heim Kurmark* in Klosterheide, one of the smallest *Lebensborn* homes.[22] A change of status in 1938 saw *Lebensborn* hived off from the *RuSHA* and its head office moved to Munich. It then belonged to the *Persönlicher Stab RFSS* (Personal Staff of the *Reichsführer SS*) and ultimately reported directly to Himmler. The *RuSHA* chairmen in office since 1936 were replaced by *SS-Oberführer* George Ebrecht, *SS-Gruppenführer* Oswald Pohl, and *SS-Standartenführer* Friedrich-Karl Dermietzel. The latter had already been in charge of health supervision at *Lebensborn*. Later *Reichsarzt SS SS-Brigadeführer* (SS chief medical officer) Ernst Grawitz and the head of the *RuSHA* were given seats on the supervisory board. Himmler placed himself at the head of *Lebensborn* as chairman of the board. *SS Oberführer* Guntram Pflaum, chief of staff in the *Sippenamt* in the *RuSHA*, who had been the official head of *Lebensborn,* remained in office as managing director, but his position was downgraded and key elements of his area of responsibility were transferred to Ebner as executive member of the board.[23]

In 1938, the internal restructuring of *Lebensborn* coincided with the expansion of its activities after the so-called *Anschluss* of Austria to the German Reich.[24] Following the opening of two new maternity homes in May 1938, *Heim Pommern* in Bad Polzin, today Połczyn-Zdrój in Poland, and *Heim Friesland* in Hohehorst,[25] *Heim Wienerwald* (until 28 May 1942: *Heim Ostmark*[26]) was established in Pernitz/Feichtenbach, 70 kilometers south of Vienna.

In order to establish *Lebensborn* in annexed Austria, Pflaum and Ebner wrote to Himmler in April 1938, requesting that the Gestapo confiscate houses, furniture, and motor vehicles.[27] In Feichtenbach, the former *Wienerwald* lung sanatorium

---

21 Karin Borchert, Wolfgang Kasparek, and Matthias Meißner, *Geboren im Lebensbornheim "Harz" Wernigerode* (Halberstadt: Kreisgeschichtskommission Landkreis Wernigerode, 2003).
22 Schmitz-Köster, *"Deutsche Mutter"*, 100.
23 Lilienthal, *Der "Lebensborn e.V."*, 40–58.
24 After the *Anschluss*, the official name used for Austria was *Land Österreich*. From 1939, the term *Ostmark* was used. From 1942, the term *Ostmark* was considered too reminiscent of the state of Austria, and the term *Alpen- und Donau-Reichsgaue* (Danubian and Alpine Reichsgaue) was chosen for the former states of Austria, which were reorganised into seven *Reichsgaue*. The *Heim Wienerwald* was located in the *Reichsgau Niederdonau* (Reichgau Lower Danube), which consisted of areas in Lower Austria, Burgenland, South-Eastern parts of Bohemia, and Southern parts of Moravia.
25 Schmitz-Köster, *"Deutsche Mutter"*; Gertrud Burmester and Herbert Perthen, *Lebensbornheim Friesland/Hohehorst. Ein Versuch zur "Local" und "Oral History". Schriftliche Hausarbeit zur Ersten Staatsprüfung für das Lehramt an Öffentlichen Schulen*, unpublished paper, Bremen 1981.
26 *Umlauf*, 24 March 1943, AA, 4.1.0/8209600, Ref. 82447881.
27 Brandt to Hoffmann, 28 January 1939, AA, 4.1.0/8209600, Ref. 82447637. The property had a size of over 33.7 hectares, of which 17 hectares were forest, and was free of mortgages. The fire insurance value was set at RM 563,000, development costs until the end of 1938 at about RM

was "aryanised" and converted to serve the purposes of *Lebensborn* from October 1938. It had been an institution specialised for diseases of the respiratory organs, owned and run by the Jewish doctors Hugo Kraus and Arthur Baer since 1904.[28] A children's home in Neulengbach near Sankt Pölten and *Schloss Oberweis* near Gmunden were also assigned to *Lebensborn*. The children's home in Neulengbach was never opened due to a lack of funds and was rented to the *Wehrmacht*. *Schloss Oberweis* also seemed at first to be unsuitable for *Lebensborn* purposes.[29]

After the *Anschluss*, the National Socialist regime initiated efforts in reproductive engineering in annexed Austria, including the establishment of *Lebensborn* facilities. Yet, the authoritarian regime in Austria between 1934 and 1938, a transitional period between democracy and National Socialism, had prepared the ground for the fascist ideals of motherhood: The end of the First Republic and democratic parliamentarianism in 1933/34 led to an end of the gender policy debates surrounding the "new woman," sexuality and contraception, the controversies concerning decriminalisation of abortion, and the reform of marriage law that had begun at the turn of the century and gained momentum after the First World War.[30] Instead, the authoritarian *"Ständestaat"*

---

100,000. *Tätigkeitsbericht der Verwaltungshauptabteilung des Lebensborn e.V.*, 14 February 1939, AA, 4.1.0./8210500, Ref. 82339797.

28  Ast, *Feichtenbach*, 62–69.

29  *"Lebensborn e.V."*, 21 June 1938, AA, 4.1.0/8210600, Ref. 82450204–82450205, and 4.1.0/ 8209600, Ref. 82447634–82447635.

30  Ingrid Bauer, "Eine frauen- und geschlechtergeschichtliche Perspektivierung des Nationalsozialismus," in *NS-Herrschaft in Österreich. Ein Handbuch*, edited by Emmerich Tálos, Ernst Hanisch, Wolfgang Neugebauer, and Reinhard Sieder (Wien: öbv und hpt, 2001), 409–43, here 410–13. For example, the rapid expansion of sexual counselling centres after the First World War represented a lasting rupture in the normative basis of gender relations, which in Austria was not resolved until the Second Republic. See Maria Mesner, "Educating Reasonable Lovers: Sex Counseling in Austria in the First Half of the Twentieth Century," in *Sexuality in Austria*, edited by Günter Bischof, Anton Pelinka, and Dagmar Herzog (New Brunswick and New Jersey: Transaction Publishers, 2007), 48–64, here 50. (Contemporary Austrian Studies 15). After 1933/ 34, restoring a very hierarchical gender order seemed necessary to achieve the Austro-fascist goal of re-Catholicizing society, which led to legislative discrimination against women. See, for example, Irene Bandhauer-Schöffmann, "Hausfrauen und Mütter im Austrofaschismus. Gender, Klasse und Religion als Achsen der Ungleichheit," *Österreichische Zeitschrift für Geschichtswissenschaft* 27 (2016) 3: 44–68. For additional information on how conservative visions of gender, including abortion rights, played a role in the "völkisch" women's movement, see Johanna Gehmacher, *Deutschnationale und nationalsozialistische Geschlechterpolitik in Österreich* (Wien: Döcker: 1998), 136–37. On questions of periodisation of the 20th century in Austria in relation to gender, see Johanna Gehmacher and Maria Mesner, "Dis/Kontinuitäten. Geschlechterordnungen und Periodisierungen im langen 20. Jahrhundert," *L'homme. Europäische Zeitschrift für Feministische Geschichtswissenschaft* 25 (2014) 2: 87–101, here 93. On the Dollfuß-Schuschnigg dictatorship see: Florian Wenninger and Lucile Dreidemy (eds.), *Das Dollfuß-Schuschnigg-Regime 1933–1938: Vermessung eines Forschungsfeldes* (Wien: Böhlau, 2013); Emmerich Tálos, *Das austrofaschistische Österreich 1933–1938* (Wien: Lit, 2017); Kurt Bauer, *Hitlers zweiter Putsch. Dollfuß, die Nazis und der 25. Juli 1934* (St. Pölten: Residenz, 2014).

continued the pro-natalist policies of the previous Christian Social-dominated governments and, for example, tightened the ban on abortion with the *Gesetz zum Schutz des menschlichen Lebens* (Law for the protection of human life).[31] After the *Anschluss*, the *Gesetz zum Schutz des menschlichen Lebens* was replaced by the *Gesetz zur Verhütung erbkranken Nachwuchses* (Law for the Prevention of Genetically Diseased Offspring), which provided for the forced sterilization and abortion on individuals found by the *Erbgesundheitsgericht* (Genetic Health Court) to be physically or mentally ill. From then on, abortion and sterilization were decisions that could only be made by the state and its representatives.[32] The pro- and anti-natalist policies that had been implemented in Germany since 1933 were applied to annexed Austria: Apart from strict abortion regulations, *Lebensborn* and other measures to promote births among the "hereditarily healthy" went hand in hand with the prevention of the birth of "undesirable" children through forced sterilization of the "unfit," the prohibition of intimate relationships between "Aryans" and "racially unworthy" partners, and "euthanasia."[33]

*Lebensborn* expanded its biopolitical intentions and activities not only after the *Anschluss* of Austria in 1938, but on a larger scale also after the outbreak of the Second World War in 1939, when the regime extended its family and racial policy goals to the European continent. For example, *Lebensborn* supported the widows of *SS* soldiers and the wives of "ethnic German" farmers in annexed Poland whose husbands had been killed.[34]

---

31  Maria Mesner, *Frauensache? Zur Auseinandersetzung um den Schwangerschaftsabbruch in Österreich nach 1945* (Wien: Jugend und Volk, 1994), 16–29. (Veröffentlichungen des Ludwig Boltzmann Instituts für Geschichte der Gesellschaftswissenschaften 23); Maria Mesner, *Geburtenkontrolle. Reproduktionsmedizin im 20. Jahrhundert* (Wien – Köln – Weimar: Böhlau, 2010), 201.

32  After the *Anschluss*, the *Gesetz zur Verhütung erbkranken Nachwuchses* came into force in early 1940, much later than other anti-natalist laws, such as the *Nürnberger Gesetze* (from May 1938) or the *Gesetz über die Vereinheitlichung des Gesundheitswesens* (from December 1938). This was not due to the activities of the Catholic eugenics movement in Vienna between the wars, which opposed forced sterilisation but advocated pro-natalist measures. The main reason for the delay was the protracted negotiations over the planned changes to the law in the *Altreich*. See Claudia Spring, *Zwischen Krieg und Euthanasie. Zwangssterilisationen in Wien 1940–1945* (Wien: Böhlau, 2009), 51–74.

33  See, for example, Herwig Czech, *Erfassung, Selektion und 'Ausmerze': Das Wiener Gesundheitsamt und die Umsetzung der nationalsozialistischen "Erbgesundheitspolitik" 1938 bis 1945* (Wien: Deuticke, 2003). (Forschungen und Beiträge zur Wiener Stadtgeschichte 41); Gabriella Hauch, "'… das gesunde Volksempfinden gröblich verletzt.' Verbotener Geschlechtsverkehr mit 'Anderen' während des Nationalsozialismus," in *Frauen im Reichsgau Oberdonau. Geschlechtsspezifische Bruchlinien im Nationalsozialismus*, edited by Gabriella Hauch (Linz: Oberösterreichisches Landesarchiv, 2006), 245–70; Gabriella Hauch, "Tabu. Verbotener Geschlechtsverkehr mit 'Anderen' während des Nationalsozialismus," in *kunst. kommunikation. macht. Sechster Österreichischer Zeitgeschichtetag 2003*, edited by Ingrid Bauer, Ernst Hanisch, Albert Lichtblau, and Gerald Sprengnagel (Innsbruck: StudienVerlag, 2004), 298–303.

34  Lilienthal, *Der "Lebensborn e.V."*, 104–05.

Within *Lebensborn*, *SS-Standartenführer* Max Sollmann, who had worked for the *Pers. Stab RFSS*, succeeded Pflaum in 1940. Sollmann once again reorganised the structure of *Lebensborn* and adopted new statutes. He made himself the sole director, assisted by a board of trustees.[35] However, the reorganisation did little to address the financial challenges *Lebensborn* faced following the opening of the new homes in 1938. *Lebensborn* founders had also failed to anticipate that many of the unwed mothers for whom *Lebensborn* was primarily intended would not take their children home after birth. By 1940, the homes were so overcrowded that the neonatal mortality rate began to rise. Therefore, following the establishment of the children's home *Heim Taunus*[36] in Wiesbaden in November 1939, Ebner recommended the creation of another home for 200 to 300 infants and children, and in 1942 *Lebensborn* opened *Heim Sonnenwiese* in Kohren-Salis. The first children at *Heim Sonnenwiese* came from *Heim Taunus*, which was to be converted into a maternity home.[37] The same month, *Lebensborn* opened another maternity home, *Heim Schwarzwald* in Nordrach.[38] In the summer of 1944, two more *Lebensborn* children's homes were opened in the *Altreich*: *Heim Franken I* and *Heim Franken II* in Schalkhausen, although *Franken II* was only in use for a few days.[39]

---

35  Ibid., 116–30.

36  Georg Lilienthal, "Das 'Lebensborn'-Heim Wiesbaden," in *Verfolgung und Widerstand in Hessen 1933–1945*, edited by Renate Knigge-Teche and Axel Ulrich (Frankfurt/Main: Eichborn, 1996), 437–46; Georg Lilienthal and Michaela Pohl, "Das 'Lebensborn'-Heim 'Taunus' in Wiesbaden (1939–1945)," in *Nassauische Annalen. Jahrbuch des Vereins für Nassauische Altertumskunde und Geschichtsforschung 103*, edited by Verein für nassauische Altertumskunde und Geschichtsforschung e. V. (Wiesbaden: Verein für Nassausche Altertumskunde und Geschichtsforschung, 1992), 295–310.

37  Susanne Hahn and Georg Lilienthal, "Totentanz und Lebensborn: Zur Geschichte des Alters- und Pflegeheimes in Kohren-Salis (1939–1945)," *Medizinhistorisches Journal* 27 (1992) 3/4: 340–58; Dorothee Neumaier, "Dr. Hildegard Feith: Ärztin im Lebensbornkinderheim 'Sonnenwiese'. Forschungsbericht," in *FernUniversität in Hagen*, 2019, https://ub-deposit.fernuni-hagen.de/receive/mir_mods_00001541, 20 October 2023. From 1940, *Lebensborn* also sponsored a *Kriegsmütterheim* in Stettin, where *Lebensborn* mothers lived together with their children, worked outside the home and left the children in the care of nurses during this time. Two years later, similar mothers' homes were opened in Munich, but were soon closed again due to bombing raids. Schmitz-Köster, *"Deutsche Mutter"*, 62 and 96.

38  Dorothee Neumaier, *Das Lebensbornheim "Schwarzwald" in Nordrach* (Baden-Baden: Tectum, 2017). (Reihe Geschichtswissenschaft 32). Dorothee Neumaier, "Das Lebensbornheim 'Schwarzwald' in Nordrach 1942–1945, in *Vom Nationalsozialismus zur Besatzungsherrschaft. Fallstudien und Erinnerungen aus Mittel- und Südbaden*," edited by Heiko Haumann and Uwe Schellinger (Heidelberg – Ubstadt-Weiher – Weil am Rhein – Basel: verlag regionalkultur, 2018), 83–101. (Lebenswelten im ländlichen Raum. Historische Erkundungen in Mittel- und Südbaden 3); Dorothee Neumaier, "Die Gemeinde Nordrach und das Lebensbornheim 'Schwarzwald'," *Die Ortenau. Zeitschrift des Historischen Vereins für Mittelbaden* 97 (2017): 341–70.

39  Dorothee Schmitz-Köster, *"Deutsche Mutter"*, 101–02.

Map 1: *Lebensborn* maternity and children's homes, established between 1936 and 1944. Not included are *Lebensborn* administrative buildings in Munich, apartments of *Lebensborn* staff used as cover addresses for mothers, and other *Lebensborn* properties such as one in Neulengbach, which *Lebensborn* rented to the *Wehrmacht* from 1938. © Esri

From 1941, in addition to existing and newly established facilities in the *Altreich* and *Heim Wienerwald*, *Lebensborn* offered women in the occupied territories of Western and Northern Europe places where they could give birth secretly and anonymously, and helped them to care for their children. The supposedly pure

"Germanic" genetic make-up of the Norwegian people made Norway a highly prized stomping ground for *Lebensborn* operations: in total, *Lebensborn* opened eleven homes in the region. The National Socialist authorities considered all children of German fathers and Norwegian mothers as German citizens, and some 200 children were taken to the *Altreich* for adoption.[40] *Lebensborn* also set up maternity and children's homes in Belgium, France, and Luxembourg.[41] Further maternity and children's homes were planned in the Netherlands, Denmark, and Poland, but were never opened.[42] (Map 1)

At the same time, *Lebensborn* became involved in the "germanization," i.e., the deportation of children from the *Warthegau*, Yugoslavia, Romania, and Czechoslovakia who displayed the desired "Aryan" qualities. The *Lebensborn* programme by the *SS* and the Third Reich's "illegitimacy" policies thus translated discrimination against unwed mothers not only into racial hygiene through the establishment of maternity homes, but also into child abduction. The first transports of children in the summer of 1942 were taken in at *Heim Hochland* and *Heim Pommern.*[43] *Schloss Oberweis* in Gmunden was then put to *Lebensborn* use: known as *Heim Alpenland*, it opened in September 1943 and took in deported children of school age. These children were to stay temporarily in *Lebensborn* facilities, "re-

40  Theresia Bauer, "Sonderfall Norwegen," in *Kinder für den "Führer"*, 145–51; Caroline Nilsen, "Romance, Marriage, and the Lebensborn Program: Gendering German Expectations and Reality in Occupied Norway," in *German-Occupied Europe in the Second World War*, edited by Raffael Scheck, Julia Torrie, and Fabian Théofilakis (London – New York: Routledge, 2019), 181–94; Kåre Olsen, *Vater: Deutscher. Das Schicksal der norwegischen Lebensbornkinder und ihrer Mütter von 1940 bis heute* (Frankfurt/Main: Campus, 2002); Kåre Olsen, "Under the care of Lebensborn: Norwegian War Children and their Mothers," in *Children of World War II: The Hidden Enemy Legacy*, edited by Kjersti Ericsson and Eva Simonsen (New York: Berg Publishers, 2005), 15–35; Sarah Rehberg, Die deutsche Besatzung in Norwegen und das Schicksal der "Kriegskinder," in *Born of War. Vom Krieg geboren. Europas verleugnete Kinder*, edited by Gisela Heidenreich (Berlin: Links, 2017), 173–90; Evi Weisssteiner, "Der 'Lebensborn' in Norwegen," unpublished dissertation, University of Innsbruck, 2001.

41  Schmitz-Köster, *"Deutsche Mutter"*, 103 and 283–84.

42  Ibid., 97; Monika Diederichs, "'Moffenkinder.' Kinder der Besatzung in den Niederlanden," *Historical Social Research / Historische Sozialforschung* 129 (2009) 34/4: 304–20.

43  Isabel Heinemann, "'Bis zum letzten Tropfen guten Blutes.' The Kidnapping of 'Racially Valuable' Children as Another Aspect of Nazi Racial Policy in the Occupied East," in *Genocide and Settler Society. Frontier Violence and Stolen Indigenous Children in Australian History*, edited by Dirk Moses (Oxford – New York: Berghahn, 2004), 244–66; Isabel Heinemann, "Fundament der Volksgemeinschaft. Familientrennungen und -gründungen in der nationalsozialistischen In- und Exklusionspolitik," in *Familientrennungen im nationalsozialistischen Krieg*, 57–80; here 69–78; Dorothee Schmitz-Köster, *Raubkind. Von der SS nach Deutschland verschleppt* (Freiburg im Breisgau: Herder, 2018). Ten children who were considered fit for "germanisation", together with seven others, were the only inhabitants of the village of Lidice who survived the SS massacre in June 1942 and were also sent to *Lebensborn*. Georg Lilienthal, "Medizin und Rassenpolitik. Der 'Lebensborn e.V.' der SS," in *Medizin im Dritten Reich*, edited by Johanna Bleker and Norbert Jachertz (Köln: Deutscher Ärzteverlag, 1993), 47–57, here 54.

educated," and then placed with German couples who would act as foster parents and raise them, thus contributing to the creation of the "master race."[44]

## III.    Statistics and Estimates: The *Heim Wienerwald* within *Lebensborn*

*Lebensborn* operated nine maternity homes and two children's homes in the *Altreich* and in annexed Austria between 1936 and 1945, where an estimated 8,000[45] to 11,000[46] children were born. Its maternity homes were intended to help prevent 100,000 of the estimated 600,000 to 800,000 abortions that were performed on German women each year.[47] According to Ebner, *Lebensborn* was a "military imperative" because "it cannot be irrelevant to Germany whether it has 600 regiments in thirty years or not."[48] *Lebensborn*, literally "spring of life," was to be a spring spurting legions of "Aryan" children. In reality, the number of children born in *Lebensborn* homes fell far short of the regime's expectations.

Within the network of *Lebensborn* maternity homes, the *Heim Wienerwald* was one of the largest in terms of the number of births. At the end of 1939 there were 49 beds available for mothers and 83 for children.[49] In 1942, as per *Lebensborn* statistics, the *Heim Wienerwald* had the largest share of births in all the homes, 234 out of a total of 950.[50] In 1943, *SS Hauptsturmführer* Hans Mackenrodt, one of four *Lebensborn* consultant doctors, emphasized in his quarterly review of the home reports that "the obstetric result [in the third quarter of 1942] is very satisfactory [...]: the *Heim Wienerwald* has done particularly well."[51] In the first quarter of 1943, too, the *Heim Wienerwald* shared

44  Ines Hopfer, *Geraubte Kindheit. Die gewaltsame Eindeutschung von polnischen Kindern in der NS-Zeit* (Wien – Köln – Weimar: Böhlau, 2010).

45  Lilienthal, *Der "Lebensborn e.V."*, 229.

46  Koop, *"Dem Führer ein Kind schenken." Die SS-Organisation Lebensborn e.V.* (Köln – Wien – Weimar: Böhlau, 2007), IX.

47  Speech by Himmler to *SS Gruppenführer*, 18 February 1937; *Ausbildungsbrief Nr. 3 des SS-Sanitätsamtes*, 31 May 1937, 44, both quoted in Lilienthal, *Der "Lebensborn e.V."*, 26 and 47.

48  *Referat vor den Ärzten des SS-Oberabschnitts Nord*, 22 March 1939, AA, 4.1.0/8209800, Ref. 82448193.

49  *Bettenzahl für Mütter und Kinder in den Heimen Hochland, Kurmark, Harz, Pommern, Friesland, Ostmark und Taunus*, 14 February 1940, AA, 4.1.0/8210400, Ref. 82449645 and AA, 4.1.0/8210500, Ref. 82449881. Target numbers and actual numbers of available beds varied over time. See, for example, *Belegszahlen der Lebensbornheime am 1. Februar 1942*, AA, 4.1.0/8210400, Ref. 82449649.

50  *Zahlen der Geburten in den Heimes des Lebensborn im Jahre 1942*, 22 July 1943, AA, 4.1.0/8210300, Ref. 82449209.

51  *Vierteljährliche Auswertung der Heimberichte für das 3te Quartal 1942*, 5 January 1943, AA, 4.1.0/8210300, Ref. 82449421. In the early days of *Lebensborn*, the medical care of the women

first place with the *Heim Pommern* for facilitating the highest number of births among *Lebensborn* maternity homes.[52]

According to the *Lebensborn* correspondence, Imogen H., born on 31 August 1943, was the thousandth child born in the *Heim Wienerwald*.[53] The 5,000th *Lebensborn* child of all the maternity homes was born on 17 September 1943.[54] Sollmann invited Ebner to one of the naming ceremonies at the *Heim Wiener-wald*, "not to celebrate the mother whose child by chance happened to be the thousandth, but to point out that Lebensborn needs to be honoured as the work of the Reichsführer-SS."[55]

Presuming that the information in this letter about the thousandth birth in the *Heim Wienerwald* is correct, it illustrates the fragmentary nature of records available today. In fact, a synopsis of all available sources shows that Imogen H. would have been only the 889th birth in this *Lebensborn* home. These sources include birth statistics from 1939 to 1941, quarterly reports, information on the number of residents at various times, the files at the registry office Pernitz II, which contain registrations made after the war, as well as an incomplete list stating the length of stay of women and children from 14 October 1938 to 2 March 1943, which was also part of the files of the registry office Pernitz II.[56] Thus, given

---

in the maternity homes was provided by paediatricians who had their practices near the homes. In addition, clinical reports were sent each month to Günter K.F. Schultze, Director of the University Gynaecological Clinic in Greifswald, for review. Later, three so-called consultant specialists were appointed for *Lebensborn*: Josef Becker, Director of the University Paediatric Clinic in Marburg, Wilhelm Pfannenstiel, Director of the Institute of Hygiene at the University Clinic in Marburg, and Hans Mackenrodt, Director of a private clinic in Berlin. As members of the SS, they worked on a purely voluntary basis and regularly inspected the homes, trained the nursing staff, and evaluated medical reports from the homes. Also see Lilienthal, "Medizin und Rassenpolitik," 51.

52  *Vierteljährliche Auswertung der Heimberichte für das 1. Quartal 1943*, 19 July 1943, AA, 4.1.0/ 8210300, Ref. 82449426.

53  Schwab to Sollmann, 2 September 1943, AA, 4.1.0/8210300, Ref. 82449577.

54  *Geburten in den Heimen des Lebensborn*, 7 October 1943, AA, 4.1.0/8210300, Ref. 82449210.

55  Excerpt from a letter from Sollmann to Brandt, 14 September 1943, quoted in *Lebens-bornheim "Wienerwald"*, 21 September 1943, AA, 4.1.0/8210100, Ref. 82448751. As both Ebner and his deputy Lang were prevented from attending the planned naming ceremony, the home's director Schwab was asked to hold the ceremony himself and "to give a speech highlighting the work of Lebensborn accordingly." Ebner to Schwab, 8 September 1943, AA, 4.1.0/8210300, Ref. 82449580.

56  *Vierteljährliche Auswertungen*, 1941 to 1943, AA, 4.1.0/8210300, Ref. 82449400, 82449408 and 82449413, as well as *Eingegangene Meldungen über Geburten in den Heimen des "Lebensborn" e.V.*, 21 August 1939 to 20 March 1941 (with gaps), AA, 4.1.0/8210300, Ref. 82449429–82449547; Statistics of *Lebensborn* admissions and births in the maternity homes, April 1939 to November 1941 (missing: Januar 1941), AA, 4.1.0/8210300, Ref. 82449212–82449387; *Aufstellung der in den "Lebensborn"-Heimen befindlichen Kinder nach dem Stande vom 1. Januar 1940*, AA, 4.1.0/8210400, Ref. 82449585–82449602; *Belegstärke der Heime nach Stand vom 28. 10. 1939*, AA, 4.1.0/8210400, Ref. 82449628; *Zusammenstellung der statistischen Arbeiten, 1. November 1941 bis 31. März 1942*, n.d. AA, 4.1.0/8210300, Ref. 82449167.

a constant birth rate between September 1943 and April 1945, a further 288 children were born in the home – in reality, the birth rate in the *Heim Wienerwald*, as in the other homes, rose steadily as the number of mothers admitted increased.[57] Adding up the numbers, more than 1,300 children are estimated to have been born in the *Heim Wienerwald* between the first registered birth of a child on 2 November 1938 and the last on 31 March 1945.[58] Günther Knotzinger came to the same conclusion on the basis of his research,[59] and Elisabeth Märker puts the figure even higher, claiming that at least 1,408 women gave birth in the home.[60] By way of comparison, there are birth registers for four institutions in Germany (within present borders) which give information on the number of women who gave birth in Lebensborn homes: *Heim Hochland* (1,409), *Heim Harz* (1,304), *Heim Friesland* (217), and *Heim Schwarzwald* (240). No exact figures are available for the following homes: *Heim Pommern,* located in present-day Poland, *Heim Kurmark,* and *Heim Taunus.*[61]

The number of women who gave birth in the *Heim Wienerwald* is smaller than the number of children born in the home. Eight twin births were recorded.[62] At least 72 women gave birth to two or more children at the home. Overall, it can be concluded from the available data that at least 1,114 women gave birth to one or more children in the *Heim Wienerwald.*

The available statistics compiled by *Lebensborn* officials before and during the Second World War are incomplete and sometimes contradictory. This also applies to data from the post-war years. Former *Lebensborn* employee Willy Ziesmer stated at the Nuremberg trials in 1947/48 that a total of about 18,000 children had been born in *Lebensborn* homes between 1936 and 1945, about 6,000 of them in Norway. He also stated that 250 children had been abducted from Eastern and South-Eastern Europe as part of the "germanization" programme, and that 200 children from Norway had been taken to the German Reich. In addition, Ziesmer stated that *Lebensborn* had cared of 14,900 widows of *SS* men and their 22,500 children and had supported 1,600 *SS* families with 9,600 children. As Georg Lilienthal has noted, the number of foreign children abducted and brought to the German Reich must have been much higher. In 1948, for example, the International Red Cross found 344 foreign children in the American zone

---

57 BIK database, *Lebensborn-Heim Wienerwald.*
58 Karl. S., 20/1945, registry office Pernitz II; list of residents, registry office Pernitz II.
59 Knotzinger, Das SS-Heim "Wienerwald", 35.
60 Märker, "Rassisch wertvoll", 393.
61 Schmitz-Köster, *"Deutsche Mutter",* 68.
62 Gertrud and Inge P., list of residents; Siegfried and Heide B., 28/1939 and 32/1939; Dieter and Heinz W., list of residents; Werner and Elke S., list of residents; Eike and Heidrun H., 127/1940 and 128/1940; Norbert and Herbert S., 164/1941 and 165/1941; Franz and Alfred L., 141/1944 and 142/1944; Ekkehard and Dietrich E., 190/1944 and 191/1944, registry office Pernitz II.

alone. At that time, the Red Cross expected to find even more children. The number of births in *Lebensborn* maternity homes, on the other hand, is likely to have been much lower than Ziesmer indicated. Another *Lebensborn* file suggests that between 1936 and the end of September 1943 a total of 5,047 children were born in the *Heime Friesland, Harz, Hochland, Kurmark, Pommern, Schwarzwald,* and *Wienerwald*, 1,004 of them in *Heim Wienerwald*.[63] According to Georg Lilienthal, it is unlikely that another 7,000 children were born before the end of war in May 1945.[64]

## IV. "There Is No Need for Her to Be Ashamed": Secrecy and Anonymity

Like Charlotte H., who became pregnant at the age of 20, Anna K. may have found herself in a difficult situation in 1939, when she was expecting a child from her 18-year-old partner.[65] Her son Heinz H., now 84, interprets his mother's situation then as an "emergency." It was "a disgrace for an unwed woman not even 17 years old to become pregnant."[66] For *Lebensborn*, Anna K.'s young age was no impediment to applying for one of their maternity homes. *Lebensborn* supported unwed expectant mothers, even if they were still minors, because, according to *Lebensborn*, there should be "no praise for a 17-year-old girl, but also no policy of burying one's head in the sand."[67] Overall, the average age of the unwed women who gave birth in the *Heim Wienerwald* was 24, but at least 196 women were under 21 at the time of birth.[68]

The centerpiece of *Lebensborn*'s activities was to provide pre- and postnatal care. For unwed mothers-to-be, its maternity facilities offered an alternative to giving birth at home or in hospital delivery and, by request, made sure that all of this was done in secret. According to the story passed down in the family, Anna

---

63 *Geburten in den Heimen des Lebensborn*, 7 October 1943, AA, 4.1.0/8210300, Ref. 82449210. See also a medical report according to which 2,368 women had given birth in the *Lebensborn* homes by 31 December 1940, of which twenty were twin births, *Ärztlicher Bericht*, n.d. (submitted 18 Juni 1941), AA, 4.1.0/8210500, Ref. 82449905–82449909; and a report on infant mortality in the *Lebensborn*, according to which 3,521 children were born to 3,487 women by 1 April 1942. 44 children were stillborn. *Bericht über die Säuglingssterblichkeit im Lebensborn*, 13 April 1942, 4.1.0/8210400, Ref. 82449733.
64 Lilienthal, *Der "Lebensborn e.V.",* 229–30.
65 Heinz K., 22/1939, registry office Pernitz II.
66 Heinz H., interviewed by Lukas Schretter, 113 minutes, 20 May 2020, 4, interview in the possession of BIK.
67 *Zum Besuch der Schwestern aus Tutzing am 13. Juni 1940 in Steinhöring*, n.d., AA, 4.1.0/ 8209800, Ref. 82448201.
68 BIK database, *Lebensborn-Heim Wienerwald*.

K., who worked as a stenographer and lived with her parents near Vienna, had revealed her pregnancy to an immediate superior with influential friends in the National Socialist party. He suggested that she gave birth in a *Lebensborn* home. At *Lebensborn*, according to her son, "there was no need for her to be ashamed."[69] Surviving *Lebensborn* statistics for the time period from 1 November 1941 to 31 March 1942 show that in this period 43.1 per cent of home admissions, or 155 cases, were made with a request of secrecy, usually by both the child's father and mother.[70]

Keeping Anna K.'s pregnancy and childbirth secret was only made possible by circumventing legal requirements. In the *Heim Wienerwald,* as in other *Lebensborn* maternity homes, there was a separate registry office so that the women did not have to report their whereabouts and the birth of their child to the registry office of their home town. If necessary, *Lebensborn* even provided the women with fake mailing addresses. When it was discovered that fake mailing addresses were being used, *Lebensborn* set up three additional registration offices in Berlin, Munich, and Vienna in 1939 to circumvent the women's obligation to register. According to Ebner, this was "necessary until the public comes round to the view, which is indispensable for population policy, that there is no stigma attached to illegitimate births."[71] Still, if a pregnant woman was absent from work for an extended period, it was inevitable that her employer would be informed. There was no blanket arrangement for secrecy measures in such cases. Ebner explained in 1943 that "at *Lebensborn,* we try to eliminate difficulties on a case-by-case basis."[72] In later years, women were even allowed to conceal their marital status, if *Lebensborn* deemed it necessary to provide them with a completely new identity for pregnancy and childbed.[73] After years of personally observing the development of the so-called "confidential cases" at *Lebensborn*, Himmler became convinced that the registry officials were the source of rumours about the cases that were supposed to be kept secret. He was prepared to make concessions only "if in general the violation of the confidential nature of illegitimate births was made punishable strictly in accordance with our criminal laws." He was thinking of "the death penalty, which of the death penalty, which would then actually have to be applied."[74]

---

69 BIK, Heinz H., 5.
70 *Zusammenstellung der statistischen Arbeiten, 1. November 1941 bis 31. März 1942*, n.d., AA, 4.1.0/8210300, Ref. 82449166. Also see Lilienthal, *Der "Lebensborn e.V.",* 80; Schmitz-Köster, *"Deutsche Mutter",* 208.
71 *Einrichtung besonderer Meldestellen für den Verein "Lebensborn",* 20 July 1939, AA, 4.1.0/ 8209800, Ref. 82448194–82448195.
72 Ebner to Röhre, 10 Juni 1943, AA, 4.1.0/8211000, Ref. 82451040.
73 Lilienthal, *Der "Lebensborn e.V.",* 82.
74 *Aktenvermerk,* 28 February 1944, Bundesarchiv Berlin-Lichterfelde (BA), NS19/3384. See also Schmitz-Köster, *"Deutsche Mutter",* 207.

It was not only women like Anna K. who wished to conceal their pregnancy and the birth of their child. This option was also available to the fathers of the children. The temporary concealment of the fathers' identity was ensured by the fact that the acknowledgement of paternity did not have to be reported immediately to the father's birth registry office and that the single mother was granted the right to refuse to testify about the child's father. The *Lebensborn* head office did not even inform the registry office and staff of its own maternity homes of the identity of the fathers.[75]

In Anna K.'s case, secrecy was requested only for the period of pregnancy and childbirth. Anna K. married the father of her son on 16 October 1939, shortly after he had been called up to the front.[76]

In 19 forces letters received from February 1942 to January 1943, Heinz H.'s father entreated his wife to remain faithful to him. He had heard from other soldiers that their wives were having affairs, and "all this reveals how little the woman at home appreciates [her husband's] enforced absence, his loneliness, the deprivations he has to bear, and his readiness to die."[77] He inquired about her and her son's well-being, for "the time I was allowed to spend with the sweet little rascal was all too short."[78] In his letters he shared his thoughts on whether he and his wife should have a second child upon his return from the war. "When this war is over and I can return to you, the first thing we will do is enjoy life and our home. Our Heinzi will not be in the way." If the future had "a princely salary in store for me, our youth should make it possible for us to have another child, who will then be supported by his big brother and us."[79] Even though separated temporarily by the war, couples continued to exchange their views on family planning. National Socialist population policy aimed to keep the birth rate of the "Aryan" population stable, and couples had to strike a balance in their family planning between individual hopes and desires, societal values and norms, population

---

75  Today, we know much less about the fathers than about the mothers. The documents about the children's fathers were kept by the *Lebensborn* head office in Munich and destroyed at the end of the war. Only a few documents have survived, such as acknowledgements of paternity. For more information, see Lilienthal, *Der "Lebensborn e. V."*, 84; Schmitz-Köster, *"Deutsche Mutter"*, 265–79; Dorothee Schmitz-Köster, *Unbrauchbare Väter. Über Muster-Männer, Seitenspringer und flüchtende Erzeuger im Lebensborn* (Göttingen: Wallstein, 2022).

76  Marriages sometimes also took place in the home, performed by the home's director in his capacity as registrar. According to a compilation of statistical data from November 1941 to March 1942, 351 births took place in all *Lebensborn* homes existing at the time. Of these, 59.2 per cent of the mothers were unwed. 15 marriages took place between the children's parents, of which one third took place before the birth and two thirds after the birth. Almost half of the marriages took place in the home. *Zusammenstellung der statistischen Arbeiten, 1. November 1941 bis 31. März 1942*, n.d. AA, 4.1.0/8210300, Ref. 82449167.

77  Private collections Heinz H., forces letter by Gottfried H. to Anna H., 8 January 1942, 3.

78  Ibid., 13 February 1942, 2–3.

79  Ibid., 18 November 1942, 4–5.

policy, and the demands of the war. Allowing families to fulfill their function as reproductive communities was one reason for granting furloughs.[80] Anna K. and her husband eventually decided not to have another child. Heinz H. believes that, as the war progressed, his parents felt that the age difference between him and a potential sibling would have been too great.[81]

## V. "Someone Like That Does Not Belong in Lebensborn": Admission and Rejection

In April 1938, a few months before the opening of the *Heim Wienerwald*, Ebner summarised the admission criteria for *Lebensborn* as follows: wives and brides of SS members were eligible. Other expectant mothers would only be admitted if they met the selection criteria of the SS. In particular, *Lebensborn* would accept women whose childbirth had to be kept secret for certain reasons. At any rate, paternity had to be properly established and acknowledged. Applicants would also have to provide proof of "congenital health" and "Aryan" descent.[82]

How did pregnant unweds find out about *Lebensborn* and the possibility of giving birth in one of its homes? There is little to be found in the interviews with children of women who were unwed at the time of conception and chose *Lebensborn* to give birth anonymously. Information about the application process does not seem to have been passed on within the families.[83] Sometimes personal contacts may have played a role – in the case of Anna K., according to the family story, it was her superior who put her in touch with *Lebensborn*, and in the case of Charlotte H., it was the connections of her godmother and the child's father.

Pamphlets informed single mothers that "the *Schutzstaffel* does not approach existing problems with theoretical discussions, but tries to solve visible difficulties p r a g m a t i c a l l y [emphasis in original]." *Lebensborn* would intervene

---

80 Katharina Piro, "Projekt 'Monika.' Kriegstrennung und Familienplanung – das Beispiel eines deutschen Ehepaares 1939–1941," in *Familientrennungen im nationalsozialistischen Krieg*, 119–46; Christian Packheiser, "Personal Relationships between harmony and alienation. Aspects of home leave during the Second World War," in *Private Life and Privacy in Nazi Germany*, 233–56.

81 BIK, Heinz H., interview, 34.

82 *Aufnahmekriterien*, Ebner to Irmgard L., 27 April 1938, AA, 4.1.0/8209800, Ref. 82448190.

83 Of the thirty-four interviews conducted between 2021 and 2023 with former *Lebensborn* children from the *Heim Wienerwald*, not one provided detailed information on why and how the mother applied for admission to *Lebensborn*. Some of the former *Lebensborn* children whose parents were married, such as Helmut P., point out that it was the father's SS membership that determined why the child was born in the *Heim Wienerwald*: "Yes, and because he was in the SS, of course I was born in the SS maternity home in Feichtenbach." BIK, Helmut P., interview conducted by Lukas Schretter, 25 June 2021, 3.

"wherever it is necessary to preserve valuable life for our people and to promote it to the best of its ability. For if today the state excludes people with hereditary diseases from procreation, t h e n   o n   t h e   o t h e r   h a n d   e v e r y   h e a l t h y   l i f e   o f   g o o d   b l o o d   t h a t   c o m e s   i n t o   t h e   w o r l d   m u s t   b e   p r o m o t e d   a n d   p r e s e r v e d   a t   a l l   c o s t s [emphasis in original]."[84] *Lebensborn* intended to spare pregnant women from prying eyes by offering them a safe refuge during the period of their visible pregnancy and a "respectable return" to mainstream society after the delivery, but it refrained from aggressively advertising itself on radio or in the print media.

Lack of personal means was not an obstacle to being admitted to *Lebensborn*. The services of *Lebensborn* were financed to a large extent by membership fees: *SS-Führer* were required to become members of *Lebensborn*, with contributions based on age, rank, marital status, and number of children. Donations were also made by associations, companies, party, and state offices. Sometimes real estate was also donated, and some of houses and plots of land on which the homes were established, as in the case of the *Heim Wienerwald*, were "aryanised." However, as mentioned above, the majority of *Lebensborn*'s funding was provided by the *NSV* until 1940, when it was taken over by the *Reichsfinanzministerium* (Reich Ministry of Finance).[85] Costs of the home stay covering bed and board for mother and child were defrayed by the fathers, who had to acknowledge their paternity and whose contributions were to exceed the legal minimum if possible.[86] In addition, the women had to agree to cede maternity benefits to *Lebensborn* as soon as they were able to make claims on their health insurance.[87] In late 1941 and early 1942, 40 per cent of the women taken in by *Lebensborn* were commercial employees; in 25.8 per cent of the cases, the father of the child was a full-time *SS* employee, in 25 per cent of the cases a member of the *Waffen-SS*. In 36 per cent of cases he was a member of the *Wehrmacht*. The average income of the mother-to-be was RM 132, that of the father-to-be RM 330.[88]

Unwed pregnant women usually applied for admission to *Lebensborn* at its Munich head office between the fourth and eighth month of pregnancy.[89] They had to provide the following documents to prove that they were "Aryan" and healthy: an *Ahnenpass* (proof of ancestry, pedigree) for "racial" suitability, which had to go back to 1800 or to their grandparents, and a congenital health questionnaire about genetic defects in the family. This was accompanied by a medical

---

84  *Lebensborn* brochure, n.d., AA, 4.1.0/8209700, Ref. 82448969.
85  Lilienthal, *Der "Lebensborn e.V."*, 124–30.
86  Ibid., 124.
87  Ibid.
88  *Zusammenstellung der statistischen Arbeiten, 1. November 1941 bis 31. März 1942*, n.d., AA, 4.1.0/8210300, Ref. 82449170.
89  Ibid., Ref. 82449166.

check-up form. In the early years of *Lebensborn* programme, this check-up was carried out by an *SS* doctor. During the war years, when the *SS* suffered from a shortage of doctors due to conscription for military service, the examination, including pelvic measurement,[90] could be carried out by any general practitioner accredited in the German Reich. Applications also included a questionnaire asking the women not only about their profession, health insurance, and party affiliation, but also about their intentions to marry the father of their children. Lastly, a handwritten curriculum vitae, a full body photograph of the applicant, and an affidavit stating that the man named by the woman was indeed the biological father of the child were required.[91]

The father-to-be had to submit analogous documents, otherwise the mother-to-be was denied admission to *Lebensborn*.[92] In 1941, *Lebensborn* considered whether and how it could gain access to the health certificates of the prospective fathers via the health authorities in order to check their suitability.[93] For example, Ortrud B.'s application from 1940 demonstrates that it was not only the physical suitability of the child's father that mattered, but also how his character was assessed. Ortrud B. herself met the *SS* selection criteria, but the father of the child, as *Lebensborn* found out, had been arrested for fraud and had deliberately concealed his married status from Ortrud B. In addition, he would have had a bad reputation. Therefore, she "could not possibly be admitted to a Lebensborn home."[94] However, *Lebensborn* intended to direct her to other places where she could give birth.[95]

Sources rarely mention women who were rejected. Those with familiy connections to Jews, with disabilities or genetic diseases, or with a connection to any other "undesirable" minority were not accepted.[96] Some files show Ebner himself weighing up whether an applicant was suitable for *Lebensborn:*

---

90  *Beckenmaße*, 14 February 1941, AA, 4.1.0/8211100, Ref. 82451193.
91  Lilienthal, *Der "Lebensborn e.V."*, 90–91.
92  Ibid., 91.
93  Viermetz to Ebner, *Erbringung der Gesundheitsnachweise durch die Kindsväter*, 13 May 1941, 4.1.0/8211100, Ref. 82451195.
94  Ebner to Becker, *Fräulein Ortrud B.*, 23 April 1940, AA, 4.1.0/8211100, Ref. 82451215.
95  Ibid. Similarly, in the case of Ilse F. the father, an *SS-Rottenführer*, did not pass muster with *Lebensborn*. He had made out to Ilse F. that he was single, when he was in fact married and had two children. In addition, he was currently in custody for theft. According to *Lebensborn*, he was feigning insanity to get off scot-free. *Heimaufnahme von Fräulein Ilse F.*, 8 August 1940, AA, 4.1.0/8211100, Ref. 82451216. See also AA, 4.1.0/8211100, Ref. 82451213.
96  According to Georg Lilienthal, the racial and congenital health screening of future parents was conducted first by *Lebensborn* staff, then by an *SS* doctor, and, finally, by the director of the home. According to Heinemann, this is correct as far as the congenital health screening is concerned, an issue within the discretion of a medical doctor; it is not correct for the racial screening, which was carried out until 1938 by *RuSHA* staff and reverted to them in 1941. Who was responsible in the period from 1938 to 1941 is in Isabel Heinemann's view one of the

In 1940, Johanna D., who had become pregnant by a police sergeant, applied for admission to keep the birth secret. The medical examination showed that her pelvis was narrow according to *Lebensborn* criteria, but otherwise she would have made a good impression. However, in view of possible complications – an aunt of hers had committed suicide – she was rejected.[97]

In March 1941, Maria L.'s application to give birth in one of the *Lebensborn* homes was rejected on the grounds that schizophrenia had apparently occurred among her close relatives and that there was a distinct possibility that it was congenital. In addition, Ebner noted that the expectant mother was not "Nordic," as she claimed in the questionnaire enclosed with the application, "but purely Mediterranean and looks Jewish. Someone like that does not belong in Lebensborn." Furthermore, the mother-to-be had stated that she wanted to keep her stay in the home as short as possible. Thus, Ebner suspected, "she would like to run away after three weeks and leave the child to us. On behalf of Lebensborn, I reject a mother who is so little committed to her motherly duties that she does not express the will to breastfeed her child properly from the outset."[98]

In June 1941, Melanie P. was rejected by *Lebensborn* because "among other deficiencies" she suffered from Graves' disease. "Experience has shown that such patients are always perceived as repulsive by other inmates because of their nervous nature. They are therefore not suitable for a Lebensborn home."[99]

In 1944, Emmi B. enquired why her application was turned down. Ebner replied that one of her sisters had a foot deformity and "under certain circumstances, hereditary defects in relatives may lead to a mother's rejection." However, Ebner wrote that this did not mean that the foot deformity would necessarily resurface in Emmi B.'s child. This was not to be expected, especially as the child's father was healthy. He concluded: "So you really do not need to worry about it."[100]

Admission regulations appear to have been more relaxed during the war, as the birth rate in the *Lebensborn* homes was not to drop under any circumstances.[101] This, and the fact that many women left the homes without their children, led to higher occupancy rates, which in turn led to a poorer state of health of the children.[102] However, the claim to raise a "master race" was not to be abandoned, especially after infant mortality in the homes had risen from April

---

topics for future research. Isabel Heinemann, *Rasse, Siedlung, deutsches Blut. Das Rasse- und Siedlungshauptamt der SS und die rassenpolitische Neuordnung Europas* (Göttingen: Wallstein, 2003), 107, Footnote 159.

97  *KM Johanna D.*, 4/5 December 1940, AA, 4.1.0/8211100, Ref. 82451222–82451223.
98  *Heimaufnahme KM Maria L.*, 8 March 1941, AA, 4.1.0/8211100, Ref. 82451229.
99  *Aufnahme der Frau Melanie P.*, 5 June 1941, AA 4.1.0/8211100, Ref. 82451235.
100  Ebner to Emmi B., 20 June 1944, AA, 4.1.0/8211100, Ref. 82451265.
101  Lilienthal, *Der "Lebensborn e.V."*, 91–95.
102  Ibid., 105–16.

1940, and appropriate measures were to be taken.[103] In May 1941, *Lebensborn* consultant paediatrician *SS-Sturmbannführer* Becker demanded not only hygienic and structural improvements, but also a strict selection of applicants. Ebner also announced that admission would be made more difficult in the first half of 1941, at a time when the Third Reich leadership expected the war to end soon.[104] Overcrowding in the maternity homes eventually led to the establishment of additional *Lebensborn* children's homes and maternity homes – although the establishment of the children's homes completely reversed the idea of children growing up in the care of their mothers.[105] In 1943, as more and more children born in the homes were left behind by their mothers, Ebner suggested that suitable nursing homes should be established to accommodate nursing mothers near maternity homes such as the *Heim Wienerwald*.[106] Yet, at the same time, Himmler defended the easing of admission restrictions on account of the possibility that the heavy toll of the war, which had already spread across the European continent, might cause a birth deficit that would undermine his racial plans. With Himmler's personal permission, also women from the conquered Eastern territories who were expecting a child from an *SS* member were allowed to give birth in a *Lebensborn* home.[107]

Overall, the conditions for admission remained in force until the very end. From 20 August 1944, the medical examination of a prospective mother had to be carried out in the home itself by the home's director, not least owing to the work overload of the general practitioners. *Lebensborn* continued to reject supposedly "purely Mediterranean, purely Eastern, and purely Baltic women" as failing to meet the *SS* criteria. However, if "dark racial influences (Eastern, Mediterranean, Dinaric) were found in racially good-looking mothers," the pregnant woman could still be admitted. The minimum height for women was 155 centimeters, but height "need not be decisive for any rejection, especially in cases of strict secrecy or in cases where it is a matter of a wished-for child." In any case, "on medical grounds, women with serious physical deformities or mental defects, repulsive skin rashes, pulmonary tuberculosis, and venereal diseases" should be rejected. Any such rejection must "of course be carried out with great delicacy; the mother

---

103  By the end of 1939, the infant mortality rate in the homes was 3 per cent according to *Lebensborn*, in mid-1940 it was 4.7 per cent and one year later it was 4.23 per cent. In the German Reich, on the other hand, the rate was 6 per cent. It is doubtful whether these figures are correct. After the war, a statistician who had worked for Himmler stated that, according to his calculations, the infant mortality rate in the homes was eight per cent – two per cent higher than in the Reich. Schmitz-Köster, *"Deutsche Mutter"*, 358.

104  Ebner to Himmler, 21 July 1941, AA, 4.1.0/8210000, Ref. 82448654.

105  Lilienthal, *Der "Lebensborn e.V."*, 107–09.

106  *Unterbringung der Lebensborn-Mütter*, 6 September 1943, AA, 4.1.0/8209200, Ref. 82448991.

107  Lilienthal, *Der "Lebensborn e.V."*, 93.

in question is to be handed over to the nearest NSV office."[108] If women did not meet the required criteria, they were not accepted by *Lebensborn*; evidence of this can be found not only in the cases of rejected applicants but also in the racist assessments of the mothers and their children during their stay in the home, and in the children who were born disabled and in few cases sent to the Nazi child "euthanasia" programme, where they were poisoned or starved to death.[109]

The expectations of male and female "Aryan" sexual bodies in the Third Reich were clear, just as were the National Socialist attitudes towards gender and gender roles in line with their ideological and racist ambitions. *Lebensborn* did not accept at any time married "Aryan" women who had become pregnant outside marriage, as this could have had to be contrued as *Lebensborn* approving of female infidelity.[110] The opposite case, the admission of a single woman who had become pregnant by a married man, should not pose a problem.[111] In late 1939, after the war had begun, Himmler even called on SS men to have children outside marriage before going to the front, promising that the party and *Lebensborn* would then take care of mother and child if necessary.[112] When parts of the *Wehrmacht* leadership read this as a call for SS men to cuckold married German men, Himmler had to issue a clarification in 1940.[113] When two women gave birth at the same time in a *Lebensborn* home, citing the same father, *Lebensborn* criticised the father of the child for poor planning.[114] In January 1941, Sollmann ordered staff to check with all applicants whether another woman who was expecting a child fathered by the same man had already been placed in the *Lebensborn* home. If so, the newcomer was to be placed in another home. In cases of gross negligence, the *Lebensborn* staff member in question was dismissed without notice. The order was promted by a case from the *Heim Kurmark*, where *Lebensborn* had actually been at risk of concurrently housing two women who had become pregnant by the same man. Only at the last minute was one of them transferred to *Heim Pommern*.[115]

---

108 *Ärztliche Anordnung Nr. 104*, 20 August 1944, AA, 4.1.0/8209600, Ref. 82447827–82447828.
109 For more information, see Sabine Nachbaur's article in this volume.
110 More general, see Birthe Kundrus, "'Die Unmoral deutscher Soldatenfrauen.' Diskurs, Alltagsverhalten und Ahndungspraxis 1939–1945," in *Zwischen Karriere und Verfolgung*, edited by Heinsohn, Vogel, and Weckel, 96–110.
111 Schmitz-Köster, *"Deutsche Mutter"*, 191; Lilienthal, *Der "Lebensborn e.V."*, 149.
112 *SS-Befehl für die gesamte SS und Polizei*, 28 October 1939, Vienna Provincial Police Directorate (LPD), Offical Libaray, box 1939/2, folder "Miscellaneous 1939" and BA, NS 2/276. Quoted in Bastian Hein, *Die SS. Geschichte und Verbrechen* (München: Beck, 2015), 57–58;
113 *An alle SS-Männer und ihre Angehörigen. Ausführungsbestimmungen zum Befehl des Reichsführers SS vom 28.10.1939*, 19 June 1940; BA, NS 2/276.
114 Schmitz-Köster, *"Deutsche Mutter"*, 191.
115 *Anordnung*, 15 January 1941, AA, 4.1.0/8211100, Ref. 82451191.

## VI.    "She Was Allowed to Work There, Earn Money, and I Was Well Looked After": Institutional Protection and Economic Security

In 1942, Maria B., born in 1923, a secretary with the police in Vienna, got pregnant by her superior Helmut S., *Hauptmann* of the *Schutzpolizei* at the police headquarters at Schottenring. Helmut S. was married and had two children with his wife. His wife was pregnant with their third child when Maria B. learned of her own pregnancy. Helmut S. then arranged for his pregnant secretary to be admitted to the *Heim Wienerwald*. After the birth of their daughter Helga in May 1943, it would have been impossible for Maria B. to return to her former workplace, and it would have been difficult for her to find a new job and care for her daughter at the same time.[116]

*Lebensborn*'s activities were not limited to providing unwed mothers like Maria B. with a carefree and, if they wished, secret childbirth. It also provided institutional protection and economic security. If a woman wished to keep her child and the child's father secret after giving birth, but had to terminate her sojourn in order to work and care for her child and herself, to complete education, or to settle her family situation, she could leave her child in the *Lebensborn* home for one year.[117] Moreover, a legal guardian had to be appointed for "illegitimate" children. Thus, after 1938, when the new statutes were passed, *Lebensborn* accepted guardianship of newborn children, and required unwed mothers to apply for guardianships before giving birth. However, this was on condition that they met the racist selection criteria.[118] Youth welfare offices were banned from assessing the children's living conditions, and in 1942 *Lebensborn* succeeded in removing children completely from the control of the youth welfare offices.[119] *Lebensborn* also made sure that the fathers fulfilled their legal obligation to pay child support. To support the so-called "nobility of the future,"[120] *Lebensborn* set up ward savings accounts and provided financial and material support for mothers and children.[121]

Furthermore, *Lebensborn* intended to monitor and control the children's further development. In 1939, Himmler complained that there were no statistics on the physical condition of the children after they left the maternity homes. He suggested that *SS* doctors weigh each child on the day before their birthday until

---

116 Helga B., 121/1943, registry office Pernitz II.
117 Lilienthal, *Der "Lebensborn e.V."*, 69.
118 Ibid., 70–76.
119 Ibid., 86–89.
120 *Lebensborn e.V. in München*, brochure, Miesbach, 5. Provincial Archives of Lower Austria (NÖLA), Office of the Lower Austrian Provincial Government, Provincial Office I/2, number 33/1975.
121 Ibid., 8.

they were 20 or 21 years of age. The children were to "receive RM 1 or something along those lines from the *Lebensborn* association on his or her birthday."[122] With this ploy, it should be possible to obtain statistical data. The proposal was postponed until after the end of the war, probably because of the organisational and financial effort involved.[123]

In principle, *Lebensborn* wanted the children born in the maternity homes to grow up in the family environment of their biological mothers. Plans of handing over those children who were left behind in the maternity homes and could not be cared for by their own mothers to SS families were not pursued any further.[124] Only when it was impossible for a mother to raise her child did *Lebensborn* take the children into its children's homes or place them in the care of foster families or, in rare cases and only with *Lebensborn*'s explicit consent, of adoptive parents.[125] For the *Heim Wienerwald* this was recorded in 44 cases, i. e. 3.7 per cent of the children born in the home – compared to a total of twenty-five to thirty adoptions of children up to 1940, and 260 adoption proceedings initiated in the post-war period, according to the testimony of former *Lebensborn* staff.[126] According to Himmler, offering a child for adoption would "give succour to frivolous girls who quickly rid themselves of their child in this way; on the other hand, the possibility of adoption may save marriages that are in danger of breaking up after a certain time because of the infertility of one or the other partner." The fact that "a child then comes into the marriage puts an end to searching for a way out, either in the direction of a divorce or in the direction that the infertile part in question generously allows the other to have children with other healthy partners, with the proviso that the marriage remains upright."[127]

*Lebensborn* offered work placements so that unwed women could find suitable work after giving birth. By 1939, 52.9 per cent of unwed women had taken up the offer and the majority were actually able to find work. The *Lebensborn* head office made sure that the workplaces were not too far away from the homes so that the mother could see the child regularly.[128]

To Maria B. and others who depended on it, the association even offered a job in *Lebensborn* so that they could provide for their children. Hiring women who had given birth in *Lebensborn* homes began in 1938, when the expansion of

---

122 *Vorschlag zum Messen und Wiegen von Lebensborn-Kindern*, 12 December 1939, AA, 4.1.0/ 8209900, Ref. 82448318.

123 Ibid., 18 March 1940 and 20 March 1940, AA, 4.1.0/8209900, Ref. 82448318.

124 Lilienthal, Der *"Lebensborn e.V."*, 75.

125 Schmitz-Köster, *"Deutsche Mutter"*, 54, 203, and 357.

126 Lilienthal, Der *"Lebensborn e.V."*, 77–78.

127 *Reichsführer-SS Heinrich Himmler an Sollmann*, 3 April 1942, AA, 4.1.0/8209900, Ref. 82448359.

128 Lilienthal, Der *"Lebensborn e.V."*, 69.

*Lebensborn* increased the need for additional skilled workers.[129] An order to home directors, dated 30 August 1939, specified:

> "In recruitment, our own mothers are to be taken into consideration as far as possible. Before they first report for duty, they are to acknowledge and at the same time to be instructed in detail that, as employees of the "Lebensborn e.V.", they have no rights as mothers but must fulfill their duties and comply with the orders issued. In particular, they are to be informed that they may only look after their own children in their free time. Under no circumstances can they be allowed to favour their own child in any way. This behaviour is against the spirit of the home community and will inevitably result in dismissal."[130]

Helga S., the daughter of Maria B., assesses the fact that her mother gave birth and got a job at the *Heim Wienerwald* as follows: "It was a great relief for my mother that she was allowed to work there, earn money, and I was well looked after. [...] I was cared for by the nurses and grew up in a very sheltered and happy environment."[131] The *Heim Wienerwald*, where she lived with her mother until the end of the war, offered her mother the possibility of anonymous childbirth, and, in her opinion, the children living there had "many opportunities to be outside, romp around, go for walks, and celebrate festivities,"[132] in other words, to enjoy a carefree early childhood.

There are considerable differences in the way former *Lebensborn* children process the fact that they were born in of the association's maternity homes. While some former *Lebensborn* children, such as Helga S., state that the racial-ideological background of *Lebensborn* was of little significance but emphasize the support their unwed mothers received from *Lebensborn*, others state that their (single) mothers had chosen this place for childbirth solely for practical reasons, for example because it was close to their hometown. For others, the feeling that "something was wrong" accompanied them from an early age and throughout their adult lives. Confronting the fact that they were born in a *Lebensborn* home has been part of their own historical family research and individual coming to terms with their parents' past.[133] In the case of Helga S., her father, Helmut S., enlisted for the front a few weeks before she was born. Helga S. says that in the letters he wrote to her mother, he urged her to give the child to

---

129 Ibid.
130 *Allgemeine Anordnung, Nr. 147*, 30 August 1939, AA, 4.1.0/8210500, Ref. 82449989.
131 Helga S., interviewed by Lukas Schretter, 50 minutes, 5 June 2020, 3, interview in the possession of BIK.
132 Ibid.
133 Dorothee Schmitz-Köster, "A Topic for Life: Children of German Lebensborn Homes," in *Children of World War II*, 213–28; Schmitz-Köster, *"Deutsche Mutter"*, 258–64 and 311–50; Tatjana Neef, "Lebensborn-Kinder – die schmerzhafte Suche nach der eigenen Identität," in *Kinder für den "Führer"*, 195–208; Lilienthal, *Der "Lebensborn e.V."*, 231–62

foster parents. He also complained about the costs he had to bear for the delivery of the child in the *Lebensborn* home. The birth of his legitimate son, who had been born in a hospital home six months before Helga S. was born, would have been considerably cheaper.[134] In March 1944, the *Auskunftsstelle für Krie-gerverluste der Waffen-SS* reported that Helmut S. had "died a hero's death in Russia on 30 December 1943."[135] In 1945, just before the end of the war, when Helga S. was almost two years old, the employees, mothers, and children in *Heim Wienerwald* were transferred to *Heim Hochland* in Steinhöring in anticipation of the advance of Soviet forces. According to the family account, Maria B. fled alone with Helga S. and was sick when they arrived in Steinhöring on 13 April 1945.[136] When U.S. troops arrived in Steinhöring, 18 of the 162 children found and registered there had been born in the *Heim Wienerwald*; Helga S. was probably one of them.[137]

## VII. "It Would Therefore Be a Great Comfort for Me to Know That My Wife Is in Good Care:" Married Women in *Lebensborn*

On 16 February 1941, the assistant physician *SS-Untersturmbannführer* Gerhard W. approached Norbert Schwab, the head of the *Heim Wienerwald* from 1941 to 1944, and asked for his wife to be admitted:

"My wife, who lives at home in G., is due to give birth around 12 June. When I enlisted at the beginning of the war a representative of the KVD [Kassenärztliche Vereinigung Deutschland] had been installed [in my district], but he left on 1 January 41 and since then there has been no doctor here, only his very unimpressive midwife. However, since my wife is a forty-year-old nulliparous woman, complications during childbirth, which would make medical intervention seem necessary, cannot be ruled out, despite her good pelvic measurements and the fact that the pregnancy has so far been completely free of complications, and my wife is fully aware of this. However, it is doubtful whether I can get leave when my wife gives birth, as I am currently again with a field troop and can be deployed at any time. It would therefore be a great comfort to me to know that my wife is in good care and in an environment permeated by our spirit, especially during this time. As we cannot get a maid at home with the current shortage of labour, I would like to send my wife to you as early as the beginning of June and leave her with you until mother and child are fully fit to travel. I would therefore ask you to advise me about the conditions of

---

134  BIK, Helga S., 11.

135  *Auskunftsstelle für Kriegerverluste der Waffen-SS*, 18 March 1944, BA, VBS 1069 (R19).

136  BIK, Helga S., 12–13.

137  Rudolf Oswald, *Den Opfern verpflichtet. Katholische Jugendfürsorge, Caritas und die SS-Organisation "Lebensborn" nach 1945* (München: Sankt Michaelsbund, 2020), 53. See also list of all children present when the U.S. troops arrived in Steinhöring, AA, 4.1.2/81796213, Ref. 8321126.

admission, the fee, and other things to be taken into consideration, such as the time of registration, items and linen to be brought along and the like. I would appreciate it very much if you could also send me pictures of the home and the surrounding area."[138]

SS wives were not peripheral to the organization conceived as entirely male, but rather SS couples were understood as the cell of elite "Aryan" society. Thus, in addition to unwed women, wives of members of the SS and the German police were admitted to *Lebensborn* to give birth to their children. Admission criteria were easier for married women like Gerhard W.'s wife. When Ebner learned of this case, he informed the *Lebensborn* admissions department that he had no objection to the admission of Gerhard W.'s wife, although complications might occur during childbirth.[139]

The documents that unwed parents normally had to submit for a *Lebensborn* application were not needed if the father of the child was an SS member, such as Gerhard W., and a marriage permit had already been issued by the *RuSHA*. Well before the war, SS members were constantly exhorted to choose their wives on the basis of "racial" and biological health, following Himmler's 1931 *Heiratsbefehl* (marriage decree), and to produce children for the Fatherland. Thus, in order for the *RuSHA* to give consent to an SS marriage, the couple would have already undergone a comprehensive screening, including an assessment of their fertility.[140] However, to be admitted to *Lebensborn*, women who were married to SS men or members of the police were not entirely exempt from a medical check-up either.[141] When, from August 1944, the home directors themselves had to fill in the health forms, the *Lebensborn* head office stated that "in the admission of married women of members of the SS and the police [...] it is possible to proceed generously with regard to racial and health assessment."[142]

Internal *Lebensborn* regulations instructed staff "to refrain from rejecting those [applicants] in possession of an engagement and marriage permit from the Rasse- und Siedlungshauptamt-SS in Berlin, since Lebensborn cannot be seen to be more particular than the Rasse- und Siedlungshauptamt-SS itself."[143] In a few cases where there were objections because of hereditary diseases, *Lebensborn* took in the pregnant wives of SS men, not least because it did not have to assume

---

138 Gerhard W. to Norbert Schwab, 14 February 1941, AA, 4.1.0/8213000, Ref. 82458574.
139 Gregor Ebner to *Lebensborn* Home Admission Department, 26 February 1941, AA, 4.1.0/ 8213000, Ref. 82458575.
140 Gudrun Schwarz, *Eine Frau an seiner Seite. Ehefrauen in der "SS-Sippengemeinschaft"* (Hamburg: Hamburger Edition, 1997), 27–28.
141 See, for example, *Ehefrau des SS-Mannes Walter R.*, 30 November 1940, AA, 4.1.0/8211100, Ref. 82451217–8.
142 *Ärztliche Anordnung 104*, 20 August 1944, AA, 4.1.0/8209600, Ref. 82447827.
143 *Heimaufnahme der Ehefrau des SS-Scharführers Johann d. W.*, 12 December 1940, AA, 4.1.0/ 8211100, Ref. 82451224.

guardianship of the children of married couples. This led, for example, to the wife of SS *Scharführer* Johann d. W. being admitted to one of *Lebensborn*'s maternity homes, even though "the child's father showed a most severe impairment, so that damage to his genetic make-up may be assumed."[144]

Whereas single women were admitted to *Lebensborn* as early as the seventh month of their pregnancy or even earlier if they wished to conceal their pregnancy, and stayed for a longer period, married women usually came to *Lebensborn* shortly before giving birth and only stayed for postnatal care.[145] Married women did not have to keep their pregnancy a secret and used *Lebensborn* primarily to give birth in a protected environment. On average, married women stayed in the *Heim Wienerwald* for 48 days, compared to 95 days for unwed women.[146] *Lebensborn* sought to ensure that married women did not stay in the home any longer than necessary. A case in point was the sister-in-law of the home's director, a married woman who wished to stay in the home for a few more months after the birth to her son in November 1939, on account of the great housing shortage. Ebner only allowed her to stay until the end of the year.[147]

| | Average Number of Births per Month and Home | | | | | |
|---|---|---|---|---|---|---|
| | Hochland | Friesland | Schwarwald | Harz | Wienerwald | Total |
| 1939 | 11 | 7,1 | 8,1 | 9,3 | 5,9 | 63,6 |
| 1940 | 15,7 | 9,6 | 9,1 | 9 | 14,25 | 86,4 |
| 1941 | 12,9 | - | - | 12 | 12,6 | 74,2 (1 Jan 1941– 1 Apr 1942) |
| 1942 | 14,4 | - | - | 12 | 14 | 79,2 |

---

144 *Heimaufnahme*, AA, 4.1.0/8211100, Ref. 82451225. See also *Heimaufnahme Frau Elfriede L.*, 7 May 1941, AA, 4.1.0/8211100, Ref. 82451232; *Aufnahme der Frau Erika P.*, 30 May 1941, AA, 4.1.0/8211100, Ref. 82451233. By contrast, Ingeborg B., who had planned to arrive at the *Heim Harz* in January 1944, was rejected because she had had three miscarriages and would have needed special care. Ebner recommended a hospital instead of a *Lebensborn* home, as the *Lebensborn* homes did not have the appropriate staff. Ebner to the *Lebensborn* Home Admissions Department, 9 August 1943, AA, 4.1.0/8211100, Ref. 82451241.

145 Lilienthal, *Der "Lebensborn e.V."*, 65.

146 BIK database, *Lebensborn-Heim Wienerwald*. In the winter and spring of 1941–1942, according to a statistic of *Lebensborn* for all maternity homes, married women on average remained in the home for 45.7 days after giving birth (age of the child: 27.1 days), unwed women for 77.5 days (age of the child: fourty-four days). When child and mother were discharged separately, the average stay of "illegitimate" children lasted almost ten months. *Zusammenstellung der statistischen Arbeiten, 1. November 1941 bis 31. März 1942*, n.d., AA, 4.1.0/8210300, Ref. 82449166. By comparison, single women stayed in the Pomeranian home for 100 days in 1938 and married women for sixty-four days; in 1942, single women stayed for eighty-one days and married women for fourty-one days. Schmitz-Köster, *"Deutsche Mutter"*, 359, footnote 50, and 372, footnote 55.

147 *Heimaufenthalt Frau Helene v. H.*, 24 November 1939, 2 December 1939, and 6 December 1939, AA, 4.1.0/8211100, Ref. 82451295–82451297.

*(Continued)*

| | Average Number of Births per Month and Home | | | | | |
|---|---|---|---|---|---|---|
| | Hochland | Friesland | Schwarwald | Harz | Wienerwald | Total |
| 1943 | 16 | - | - | 13,1 | 14,25 | 87,2 (1 Apr 1942–30 Sept 1943) |
| 1944 | 18 | - | - | 14,2 | 16,7 | - |
| 1945 | - | - | - | 15,2 | 3,1 | - |

The data on the average number of births in *Heim Hochland, Friesland, Schwarzwald* and *Harz* are taken from Schmitz-Köster, *"Deutsche Mutter"*, 359. The data on the average number of births in all *Lebensborn* homes are taken from Lilienthal, *Der "Lebensborn e.V."*, 112, based on an analysis of *Lebensborn* statistics. The data on the average number of births in the *Heim Wienerwald* are taken from the BIK database *Lebensborn Heim Wienerwald*. They are based solely on the files of the registry office Pernitz II, which contain registrations made after the war, and on an incomplete list of the length of stay of women and children from 14 October 1938 to 2 March 1943, which was also part of the files of the registry office Pernitz II.

During the war, mothers' sojourns at the home were shortened, not least due to overcrowding, and the frequency of births increased.[148] As a rule, however, according to a 1939 decree for *Lebensborn* maternity homes, the length of stay usually depended on the mother's state of health and on the duration of breastfeeding. Married mothers were discharged 14 days after the birth of the child, if this was advisable in the medical opinion of the home's director. It did not seem reasonable to allow these mothers to extend their stay, given that room was always needed for newly admitted pregnant women. By contrast, unwed mothers were to be discharged from the home six to eight weeks after the birth of their child, provided that they breastfed during that period. If a mother was still exclusively breast-feeding after eight weeks and intended to leave the home without her child, she should not suddenly wean the child "because her time is up."[149] Rather, she should be given the opportunity to continue breastfeeding by prolonging her stay. Mothers who had little milk after six to eight weeks and whose infants were fed mainly on formula could, provided the infants were not weaklings "for whom every drop of breast milk is precious, wean their children after the specified time"[150] and be discharged. As the war progressed, attention was paid ensuring that the length of the children's stay did not become excessive:

---

148 In 1940, according to a report on child mortality, there were two to three times as many children in the *Lebensborn* homes at the same time as originally planned; in the *Heim Wienerwald* this number was sixty-five children. *Kindersterblichkeit in den Lebensborn-Heimen*, 17 May 1940, AA, 4.1.0/8210400, Ref. 82449711. Lilienthal, *Der "Lebensborn e.V."*, 114.

149 *Anordnung*, 23 August 1939, AA, 4.1.0/82111100, Ref. 82451271.

150 Ibid. For the importance the *Lebensborn* attached to breastfeeding, also see also see the article of Barbara Stelzl-Marx in this volume.

on 5 September 1942, Schwab wrote to Ebner that "our home is now fully occupied. I would therefore ask you to urgently arrange for the further discharge of
children over half a year."[151]

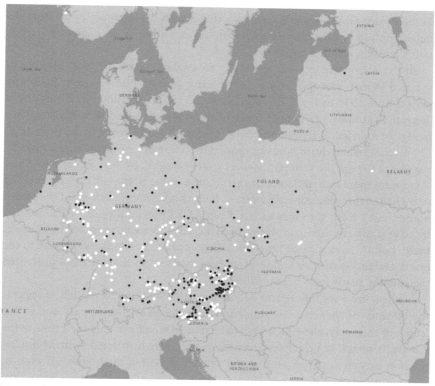

Map 2: The map shows the places of residence of those mothers for whom information was
recorded in the registry office Pernitz II. The places of residence were not always the places where
they were born or grew up, but the places where they lived temporarily during the war. The
information comes from both files created during and after the end of the war. Black dots
indicate the place of residence of married women who gave birth to a child in the *Heim Wienerwald*, white dots indicate the place of residence of unwed women. © Esri

To a certain extent, the differences between married and unwed women also
made themselves felt with regard to where they respectively came from. The
*Lebensborn* homes were not supposed to become maternity wards for women
from immediate vicinity;[152] Gerhard W.'s wife came from about 100 kilometers

---

151 Schwab to Ebner, referring to *Ärztliche Anordnung Nr. 72*, 5 September 1942, AA, 4.1.0/
    8211100, Ref. 82451306.
152 As a rule, admission to a *Lebensborn* home of a married woman whose husband was neither a
    member of the SS nor of the German police and who applied because of the proximity of the

away. In actual fact, in the *Heim Wienerwald* the married women more often came from close vicinity, while unwed women more often would travel hundreds of kilometres to give birth at this *Lebensborn* facility – to ensure secrecy, *Lebensborn* did not always place the unwed mothers in the maternity home closest to their place of residence. (Map 2) A a rule, staff did not usually come from the neighbourhood of the home either, with the exception of the student nurses as well as the kitchen and house staff.[153]

At the *Heim Wienerwald*, according to available data, the total number of married women was approximately the same as that of unweds over the entire period from 1938 to 1945. This corresponded to the situation in *Lebensborn* in general. In January 1939, Ebner spoke of about half of the mothers in *Lebensborn* being not married.[154] He reiterated these figures 1943.[155] While in the early years of *Lebensborn* and during the war more unwed women used its services, towards the end of the war the situation seems to have changed. In 1944, Ebner noted that there were more married than unwed women in the homes. It is likely that the wives had become increasingly aware of the advantageous location of *Lebensborn* homes, away from the cities at risk from Allied bombing raids.[156] The women listed as unwed in the *Heim Wienerwald* include those who married the father of their child there or a short time later. They also include those who came to the home as fiancées of their children's fathers, whose deaths at the front prevented the couples' plans from being realised.[157]

While there were differences between married and unwed women as regards the distance of their normal residence from the *Heim Wienerwald* and in the length of their stay, all women were to be treated equally during their time in the maternity home. In principle, *Lebensborn* staff were instructed to make no distinction between married and unwed women.[158] Within the homes, all women, whether married or not, were addressed as *Frau* (Mrs.) and by their first name. This form of address was also to be used by the women among themselves, not

---

home to her place of residence, was to be refused. In 1940, Ebner, referring to the application from a man from the vicinity of the *Heim Hochland* he ran, stated that he had always refused to admit women from the immediate vicinity of the home because otherwise the home would be overrun by women in that category. *Heimaufnahme*, AA, 4.1.0/8211100, Ref. 82451227.

153 For more information see the article of Nadjeschda Stoffers and Lukas Schretter in this volume.

154 *Zwei Jahre Lebensborn-Arbeit*, Speech by Gregor Ebner on the occasion of an *SS Gruppenführer* meeting, 25 Januar 1939, quoted in Lilienthal, *Der "Lebensborn e.V."*, 63.

155 Ebner to Rudolf Müller, 13 July 1943, AA, 4.1.0/9210200, Ref. 82448953.

156 Lilienthal, *Der "Lebensborn e.V."*, 63 and 71.

157 In at least forty-three cases, the fathers of the children born in the *Heim Wienerwald* died at the front or of natural causes. Of these, twenty-five were married to the mothers of the children, in five cases they were not married, and in thirteen cases this is not known. BIK database, *Lebensborn-Heim Wienerwald*.

158 Lilienthal, *Der "Lebensborn e.V."*, 63; Schmitz-Köster, *"Deutsche Mutter"*, 61 and 176.

least in order to fulfill the ideal that all women should be treated with respect and without distinction. The equal treatment of unwed and married mothers also harboured conflict material: SS members complained that their wives, who felt they belonged to an elite, were treated the same way as unwed mothers, and perceived this as demeaning. In the early years of the *Lebensborn* programme in particular, married women seem to have hesitated to apply for *Lebensborn* "because they were equated with unwed mothers. The prevailing opinion about Lebensborn e.V. was that this organisation was somewhat dark and mysterious." There were fears that "it did not make a good impression on the women if the brochures always talked about the secrecy of giving birth."[159] In 1938, several *SS-Unterführer* therefore even resigned their membership from *Lebensborn*.[160] Ebner countered that the homes welcomed "valuable unwed mothers" and that the "wives of SS leaders are welcome at any time if they are willing to adapt to the milieu of the home."[161]

## VIII.  "Predominantly Eastern With All the Associated Mental Characteristics": Assessment of Mother and Child

Franziska L., born in 1919 in Z. in Austria, unwed, gave birth to her daughter Hildegard on 17 March 1940 in the *Heim Wienerwald*. The father of the child, Richard R., born in 1914 in Vienna, was a machine fitter by profession.[162]

Like all women and newborns in the home, Franziska L. and her daughter were closely monitored by the home's doctor and the head nurse.[163] Without the child's mother being aware of this, they entered their subjective assessment into the *Reichsführer SS-Fragebogen* and sent it to the *Lebensborn* head office in Munich. In addition to the mother's personal details, the questionnaire contained information about her "racial appearance" and her behaviour in the home and towards the child. Furthermore, the director and the head nurse passed judgement on whether the mother's racial, ideological, and character traits corresponded to the SS selection criteria and whether she "desired more children

---

159 *Aktenvermerk*, 30 August 1938, AA, 4.1.0/8210200, Ref. 82448910 and BA, NS 48/29. For more information on myths on rumors about *Lebensborn* before and after the end of the war, see the editorial by Lukas Schretter and Barbara Stelzl-Marx in this volume.
160 *Austritt aus dem Lebensborn e.V.*, 3 October 1938, AA, 4.1.0/8210100, Ref. 82448799–82448801.
161 *Aktenvermerk*, 30 August 1938, AA, 4.1.0/8210200, Ref. 82448910.
162 Hildegard L., birth certificate, 89/140, registry office Pernitz II.
163 For more information, see the article of Nadjeschda Stoffers and Lukas Schretter in this volume.

in accordance with the SS selection principle."[164] Other criteria were her qualities as a housewife, her "behaviour during pregnancy and birth"[165] and her willingness and ability to breastfeed her child.[166] No information about the father can be found in this draft questionnaire kept at the registry office Pernitz II. At the *Lebensborn* head office, the submitted document was supplemented with some information about the child's father and the child, checked, and given a final racial score.[167] Marked "confidential," the questionnaire was intended for Himmler personally. From January 1941, the assigned grades to the individuals profiled by the questionnaires were: "I = completely in accordance with the SS selection, II = good average, III = no longer in accordance with the selection."[168] A fourth grade was added in January 1942.[169]

Implementation of this assessment system in *Lebensborn* in 1938 roughly coincided with the establishment of the *Heim Wienerwald*, where the system was applied from the word go.[170] On 17 March 1939, the questionnaires submitted to Munich were returned to the *Heim Wienerwald* because of the poor quality of their completion.[171] The home directors and head nurses of the *Lebensborn* homes were repeatedly instructed on how to fill in the questionnaires correctly. For example, a negative character assessment could not be paired with the assessment "good National Socialist" as, according to Sollmann, "National Socialism is a character issue like no other."[172] With regard to questionnaires sent in 1943 to the *Lebensborn* headquarters from the *Heim Wienerwald*, the home's director Schwab was told that the description "clean but untidy"[173] was self-contradictory. Schwab explained that he had meant to say that the "mother in question is clean and well-groomed in appearance, but sorely lacking in orderliness in her room."[174] Initially, the questionnaires only concerned unwed women, but soon the information had to be provided for every woman admitted.[175]

---

164 Franziska L., *RF-Fragebogen*, draft, handwritten information, n.d., 89/140, registry office Pernitz II.
165 Ibid.
166 Ibid.
167 *Fragebogen für den Reichsführer SS*, 7 December 1938, AA, 4.1.0/8211100, Ref. 82451310.
168 *Aktenvermerk über die Besprechung beim Reichsführer-SS am Sonnabend den 11. Jänner 1941 mittags um 1 Uhr*, AA, 4.1.0/8209900, Ref. 82448330.
169 Copy of Himmler's letter from 26 January 1942, signed by Ebner, 20 March 1943, AA, 4.1.0/8211100, Ref. 82451198 and 82451317; Lilienthal, *Der "Lebensborn e.V."*, 95–99.
170 Schmitz-Köster, *"Deutsche Mutter"*, 218.
171 *Fragebogen*, 17 March 1939, AA, 4.1.0/8211100, Ref. 82451312–82451313.
172 *Rundschreiben* by Sollmann, 11 April 1942, AA, 4.1.0/8211100, Ref. 82451200.
173 Ebner to Schwab, 9 March 1943, AA, 4.1.0/8211100, Ref. 82451323.
174 Schwab to Ebner, *RF-Fragebogen*, 19 March 1943, AA, 4.1.0/8211100, Ref. 82451324.
175 Lilienthal, *Der "Lebensborn e.V."*, 95–96.

The director of the *Heim Wienerwald* from 1938 to 1941, Karl Sernetz, and the head nurse approached Ebner about Franziska L. because they were not satisfied with her appearance and behaviour. On 9 February 1940, Ebner informed Sernetz that he had examined Franziska L.'s file in the *Lebensborn* admissions department. The photograph she had submitted displayed "Eastern racial characteristics" but did not make her appear deficient in height.[176] The information on her height provided by the examining physician had patently been inaccurate. In view of her reproductive potential, the physician had described the overall impression she had left him with as good. The curriculum vitae written by Franziska L. was orthographically correct and neatly written. There had been no particular reason for *Lebensborn*'s admissions department to reject her. Ebner noted: "However, the case gives me reason to advise staff at the head office to examine as strictly as possible in future."[177]

In Franziska L.'s *Reichsführer SS-Fragebogen*, both the home's director and the head nurse assessed her negatively. Her "racial appearance" was "predominantly Eastern with all the associated mental characteristics."[178] She did not "take to the ideas of National Socialism." In terms of character, she was described as "friendly, not very intelligent, needy, helpful, requires guidance." In the home community, she "sticks out disagreeably with her simple-minded remarks, otherwise she fits in well." This was followed by: "Under guidance capable of achieving satisfactory results; competence in all fields average."[179] Before giving birth she had been "anxious, during the birth calmer."[180] The questionnaire also stated that she was very attached to her daughter; in general, although she appeared to be physically healthy, she had a weak constitution. According to the director of the home and the head nurse, the blonde, blue-eyed child was also rather weak, due to a birth weight of no more than 2,800 grams. They stated that Franziska L.'s plans for the time after her discharge were rather vague; it was certain that she could not return to her former home because of her child. The marriage with the child's father that she had been hoping for was thwarted by his death. In her view, having additional children would be dependent on being married. In the light of its selection principles, the SS felt that not only should she not be encouraged to become pregnant again, but also that she and her child did not deserve any support. An interim conclusion stated that "a tragic fate un-

---

176  Ernetz to Ebner, *Frau Franziska L.*, 9 February 1940, AA, 4.1.0/8213000, Ref. 82458469.
177  Ibid.
178  Franziska L., *RF-Fragebogen*, 1, handwritten draft, n.d., 89/140, registry office Pernitz II. This is not the full *RF SS* questionnaire, but a handwritten draft. It is not known whether the information in the draft actually corresponded to the final document.
179  Ibid., 2.
180  Ibid.

doubtedly awaits the mother but from the SS' point of view she must be rejected."[181]

When Ebner visited the *Heim Wienerwald* on 9 April 1940, he got to know Franziska L.[182] He initially concluded that her appearance was indeed "purely Eastern." However, he noted, the intelligence deficits that had been apparent during her pregnancy had become much less pronounced since the birth and Franziska L. had also integrated well into the home community, having shed her initial shyness. In Ebner's opinion, given her rural background, it was no wonder that she initially had problems adjusting to the milieu of the home. In addition to the death of her fiancé, one of her sisters had recently died, which, according to Ebner, caused her great grief. Ebner suggested that, despite the reservations, the *Lebensborn* should become the child's guardian. The child was also to bear the name of the deceased father, as the parents had been about to marry.[183] Per a decision of 1941, the child acquired the legal status of a "legitimate" child.[184]

The aforementioned statistics from the *Lebensborn* head office for the months of November 1941 to March 1942 show how many of the previously accepted women no longer satisfied the SS selection principle after giving birth and during their stay in the maternity homes. As many as 17.2 per cent "did not" meet the selection principle, 14.1 per cent "did not fully," and 68.7 per cent "fully." The fathers fared better. Of these, 73.3 per cent complied with the selection principle, 19.9 per cent did not fully comply and 7.1 per cent did not comply at all.[185] As Dorothee Schmitz-Köster concludes, mothers were scrutinised more closely during their stay in the home and were probably measured against higher standards because they were ultimately responsible for maintaining the "racially desirable" population.[186]

Regardless of the fact that assessments of the women by the home's director and the head nurse did not always match those made by *Lebensborn* head office, as was the case with Franzsika L., the assessments had far-reaching consequences for mother and child.

Provided the assessment was positive, *Lebensborn* supported them. Himmler personally took over guardianship of those children born on his birthday.[187] Recommendations were made, such as for Margarete F., who gave birth in the *Heim Wienerwald* in 1940, for whom Ebner informed the military superiors of her future husband that "she has an excellent reputation, is honest and her

---

181 Ibid.
182 *Frau Franzsika L.*, 5 April 1940, AA, 4.1.0/8213000, Ref. 82458470–82458471.
183 *Frau Franzsika L.*, *Heim Wienerwald*, 12 April 1940, 4.1.0/8212800, Ref. 82457556.
184 Franziska L., *Beschluss*, 4 February 1941, 89/1940, registry office Pernitz II.
185 Schmitz-Köster, *"Deutsche Mutter"*, 223.
186 Ibid.
187 *Rundschreiben*, AA, 4.1.0/8211100, Ref. 82451383; Lilienthal, *Der "Lebensborn e.V."*, 99.

attitude towards the National Socialist leadership is impeccable," and that her "parents are, as can be seen from the files, respectable and loyal to the state. I do not know them personally."[188] Mothers awarded grades I and II were eligible for jobs as typists in SS offices.[189] In contrast, an unfavourable assessment, such as the one given to Franziska L. and her child, could lead to their rejection if they became pregnant again and applied to *Lebensborn*.[190] A negative assessment could be counted on when mothers complained or showed themselves dissatisfied with arrangements in the home. Worth mentioning in this context is the case of Agnes S. from 1943, who caused a stir in the *Heim Wienerwald* when she told other mothers about her work with the *Gestapo* in Smolensk and mentioned that mass executions of Jews had taken place and even infants had been shot in the neck. She apparently also complained about the food in *Heim Wienerwald*, saying that she had eaten better in the Eastern territories. According to the home's director, she was to be removed from the home as soon as her child's medical condition permitted.[191] Ebner produced report, stating "that any mother who speaks out with such hatred about *Lebensborn* must be prevented from being again admitted to a *Lebensborn* home in future."[192] It is unknown how many women faced the consequences of a negative assessment, and what these consequences were in detail, but the secrecy of pregnancy and childbirth was irrevocably compromised when a woman was dismissed from *Lebensborn* and *Lebensborn* refused to accept guardianship of the child.

## IX.  Conclusion

In October 1938, six months after the *Anschluss* of Austria to the German Reich, *Lebensborn* opened the *Heim Wienerwald* with the aim of bringing the situation of unwed mothers and their children largely on par with marital status, thus increasing the birth rate among the "Aryan" population. Founded in 1935, *Lebensborn* had by then become an integral part of National Socialist racial and population policies, whose attempts to control reproduction ranged from incentives to marry and have children for the racially and eugenically "fit" to disincentives and compulsory sterilization. Throughout the war, *Lebensborn*

---

188  *Fräulein Margarete F., Heim Wienerwald*, 27 June 1940, AA, 4.1.0/8211000, Ref. 82451131.
189  Lilienthal, *Der "Lebensborn e.V."*, 98.
190  *Zweiter Antrag auf Heimaufnahme*, 14 February 1941, AA, 4.1.0/8211100, Ref. 82451192.
191  Schwab to Ebner, *KM Agnes S.*, 16 April 1943, AA, 4.1.0/8210200, Ref. 82448949.
192  Ebner to the Chief of the Reich Security Main Office, *SS Mütterheim Wienerwald*, 4 May 1943, AA, 4.1.0/8210200, Ref. 82448947. Also see Astrid Eggers, "Ich war die Marionette meiner Mutter," in *Verschwiegene Opfer der SS. Lebensborn-Kinder erzählen ihr Leben*, edited by Astrid Eggers and Elke Sauer (Leipzig: Engelsdorfer, 2015), 134–50, here 143.

planned to expand its sphere of influence, for example by restructuring the association and establishing children's homes as well as additional maternity homes. In terms of the number of children born between November 1938 and March 1945, the *Heim Wienerwald* was one of the key *Lebensborn* facilities. It was one of only two *Lebensborn* facilities opened in the territory of present-day Austria, the other being *Heim Alpenland,* which was opened in 1943 for *Lebensborn* children abducted from Eastern and Southeastern Europe.

Mothers-to-be, such as Charlotte H., Anna K., Maria B., and Franziska L., were accepted by *Lebensborn* to the *Heim Wienerwald* because they were considered "Aryan" women and could prove that their children had "Aryan" fathers. If necessary, *Lebensborn* kept the women's stay in the home and the birth of their children secret. It took over guardianship on request, but only if the children met the racist criteria of the *SS*. It also made sure that fathers acknowledged paternity and paid child support. If necessary, *Lebensborn* offered to place the children in the *Heim Wienerwald* or in children's homes after the mothers had been released, and to help the mothers find work. Sometimes *Lebensborn* even placed the mothers to work in the *Heim Wienerwald,* in other *Lebensborn* maternity homes, or at the *Lebensborn* head office, which had been relocated from Berlin to Munich in 1938. However, not all unwed mothers were in need of these support services. For example, it was not necessary for *Lebensborn* to accept guardianship if a child's parents were about to marry. Only in rare cases children from the *Heim Wienerwald* were placed with foster parents and adoptive families. Furthermore, wives of *SS* men and members of the German police gave birth to their children in the *Heim Wienerwald*, relieving them of existential worries. To married women, the "selection" process was applied somewhat more loosely.

The intention of *Lebensborn* was that most of the children born in the *Heim Wienerwald* would grow up with their mothers. This was in stark contrast to the "germanisation" of children from Eastern and Southeastern Europe, where children were torn from their families, and to the activities of *Lebensborn* in Norway, where children were given up for adoption in the *Altreich*, sometimes without their mothers' knowledge.

Yet, the primary aim of *Lebensborn* was not to support unmarried mothers in *Heim Wienerwald* so that they would be able to establish themselves. Rather, the plight of mother and child was exploited in favour of National Socialist racial ideology. Those mothers and their newborns who did not meet the expectations of the home management or *Lebensborn* leadership during their stay in the home forfeited the privileges they had enjoyed, or were even expelled. During war years, *Lebensborn* wanted to further increase the birth rate, which meant turning away from the strict "selection criteria" of the pre-war years. Still, only "hereditarily healthy" applicants were allowed to give birth in the *Heim Wienerwald* and other *Lebensborn* maternity homes. Moreover, during war years, *Lebensborn* argued in favour of a short sojourn of mothers on the one hand, and a long mother-child phase on the other, so that mothers could breastfeed their children for as long as *Lebensborn* expected them to do so. Despite these changes and contradictions, at no time did *Lebensborn* pause to monitor whether mothers in the *Heim Wienerwald* met the racial, ideological, and characterological selection criteria of the *SS*; using the *Reichsführer* SS questionnaires, the assessment of these women and their children was carried out continously from 1938 to 1945.

Barbara Stelzl-Marx

# Lebensborn as a Blueprint for the "Nobility of the Future". Daily Life and Ideology in the *Heim Wienerwald*

## I.   Introduction

"Heilig soll uns sein jede Mutter guten Blutes" [Hallowed be every mother of good blood] was the mission statement of the *Lebensborn* association, established in Berlin in 1936 on the orders of Heinrich Himmler.[1] This motto prefaced the association's own brochures, entitled simply *Lebensborn*, which outlined the regulations of this key "instrument of National Socialist racial policy".[2] Its "ideological orientation", as the introduction stated, was provided by Himmler, who personally led the association as a part of the *Schutzstaffel (SS)*. Its tasks primarily fell within the area of "population policy", which in practical terms meant that "*Lebensborn* is tasked with contributing to a high birth rate among the SS, protecting and caring for every mother of good blood, and providing succour for mothers and children of good blood in need." The aim was for this endeavour to produce an "elite youth, equally valuable in body and mind, the nobility of the future".[3]

Himmler's aforementioned credo illustrates how thoroughly the National Socialist ideology permeated every aspect of *Lebensborn*, imbuing everyday life in its homes with a pseudo-religious character. Far from women per se being considered "sacred", this distinction was exclusively reserved for "German"

---

1   Niederösterreichisches Landesarchiv (Archives of the Province of Lower Austria, NÖLA), Office of the Provincial Government of Lower Austria, State Office I/2, Number 33/1975, Lebensborn e. V., an association registered in Munich, publisher of *Lebensborn*, Miesbach, n. d., 3. The contribution's realization was supported by the Jubilee Fund of the Austrian National Bank, the Future Fund of the Republic of Austria, and the Province of Lower Austria. Associated research was conducted at the Ludwig Boltzmann Institute for Research on Consequences of War (BIK), Graz – Vienna – Raabs, in collaboration with the Institute of History of the University of Graz.
2   Georg Lilienthal, *Der "Lebensborn e. V.". Ein Instrument nationalsozialistischer Rassenpolitik.* 2nd ed. (Frankfurt am Main: Fischer, 2008).
3   NÖLA, Office of the Lower Austrian State Government, Landesamt I/2, No 33/1975, *Lebensborn*, ed. by Lebensborn e.V. in München, 5.

women in their role as child-bearers, with the additional proviso that their children were also of "good blood". In this case the mothers were seen as "vessels for genetically healthy" German progeny. If they complied with the "strict genetic selection principle of the *Schutzstaffel*," they were deemed worthy of protection and care.[4] Conversely, if they did not, they had no claim to "care". In that case, an even worse fate could have been in store for them, as was hinted at between the lines.

The commingling of sexual and population policies, combined with a hierarchy of blood elevated to an ideology, must be seen as a specific characteristic of National Socialism. In the Third Reich, sexual matters were dealt with dictatorially at the highest level, as they touched on the foundations of the system. Consequently, "racial disgrace" or "prohibited interaction with foreigners and prisoners of war"[5] was severely punished. For German women in general, and particularly for those in *Lebensborn* homes, the emphasis was on their importance for procreation and the advancement of the "Aryan" race in general and the "German *Volksgemeinschaft*" in particular.[6] There was a dialectic of "seeding" and "weeding out", of pro- and anti-natalist measures. The *Lebensborn* maternity homes were facilities where, according to their charter, children "valuable in mind and body", the "nobility of the future" as envisioned by the SS, were to be born. The following discussion of the *Lebensborn-Heim Ostmark/ Wienerwald* illustrates the extent to which the organisation and daily routines of this maternity home were imbued with National Socialist ideology.[7]

---

4 Ibid.; Dorothee Schmitz-Köster, *"Deutsche Mutter, bist du bereit …"*. *Der Lebensborn und seine Kinder* (Berlin: Aufbau Taschenbuch, 2011), 189.

5 Karl Fallend, "Zwangsarbeit – Sklavenarbeit in den Reichswerken Hermann Göring am Standort Linz. (Auto-)Biographische Einsichten," in: Oliver Rathkolb (ed.), *NS-Zwangsarbeit: Der Standort Linz der Reichswerke Hermann Göring AG Berlin, 1938–1945*. Vol. 2. (Vienna – Cologne – Weimar: Böhlau, 2001), 105.

6 See also Brigitte Halbmayr, "Sexzwangsarbeit in NS-Konzentrationslagern" in: Dokumentationsarchiv des österreichischen Widerstands (ed.), *Jahrbuch 2005. Schwerpunkt Frauen in Widerstand und Verfolgung* (Münster et al.: Lit Verlag, 2005), 96–115, here: 96–7; Barbara Stelzl-Marx, "'Zum Schutze der deutschen Frau'. Das Largerbordell für NS-Zwangsarbeiter in Graz," in: Barbara Stelzl-Marx (ed.), *Das Lager Liebenau. Ein Ort verdichteter Geschichte* (Graz – Vienna: Leykam, 2018), 77–84, here: 77–8.

7 The basis for this paper is the evaluation of archived and currently accessible documents in the Arolsen Archives (AA), drawn from the field of activity of Gregor Ebner, whose functions as a board member and head of the Health Department, among others, made him a key official of the *Lebensborn e.V.* These files allow a qualitative, exemplary analysis of different aspects of everyday life in the various *Lebensborn* homes, including the *Wienerwald* home. For the latter, they were analysed for the first time for this article. In some cases, these examples are supplemented by an analysis of the 946 surviving files of the registry office Pernitz II, including the so-called *Reichsführer SS Fragebögen* (*Reichsführer SS* Questionnaires), of which 346 drafts have been preserved in the Pernitz municipal office. These files and questionnaires were entered into a separate database for the project: BIK, Database *Lebensbornheim Wienerwald*.

## II.    The Name-Consecration Ceremony: An Induction into the *SS-Sippengemeinschaft*

In the *Lebensborn* institutions, the focus was not on the mother, but on the child. It was the child who was at the centre of all ideological considerations and actions. The comprehensive medical aid and balanced nutrition the mother received was provided solely for the child's sake.[8] It was because of the child that the mother was honoured as a "source of strength and hub of life" and given thanks for the joy she had given through her "silent heroism".[9] The child was perceived as the "fair reward for the efforts expended". This perspective was most clearly demonstrated in the so-called name-consecration or naming ceremony, in which the child was ceremoniously admitted into the *SS-Sippengemeinschaft* and – notionally – irrevocably linked to National Socialism. The question the director of the *Lebensborn* home asked during this pseudo-religious ceremony was, "German mother, are you willing to raise your child in the belief in Adolf Hitler?" Affirmation and a handshake sealed the deal.[10]

Nowhere else did the National Socialist state's total claim to control over the individual, including spirit and soul, manifest itself more clearly on a symbolic level than in the name-consecration ceremony, Himmler's *ersatz* baptism. It was interpreted later as an instance of the "blasphemous idolatry" that Heinrich Himmler sought to instil in the SS as the "new faith" in lieu of Christianity. Essentially, the ceremony was a secularised form of Christian baptism.[11]

All *Lebensborn* homes, including the home *Ostmark/Wienerwald*, conducted naming ceremonies according to a standardised model that, while retaining key elements of the ecclesiastical rite, sought to replace Christian baptism. The recreation room, where these celebrations usually took place, was festively decorated with a bust of Adolf Hitler, an image of his mother, SS flags, laurel trees, and flowers.[12] The ceremonies started and ended with a piece of music, during which the mother would enter and exit the room with her child. After this, typically "a solemn declaration relating to purity of blood, our people, or our ancestors" was recited by a pre-school girl in the *Bund Deutscher Mädel* (League

---

Further quantitative analyses of the various topics covered in the database will be carried out in a separate publication. For more information on these sources also see the editorial of this volume.

8    Lilienthal, *Der "Lebensborn e.V."* (Frankfurt am Main: Fischer, 1993), 99.

9    Guidelines for Naming Ceremony, 3 March 1940, 109, Arolsen Archives (AA), 4.1.0/82453237.

10    Letter from the director of the *Kurmark* home to Ebner regarding marriages and naming ceremonies, 10 May 1940, AA, 4.1.0/82453234.

11    Josef Ackermann, *Heinrich Himmler als Ideologe* (Göttingen – Zürich – Frankfurt am Main: Musterschmidt, 1970), 84–86; Lilienthal, *Der "Lebensborn e.V"*, 100; Schmitz-Köster, *"Deutsche Mutter bist du bereit …"*, 164.

12    Lilienthal, *Der "Lebensborn e.V."*, 99.

of German Girls, BDM) attire, followed by a song. The director of the home would then deliver a sermon-like speech, tailoring its content to the specific circumstances. The climax was the naming ceremony itself, involving the aforementioned question to the mother and a question to the godparent about their readiness to "commit themselves to this child and its mother in life's struggle" and watch over the child in line with the *SS* clan ethos. After the reading of a quotation, often drawn from the utterances of the *Führer* and presented by the director of the home as a guiding principle for the child's life, he would lift an *SS* dagger above the child and say, "You shall bear the name …". The ceremony ended with the *SS* loyalty song and the presentation of a certificate to the mother. It concluded with a coffee snack for the mothers and godparents.[13]

The direct rivalry of this ceremony with baptism is evident in a letter from *SS-Standartenführer* Guntram Pflaum, the managing director of *Lebensborn* until 1941, to *SS-Oberführer* Dr. Gregor Ebner, the chief physician and director of *Lebensborn*, dated 6 August 1939: "Dear Ebner, There has not even been one naming ceremony at the *Wienerwald* home yet," he complained. "But there are a many necklaces with little crosses to be seen here. I therefore beg you to conduct the first naming ceremony yourself, like in the other homes." Pflaum suggested 27 August, a Sunday, as the date.[14]

Ebner responded promptly, not only confirming his personal attendance at this first naming ceremony at the *Wienerwald* home, but also providing detailed instructions on the necessary procedure. Thus, each mother was to choose a godparent from her acquaintance, who, needless to say, had to be "ideologically flawless". In exceptional cases, as Ebner emphasised, a female godparent could also be permitted. Every godparent was required to donate five *Reichsmark* to the home, in return for which the child would receive a silver spoon engraved with the location and date of the naming ceremony. These spoons needed to be requested from headquarters in good time.[15] Along with silver cups "from godfather H. Himmler", who himself assumed godparent responsibilities,[16] the silver spoons were the *SS* equivalent or substitute for traditional Christian christening mugs.

Ebner was explicit in stating that, "obviously, only those children who were not in line for Christian baptism could participate in the naming ceremony". However, he insisted, mothers "should not be coerced in any way" to submit their

---

13  Letter from the director of the *Kurmark* home to Ebner regarding marriages and naming ceremonies, 10 May 1940, AA, 4.1.0/82453234f.; Dorothee Neumaier, *Das Lebensbornheim 'Schwarzwald' in Nordrach* (Baden-Baden: Tectum, 2017), 274.

14  Letter from Pflaum to Ebner regarding the naming ceremony, 6 August 1939, AA, 4.1.0/82453210.

15  Letter from Ebner to the *Wienerwald* home regarding the naming ceremony, 11 August 1939, AA, 4.1.0/82453209.

16  Schmitz-Köster, "'Deutsche Mutter, bist du bereit…'", 253.

child for the naming ceremony: "Each mother should be free to choose whether or not she wants her child to be baptised", were the exact instructions. The pseudo-religious significance of this act is highlighted by Ebner's guidance that children who had undergone the naming ceremony should not be "presented to a religious community for a subsequent baptism once they were released from the home".[17]

The number of children who were still baptised despite having undergone the naming ceremony is difficult to ascertain. Nevertheless, aside from the fact that only about half of the children in all *Lebensborn* homes underwent this *SS* ritual, some mothers set up an "ideological counterpoint" during their stay in the home by having their new-borns baptised secretly.[18] This was not easy to accomplish, as children were mostly under the care of the nurses on the infant ward and their mothers saw them for only a few hours a day, usually for breastfeeding. Taking them to the church involved the risk of being seen, which could result in the loss of privileges. There is the documented case of an unmarried woman who had given birth to a son in the *Wienerwald* home in early 1943 and subsequently had him baptised in the *Schwarzwald* home in Nordrach in Germany. By this time, the child was several months old and could be taken on short outings by his mother, who was employed in the home at the time. Nor was this an isolated case. Other women also defied the *SS*'s idea that a child should grow up *gottgläubig*, that is, unbaptised and with a belief in God without belonging to any denomination – as soon as they were released from the *Lebensborn* home.[19]

However, these were not the only problems associated with the naming ceremonies in the *Wienerwald* home that *Lebensborn* had to deal with, after the head of the Security Police and the *Sicherheitsdienst* (SD) received a complaint and forwarded it to Ebner. The corresponding letter began seemingly moderately: "The naming ceremonies are generally still in their early days, so no overly harsh criticism can be levelled here." However, there was one severe criticism, namely that the home's director, Norbert Schwab, allegedly "had the women with their small children stand to attention in front of him to listen to the formal words of the naming". This was a notable deficiency, for "if the mothers are referred to as pillars of the nation and are brought to the fore in an old Germanic celebration to show them the respect due to them as mothers, then it is perceived as incorrect and inappropriate that these mothers, who have given birth 10 to 14 days or even less beforehand, must stand to attention".[20]

---

17  Letter from Ebner to the *Wienerwald* home regarding the naming ceremony, 11 August 1939, AA, 4.1.0/82453209.
18  Schmitz-Köster, "*Deutsche Mutter, bist du bereit....*", 165, 254.
19  Neumaier, *Das Lebensbornheim 'Schwarzwald' in Nordrach*, 275–76.
20  Letter from the head of the security police and the *Sicherheitsdienst* to *Lebensborn* regarding the *SS* Maternity Home *Wienerwald*, 14 April 1943, AA, 4.1.0/82448933.

Ebner's response is noteworthy. He ordered a review of all complaints and emphatically requested the identity of the complainant. After all, he wrote, *Lebensborn* had to present a report about this to *Reichsführer-SS* Heinrich Himmler. Based on "personal knowledge of the home", he believed he could affirm that "some of the complaints are greatly exaggerated, if not downright lies; for example, it can only be a malicious slander that the *Lebensborn* mothers have to stand to attention in front of the home director".[21]

A clarification soon followed from home director *SS-Obersturmführer* Schwab, who denied all wrongdoing. He carried out the naming procedure itself following Ebner's example. This meant that individual mothers would step forward and shake hands, promising to "raise the child in the spirit of the National Socialist worldview". He would "obviously" never demand that they stand to attention. If the mothers had recently given birth, they could give their handshake while seated in a comfortable chair. Two to three weeks after the birth, however, it would be entirely reasonable for them "as healthy women [...] to stand up and, holding their children, to give the promise standing, in accordance with the significance of the day", emphasised home director Schwab.[22] Ebner forwarded the detailed report, which also addressed other deficiencies that had been criticised in the home, to Berlin and again demanded the identity of the complainant. In conclusion, he stated that in future it must not be allowed that "a mother who speaks out against *Lebensborn* in such a malicious way is re-admitted to a *Lebensborn* home".[23]

## III.    Names: A Declaration of Loyalty to "Kin and People"

It is hardly surprising that the choice of names for the "nobility of the future" was assigned great ideological and symbolic value. Names were to be chosen before birth and given in writing to the midwife to be registered at the registry office. Subsequent alterations or the addition of further names after being recorded in the registry office was strictly prohibited, as was the use of diminutives such as Friedel instead of Elfriede. Mothers were to choose a maximum of two first names from a shortlist of "German first names". Failure to do so would lead to the child's exclusion from the naming ceremony.[24] "At the birth ceremony", as

---

21  Letter from Ebner to the head of the security police and SD regarding the *Wienerwald* home, 17 April 1943, AA, 4.1.0/82448935.
22  Letter from Schwab to Ebner regarding the report of the Reich Security Main Office, 23 April 1943, AA, 4.1.0/82448937.
23  Letter from Ebner to the head of the security police and SD regarding the *Wienerwald* home, 4 May 1943, AA, 4.1.0/82448947.
24  Suggestions for the bestowal of first names, n.d, AA, 4.1.0/82453135.

Schwab explained, "the mother commits to raising her child in the spirit of our worldview. To do this, however, she and the father must be so steadfast in their ideological stance that when choosing the child's name, it goes without saying that non-German – and especially religious or originally Jewish – names are excluded."[25]

Schwab wrote a two-and-a-half-page, densely typewritten report on the origin of the choice of names "of our people", which he hoped would provide "clarification on this topic of continued importance" for each *Lebensborn* home. He emphasised that a name should express "a declaration of loyalty to kin and people". Particularly favoured were "robust and combative names" from the "Germanic era, from the old High German sagas and songs", which in boys' names spoke "of battle and victory, honour and glory", and in girls' names "of the same combative traits or of the holy visionary powers of the Nordic woman". Conversely, with the "decline of the Reich", there had, according to Schwab, regrettably been a "broad influx of foreign names", particularly "of names from the Near East of biblical origin". As an example of "German thoughtlessness", he pointed to the name Elizabeth, with its different variations and its meaning, which in his view amounted to "God has struck me". He interpreted this as the heartless expression of disappointment "of the old Jew" over the birth of a girl instead of the wished-for boy, callously allowing the "poor unwanted girl to drag this disappointment along with her in her name all her life".[26] In fact, this Greek name of Hebrew origin means "God is abundance", which carries diametrically opposed connotations.

"Germanised names of foreign origin", like Peter, Klaus, Jürgen, Hans or Sepp, and Liesl, Grete, Karin, Hannelore, Heidemarie or Monika, were to be rejected. For with these names, children would be given "essentially alien thoughts for their journey through life", Schwab opined. By way of further explanation he added: "I believe that these children, when they later encounter the beautiful German names of their comrades in the *Hitlerjugend* (Hitler Youth, HJ) or *BDM*, will feel quite unhappy and will have little gratitude for their parents' capriciousness on this point".[27]

Conversely, the director of the home claimed that the pool of "genuine German names" was so great that only a fraction of them was sufficient to "easily replace all foreign names". He was referring to a collection of 4,500 names, the *Namenbuch* by the German writer and naval officer Bogislav von Selchow,[28] which was intended to serve as the basis for the choice of first name in *Lebens-*

---

25  Schwab on name selection, n.d., AA, 4.1.0/82453132–82453134.
26  Ibid.
27  Ibid.
28  Bogislav von Selchow, *Das Namenbuch*. (Leipzig: Koehler & Amelang, 1934).

*born.*[29] The first 15 out of about 90 favourite names were Horst, Manfred, Uwe, Alfred, Odo, Hartmut, Ottomar, Erhard, Heinrich, Heinz, Adolf, Günther, Gunther, Wolf, and Wulf for male first names. For females, these were: Ingeborg, Inge, Karen, Karin, Ingrid, Dietlinde, Brunhilde, Irmhild, Irmgard, Sigrun, Sigrid, Hilde, Hildegard, Hildegund, and Isolde. Besides the aforementioned first names of non-German origin, the following "Hebrew [hence forbidden] first names" were beyond the pale: Joachim, Michael, Josef; Elisabeth, Elsbeth, Eva, Johanna, Lisbeth, Ruth, Susanne, Gabriele, Josepha, Josephine, Zarah.[30] Lectures on name selection took place regularly as part of the ideological training in the *Wienerwald* home.[31]

However, the most frequently chosen names in the *Wienerwald* home differed slightly from the preferred list provided by *Lebensborn*. Of the approximately 500 children born there whose first names are known the girls were primarily named Ingrid, which was chosen 42 times, followed by Heide, Heidrun, Helga, Karin, Erika, Hannelore, Ingeborg, Ursula, Brigitte, Gudrun, and Sigrid. For the boys, the most popular names were Peter, Horst, Günther, Helmut, Klaus, Dieter, Manfred, Werner, Gerhard, Heinz, Hartmut, Bernd, Hans, and Herbert.[32] If a child was born on 7 October, the birthday of *Reichsführer-SS* Heinrich Himmler, the advice was for the child to be given 'Heinrich' as at least their second first name, as was the case with Manfred W. For a long time, he wondered why he carried this second first name when he had no ancestors named Heinrich: "Why is my first given name Manfred, and my second one Heinrich? It turned out that I was born exactly on the day when the boss [...] of the SS, Herr Himmler, had his birthday".[33] Oddly, some children were even given names that were forbidden in *Lebensborn*, namely Michael, Josef, Joachim, Johanna, Gabriele, and Josefa.[34]

---

29  Schwab on name selection, n.d., AA, 4.1.0/82453132–82453134.
30  Suggestions for the bestowal of first names, n.d. AA, 4.1.0/82453135–82453140; Neumaier, *Das Lebensbornheim 'Schwarzwald' in Nordrach*, 270–1.
31  Cf. e.g. Training Report at the *Wienerwald* home in October 1943, 2 November 1943, AA, 4.1.0/82454192.
32  BIK, Data base *Lebensbornheim Wienerwald*. Thanks to Martin Sauerbrey-Almasy, BIK, for the data inquiry.
33  BIK, Manfred W. interviewed by Michaela Tasotti, 10 November 2021, transcript, 3.
34  BIK, Data base *Lebensbornheim Wienerwald*.

## IV. Indoctrination: National Socialist Education and Ideological Instruction

The naming ceremony was undoubtedly a red-letter day in the calendar of a *Lebensborn* home. However, even the daily routine was imbued with National Socialist ideology, which permeated and shaped all aspects of a mother's stay in these *SS* maternity establishments. Unmarried women, in particular, who often stayed from the seventh month of pregnancy to two months after giving birth, were isolated from the outside world for many weeks. If they wished to conceal their pregnancy and childbirth from their habitual surroundings, they could be admitted earlier or discharged later. Married women typically stayed at least for childbirth and postnatal recovery, and sometimes longer. Their week or month-long stay thus provided ideal conditions for systematic indoctrination – both ideological and health-focused – which was a fixed component of daily life in the home.[35]

The aim of the ideological training courses, which were introduced in all homes from June 1938, was to "educate the mothers at the home and the patrons of *Lebensborn* in the National Socialist way and instruct them in our world-view".[36] The supervision of the training was initially the responsibility of the Race and Settlement Main Office (*Rasse- und Siedlungshauptamt*, RuSHA) and took place in coordination with the Race and Settlement Leader *(Rasse- und Siedlungs-Führer*, RuS) of the respective *SS* region. As a result of staff shortages due to the war, the ideological supervision of *Lebensborn* was eventually transferred from the *RuSHA* to the *SS* Main Office (*SSHA*) in 1942. Within *Lebensborn*, Gregor Ebner, as the head doctor and director of *Lebensborn*, was responsible for training until the end of the war.[37]

In individual homes, the medical directors were responsible for this training. This was not intended purely as a formality, but stemmed from Himmler's vision of a new medical leadership model that was first to be realised in *Lebensborn:* ideally, the doctor would be a helper, a "paternal friend and adviser to our mothers, who will only remember in an emergency that he is a doctor at all",[38] emphasised Ebner when describing the intended role of doctors in *Lebensborn*. They were responsible not only for the mothers' physical health, but also for their mental wellbeing. As "doctors for the soul", they were meant to dispense comfort to the expectant mothers like pastors.[39]

---

35 Lilienthal, *Der "Lebensborn e.V"*, 65–66.
36 Ideological Training at the *Kurmark* home, 5 December 1941, AA, 4.1.0/82454147.
37 Lilienthal, *Der "Lebensborn e.V"*, 66.
38 Ibid., 67.
39 Ibid.

That headquarters was taking an avid interest is evident from the fact that it demanded monthly reports from each home on the training it conducted. These featured – at least theoretically – film screenings, lectures, sing-alongs, readings of individual chapters of *Mein Kampf*, listening to speeches by various representatives of the National Socialist regime, and the celebration of special occasions. However, it seems that a large number of the events failed to find favour with the mothers, as appears from expressions of dissatisfaction, which are easy to understand in view of the programmes described below.[40] At the *Wienerwald* home, the mothers were "often unwilling to participate, especially during the summer season, when events are scheduled so often in the evening", as home director Schwab sympathetically noted.[41] Apparently, the *Wienerwald* home was sometimes rather lax in the way it ran the training, thereby drawing criticism from headquarters, especially in the early phase of its existence: "The training report from the *Wienerwald* home reveals that 6 singing evenings were held in August. It is requested that future training be livened up not only with singing evenings, but also with lectures, readings, etc. Heil Hitler!", as Ebner admonished the director in the autumn of 1939.[42]

The reprimand from Munich bore fruit: in January 1940, the head of the *Ostmark* home until 1941, Karl Sernetz, delivered six lectures on political topics such as "England's policy in Europe and the Near East", "The disgraceful treaty of Versailles", and "The struggle of the twentieth century", as well as health-related issues focusing on "Symptoms and prevention of rickets", "Mothers' behaviour during pregnancy" and "The advantages of natural infant nutrition". One evening was dedicated to a "community gathering to listen to the *Führer*'s speech", and there was a political news report every morning. For lighter entertainment, the head nurse still organised four singing evenings during this period.[43]

A similar routine was observed for training in February 1940, with Sernetz again focusing on English politics and preventative measures against rickets, "The Germanic peoples as bearers of culture", and "The tasks of the home front during the war". In addition to a fairy tale evening with an impromptu game, four singing evenings took place.[44] It is worth noting that one of the reports about the training in this month also mentions a name-giving ceremony that

---

40  Ibid.
41  Letter from Schwab to Ebner regarding the report of the RSHKA, 14 April 1943, 23 April 1943, AA, 4.1.0/82448937.
42  Letter from Ebner to the *Wienerwald* home regarding the training report in August 1939, 6 September 1939, AA, 4.1.0/82453784.
43  Training Report at the *Wienerwald* home in January 1940, 31 January 1940, AA, 4.1.0/82453903.
44  Training Report at the *Wienerwald* home in February 1940, 1 March 1940, AA, 4.1.0/92453916.

took place on 11 February, thus explicitly classifying this as part of the ideo-logical training.[45]

In the run-up to Christian festivals such as Christmas and Easter, it became clear how customs adapted in line with National Socialist ideology had been integrated into everyday life at the home.[46] On 23 March 1940 – Holy Saturday – Sernetz gave a lecture on "various Easter customs as traditional German folk customs", apparently intended as a replacement for the Easter liturgy.[47]

The goal of creating a National Socialist substitute religion led National So-cialist ideologues to try to replace the Christian Christmas discourse with in-terpretations of Germanic rites and myths. Like the naming ceremonies, deeply entrenched religious customs were adapted and integrated into National Socialist celebrations to convey the desired value system through emotional attachment. Christmas therefore became a celebration of the winter solstice and "of the commitment to the people and the *Führer*". It was elevated to the rank of a "festival of universal motherhood". The German mother was stylised as a sub-stitute for the mother of God. Instead of "Christ the Saviour is here!", the new slogan was "Our *Führer* the Saviour is here!" *Frau Holle*, as the "mother of life", and other German fairy tales were intended to replace the Christmas story with its Biblical elements.[48]

"The *Sippengemeinschaft*, however, is eternal, in that we live on in our chil-dren", said the director of the *Wienerwald* home in his speech at the Yule cele-bration in 1939. "Winter solstice, the celebration of the family, the clan, indeed of the people as a whole", he continued, referring to the pre-Christian roots of the festival. "When the Catholic Church forced upon us an ethnically foreign worldview, it was unable to change the festivals rooted in our nature and our mental attitude, and thus our emotional attitude towards the winter solstice. After centuries of struggle, it was forced to give in, and finally to set the [date of the] birth of Christ on the old Germanic winter solstice".[49] The speech concluded with the words: "In this sense, a triple *Sieg-Heil* to our dearly beloved *Führer!*", before everyone sang the *SS* loyalty song.[50]

In 1938, the "dignified speech" by the director of the home, *SS-Unter-scharführer* Sernetz, focused on the *Anschluss* of Austria with the Third Reich. He put particular emphasis on "the great achievement of the *Führer*, the re-integration of Austria into the motherland, Germany". "With thanks to the

---

45  Training Report at the *Wienerwald* home in February 1940, 1 March 1940, AA, 4.1.0/82453933.
46  Neumaier, *Das Lebensbornheim "Schwarzwald" in Nordrach*, 277.
47  Training Report at the *Wienerwald* home in March 1940, 31 March 1940, AA, 4.1.0/82453940.
48  Josef Thomik, *Nationalsozialismus als "Ersatzreligion"* (Aachen: einhard verlag, 2009), 25–37.
49  Copy of *Julfeier* Speech at the *Wienerwald* home 1939, n.d., AA, 4.1.0/82453396.
50  Copy of *Julfeier* Speech at the *Wienerwald* home 1939, n.d., AA, 4.1.0/82453397.

*Führer* and the pledge to work actively with him in the coming year, the director of the home concluded his speech", underlined NS head nurse Hofmann.[51]

At the *Ostmark Lebensborn* home, which went under the name of *Wienerwald* home from 1942, a speech by the director at the Yule celebration on 21 December 1939 was again a central feature. In addition, there was a Christmas celebration with "tree lighting and gift giving" on 24 December, both forming part of the ideological training.[52] The following year, as early as the end of November a separate evening was dedicated to "old Germanic customs in Yule time as preparation for the winter solstice".[53] The fairy tale *Goldmarie und Pechmarie* was apparently very popular, as it was performed twice.[54] For the winter solstice and Yule celebrations, which were to be held together on 21 December, the head of the *SS-Hauptamt* issued specific orders.[55] However, it appears that the solstice celebrations had to be cancelled, as is indicated by a handwritten note in a letter to Ebner: "Solstice celebrations cannot be held with the mothers in winter for medical reasons."[56]

Mother's Day, which was particularly hyped and instrumentalised under National Socialism for demographic policy purposes, was also categorised under ideological education. After all, motherhood was no longer considered a private matter, but was enlisted in the service of racial hygiene policy. In May 1940 – when, alongside a "celebration hour for Mother's Day", there were four singing evenings, a variety show with folk dances and shadow puppet shows, and only one lecture by home director Sernetz on "Community and comradeship" – entertainment clearly took precedence in the context of ideological re-education.[57]

In the following months, evenings of entertainment continued to dominate, but they became less frequent. For example, in June 1940 – apart from Sernetz's daily newspaper reports – there were only four singing evenings and one lecture on "Diet in pregnancy".[58] The only lecture in July was dedicated to the "home community", a subject that frequently led to conflicts in *Lebensborn* homes,

---

51 Letter from NS Senior Sister Hofmann to *Lebensborn* about the *Julfeier* in the *Wienerwald* home, 4 January 1939, AA, 4.1.0/82453371.
52 Training Report at the *Ostmark* home in December 1940, 31 December 1940; they also celebrated the *Julfeier* in other homes on 21 December. Cf. Neumaier, *Das Lebensbornheim "Schwarzwald" in Nordrach*, 277, AA, 4.1.0/82454046.
53 Training Report at the *Ostmark* home in November 1941, 1 December 1941, AA, 4.1.0/82454142.
54 Training Report at the *Ostmark* home in December 1941, 3 January 1942, AA, 4.1.0/82454254.
55 Director of the *Hauptamt* about the winter solstice and *Julfeier* 1938, 23 November 1938, AA, 4.1.0/82453351.
56 Letter from to Ebner about the winter slotice and *Julfeier*, 7 December 1938, AA, 4.1.0/82453357.
57 Training Report at the *Wienerwald* home in May 1940, 31 May 1940, AA, 4.1.0/82453970.
58 Training Report at the *Wienerwald* home in June 1940, 30 June 1940, AA, 4.1.0/82453986.

particularly in the *Wienerwald* home.[59] It was, after all, "only to be expected, in a home where over 50 mothers from all regions of the *Reich* and all social classes come together, that there will be disagreements. Unfortunately, this often includes disputes between the *Altreich* and the *Ostmark*", the director of the home noted in this context.[60] Meanwhile in August, the entire training consisted of two singing evenings led by the head nurse and a lecture by Sernetz on "The current situation in Europe".[61]

The birth of the thousandth child in the *Wienerwald* home on 1 September 1943 was a special occasion, to which a separate lecture was dedicated on the "Meaning and mission of *Lebensborn*".[62] For those children who stayed longer in the home and attended the specially established kindergarten, there were also puppet theatre shows. It is impossible to say whether this was a venue for early ideological influence.[63]

In addition to ideological training, *Lebensborn* organised training events for both mothers and staff. For instance, Ebner delivered a lecture at the home directors' meeting in July 1940 on "Infant mortality in *Lebensborn e.V.* and its prevention".[64] From July 1943, the *Wienerwald* home ran classes for mothers with a focus on homemaking and parenting issues, which both mothers and employees could attend. The focus of the nurses' training in August 1943, for example, was on combating rickets.[65] Aerial warfare gradually became an issue in the *Ostmark*, which was seen as the "air-raid shelter of the *Reich*", as is evidenced by the "First aid in air-raid protection" units for the nurses in the home.[66]

As will be shown below, nutrition in *Lebensborn* held special ideological significance. For example, as part of the training sessions, a separate course for the head chefs of the different *Lebensborn* homes on the topic of healthy cooking took place in June 1943 at the *Hochland* home in Bavarian Steinhöring, where the *Lebensborn* central office was located. Margarethe Kurz attended the training held by the *Deutsches Frauenwerk* for the *Wienerwald* home, although she apparently did not stand out for her "special knowledge and quick understanding",

---

59 Training Report at the *Wienerwald* home in July 1940, 7 August 1940, AA, 4.1.0/82454002.
60 Letter from Schwab to Ebner regarding the report of the Reich Security Main Office 14 April 1943, 23 April 1943, AA, 4.1.0/82448937.
61 Training Report at the *Wienerwald* home in August 1940, 31 August 1940, AA, 4.1.0/82454008.
62 Training Report at the *Wienerwald* home in September 1943, 4 October 1943, AA, 4.1.0/82454188.
63 Training Report at the *Wienerwald* home in November 1943, 2 December 1943, AA, 4.1.0/82454202.
64 Letter from Schwab concerning lectures about breastfeeding problems, 6 March 1941, AA, 4.1.0/82454086.
65 Training Report at the *Wienerwald* home in August 1943, 2 September 1943, AA, 4.1.0/82454176.
66 Training Report at the *Wienerwald* home in November 1943, 2 December 1943, AA, 4.1.0/82454202.

unlike the cooks from the *Kurmark*, *Harz*, *Pomerania* and *Taunus* homes. Several lectures focused on the "structure and function of the digestive organs", with emphasis on the stomach, intestine, liver, gallbladder, and salivary glands, as well as the principles of individual diets. In practical units, the cooks practised preparing the different diets.[67]

## V.    Nutrition: Eating "in the Spirit of the True *Volksgemeinschaft*"

On Hitler's birthday, 20 April 1942, the head of the health department at *Lebensborn*, *SS-Oberführer* Gregor Ebner, wrote to the directors of several *Lebensborn* homes, including the *Ostmark* home, informing them that the *Reichsführer-SS* himself requested a report on nutrition. Of special interest were such questions as "How is food cooked in the maternity homes? Do they take care to properly steam vegetables so that there is no loss of nutritional value? Are foolish boiled potatoes still being cooked, or has it strictly been ensured that only jacket potatoes are served?"[68] Heinrich Himmler also wanted to know whether the mothers were taught "proper cooking", whether enough raw food like sauerkraut was served up, and what vegetables the older children were served.[69]

Himmler's "attention to detail, combined with pettiness and distrust" clearly emerged when he concerned himself with the particulars of food preparation and distribution.[70] Every detail interested him; page after page was filled to provide information about meal plans and the consumption of coffee, sunflower seeds or cod liver oil, and even in January 1944, the *Reichsführer-SS* was instructing the *Lebensborn* Board about the correct preparation of oat porridge.[71] Nutrition was of elemental importance within *Lebensborn*.

The reason for this lies once again in National Socialist ideology and its obsession with "good German blood", the policy shaped by pronatalist and antinatalist measures as well as negative eugenics. Countless methods of "racial hygiene" implemented by the state – such as compulsory sterilisation of supposedly "hereditarily diseased" individuals under the Law for the Prevention of Hereditarily Diseased Offspring, child euthanasia, or conversely marriage loans to increase the birth rate – pursued one crucial goal: the promotion of "hereditarily healthy Aryan" offspring, coupled with the simultaneous "extermination"

---

67  Report on a Healthy Cooking Course at the *Hochland* home, 26 June 1943; Neumaier, *Das Lebensbornheim "Schwarzwald" in Nordrach*, p 231–32, AA, 4.1.0/82454244.

68  Letter from the Health Services Director to the heads of *Lebensborn* homes concerning nutrition, 20 April 1942. AA, 4.1.0/82338682.

69  Ibid.

70  Lilienthal, *Der "Lebensborn e.V."*, 67.

71  Ibid. 68.

of people defined by National Socialism as hereditarily diseased or non-Aryan. A healthy, wholesome diet combined with physical fitness and only sporadic consumption of intoxicants and luxury foods were considered pillars of health and physical strength. National Socialist scientists like surgeon and propagandist of racial hygiene Erwin Liek held poor nutrition responsible for most diseases. Conversely, a "pure and natural national diet" was considered ideal, contributing to promoting health.[72]

Against this backdrop, nutrition in National Socialism lost its private character. The entire cultural system of food ingestion was instrumentalised for political and ideological goals and used to foster the development of the *Volksgemeinschaft*. Even early on in the National Socialist era, the regime declared food supply and culture to be a national task, as shown, for example, by the introduction of "stew-Sundays" in 1933. Meals defined who belonged to the *Volksgemeinschaft* and who did not.[73] It was therefore strictly forbidden for Soviet prisoners of war to eat at the same table as locals. Violations could lead to severe penalties, but were common nonetheless.[74] This ideology also affected food as such, resulting in the rejection of foreign foods and cooking methods, and at the same time, the promotion of local foods and their names.[75] An educational guide, pushed by the National Socialists as a bestseller, used in *Lebensborn* and distributed to first-time mothers on Himmler's orders,[76] Johanna Harrer's *Die Deutsche Mutter und ihr erstes Kind* (The German Mother and Her First Child) stated: "For quenching thirst, as is already known from the maternity ward, the following are once again recommended: pure fruit juices, German [!] teas like lime blossom, rosehip, peppermint tea".[77]

The ideological instrumentalisation of nutrition also explains why it was assigned such importance in the *Lebensborn* homes. The "nobility of the future" and the mothers responsible for them were to be optimally cared for according to contemporary knowledge to maximise their healthy development. Heinrich Himmler was deeply invested in this topic, rigorously implementing his vision

---

72 Neumaier, Das *Lebensbornheim "Schwarzwald" in Nordrach*, 218; Robert N. Proctor, *Blitzkrieg gegen den Krebs. Gesundheit und Propaganda im Dritten Reich* (Stuttgart: Klett-Cotta, 2002), 33–39.

73 Neumaier, Das *Lebensbornheim "Schwarzwald" in Nordrach*, 218–19; Claus-Dieter Rath, *Reste der Tafelrunde. Das Abenteuer der Esskultur* (Reinbek bei Hamburg: Rowohlt, 1984), 179.

74 Barbara Stelzl-Marx, *Zwischen Fiktion und Zeitzeugenschaft. Amerikanische und sowjetische Kriegsgefangene im Stalag XVII B Krems-Gneixendorf.* (Tübingen: Gunter Narr Verlag, 2000), 55–6.

75 Neumaier, Das *Lebensbornheim "Schwarzwald" in Nordrach*, 219.

76 Brandt to Ebner concerning the distribution of *Die deutsche Mutter und ihr erstes Kind* in Lebensborn homes, 6 January 1944. AA, 4.1.0/82448763.

77 Johanna Harrer, *Die deutsche Mutter und ihr erstes Kind. 338–440 Tausend.* (Munich – Berlin: J. F. Lehmanns, 1941), 132.; Neumaier, *Das Lebensbornheim "Schwarzwald" in Nordrach*, 219.

within the homes. His directive to serve oat porridge instead of "bread rolls with coffee" for breakfast was to be "ruthlessly implemented", as he emphasised.[78]

Therefore, Himmler's initial inquiry about "cooking methods in the maternity homes" did not fall on deaf ears but was answered meticulously by every single one of the home directors who was contacted. *"Oberführer,"* the head of the *Ostmark* home wrote to the head of the health department at *Lebensborn* in a report reminiscent of a military briefing that "from our home's kitchen, I can report that we only cook vegetables for a short period of time. We do not steam vegetables, as we lack the necessary inserts for the large pots, and currently we are not even able to get enough pots, let alone these inserts". Following up this hint about the effects of the war on the production of consumer goods, Sernetz responded to the question of "foolish boiled potatoes", addressing the supply difficulties in the third year of the war: "Potatoes are sometimes served as boiled potatoes and sometimes as jacket potatoes. The quality of the potatoes delivered this winter was sometimes so poor that serving them as jacket potatoes was out of the question."[79]

The answers to the subsequent three questions offer interesting insights into daily life at the *Ostmark* home and the further effects of the war economy on nutrition. According to the director of the home, there had no longer been a *Mütterschule* in the *Ostmark* home for two years, meaning that mothers received no cooking lessons. However, as mothers were assigned supporting roles in the kitchen, they would have the opportunity to "watch the cooking" if they were interested. The food shortages that had become apparent since the beginning of the war were evident in the area of raw food: this was served "as far as it can be procured, mainly raw cabbage and fruit salad". The older children received vegetables daily, "as long as they can be procured, e.g., cauliflower, lettuce, carrots". At this point, in April 1942, there were only three children over two years old in the home.[80]

In addition to the emphasis on vitamin- and nutrient-rich foods and their proper preparation, *Lebensborn* first ordered "Vitaborn juices" at the beginning of 1942, namely 2410 litres for the homes and 2228 litres for the headquarters, where those in charge were apparently also mindful of ensuring a vitamin-rich diet for themselves. The vitamin juices, which – except for juniper juice – were very popular among mothers, were distributed free of charge in the homes "as a supplement to the breakfast oatmeal, as a drink to accompany meals, and as a

---

78  Neumaier, *Das Lebensbornheim "Schwarzwald" in Nordrach*, 221.

79  Letter from Sernetz to the Health Services Director at *Lebensborn* about cooking methods in the maternity homes, 28 April 1942, AA, 4.1.0/82448688.

80  Letter from Sernetz to the Health Services Director at *Lebensborn* about cooking methods in the maternity homes, 28 April 1942, AA, 4.1.0/82448689.

drink for women who had recently given birth, and for the sick".[81] It is evident from Ebner's report from May 1942 how much importance Himmler placed on the supply of vitamins: "From the fourth month of life, *Lebensborn* children are served carrots every day, chopped up and cooked. We also give carrots raw to the older children in the nursery. In addition, carrot juice is served as an accompaniment to the afternoon porridge in the nursery".[82] The focus on this particular vegetable clearly stems from the *Reichsführer-SS*'s directive that "all children in our children's homes should be given carrots (raw or cooked) <u>daily</u>".[83]

Particular attention was paid to coffee, the consumption of which had to be accurately recorded and reported to Berlin. In 1940, the homes received one kilogram of coffee beans per month by post.[84] This was increased to three kilograms at the beginning of 1941. From then on, consumption no longer had to be documented by weight, but coffee distribution – which the senior nurse in the homes took care of – was now the responsibility of the home director, who only had to submit a report on the individual recipients.[85] The coffee, doled out by the gram, was primarily used by the midwives and nurses who kept watch in the night during births.[86] However, coffee was also served at naming ceremonies – about 60 grams was used for one such celebration on 20 April 1941.[87] In mid-1943, Ebner gave Schwab, the director of the *Ostmark* home, permission to "issue a prescription for 20 g of coffee beans for each woman after childbirth".[88]

The dietary regulations and documentation in every *Lebensborn* home were thorough and informed not only by organisational principles, but also by ideological ones. Everyone dined together at fixed times, morning, noon, and night, without any segregation. Ebner considered this "one of the finest aspects of a *Lebensborn* home".[89] Everyone ate the same food, which was served commu-

---

81 Report from Ebner to the *Reichsführer-SS* concerning inquiry about Vitaborn juices and vegetable preparation in *Lebensborn* homes, 8 May 1942, AA, 4.1.0/82448694.

82 Report from Ebner to the *Reichsführer-SS* concerning inquiry about Vitaborn juices and vegetable preparation in *Lebensborn* homes, 8 May 1942, AA, 4.1.0/82448695–82448696.

83 Letter from the Personal Staff of the *Reichsführer-SS* to *Lebensborn* about nutrition in the homes, 8 April 1942, AA, 4.1.0/82448699.

84 Letter from the Head of the Main Office of Administration and Economy at the *Reichsführer-SS* to the Health Services Director at *Lebensborn* about coffee allocation in *Lebensborn* homes, 10 September 1940, AA, 4.1.0/82465104.

85 Letter from Ebner about coffee allocation for *Lebensborn* homes, 14 January 1941, AA, 4.1.0/82465113.

86 Overview of the monthly consumption of coffee allocated by the *Reichsführer-SS* at the *Wienerwald* home in August 1940, 30 August 1940, AA, 4.1.0/82465274.

87 Overview of the monthly consumption of coffee allocated by the Reichsführer-SS at the *Wienerwald* home in April 1941, 2 May 1941, AA, 4.1.0/82465294.

88 Letter from Ebner to Schwab about the use of bean coffee, 28 June 1943, AA, 4.1.0/82465312.

89 Report by Ebner on the complaint, 13 December 1943, AA, 4.1.0/82457065. Cited in: Neumaier, *Das Lebensbornheim "Schwarzwald" in Nordrach*, 222.

nally. Echoing the concept of the *Volksgemeinschaft*, these homes aimed to create a community of mothers, irrespective of their marital status. The aim was "camaraderie amongst equals, uniting for a common purpose and losing one's individuality in the larger collective".[90] It was part of the *SS*'s intent to provide protection and equal status "especially to unmarried mothers".[91]

For instance, at the *Wienerwald* home, the menu for a week in early 1943 included soup every day – such as semolina, vegetable, noodle, star-shaped pasta or egg soup – and main courses such as mashed potatoes with fried egg and salad, or beef with cabbage and potatoes. On Sundays, there was smoked meat with mashed potatoes and sauerkraut. Twice a week, a dessert was served, such as yeast pastry with vanilla sauce or semolina pudding with compote. Evening meals often featured potatoes prepared in various ways, accompanied by bread, tea, and cabbage salad, or by cocoa, rolls, butter, and even oranges. Coffee and cake were always available on Sundays.[92] Ulrike Z., born in the *Wienerwald* home, recalls her mother describing the accommodation and care as "fantastic", comparable to "being in a luxury hotel".[93]

Weekly meal plans for the *Wienerwald* home submitted by Ebner to the *Lebensborn* headquarters in Steinhöring have been preserved, at least until the autumn of 1944.[94] These were substantial meal plans for wartime. The mothers still regularly lodged complaints, for instance, about the excessive offer of gas-inducing cabbage.[95] The oatmeal served for breakfast also frequently provoked dissatisfaction amongst the women, who expressed concerns about gaining weight from it. The *Lebensborn* headquarters dismissed these concerns as groundless and insisted that the homes should simply make the porridge more palatable.[96]

It appears there were complaints about the way mothers and employees at the *Wienerwald* home were summoned to meals. Up to that point, as Ebner reported, "a cowbell with an unbearable sound had been used, which was so loud that it always startled children and women who had just given birth from their sleep".[97] He requested a suitable gong from the head of the *Lebensborn* administration, *SS-Obersturmführer* Alfred Wehner,[98] who promptly replied, "*SS-Sturmbannführer*

---

90  Schmitz-Köster, *"Deutsche Mutter, bist du bereit ..."*, 148.
91  Ibid, 210.
92  Menu for the *Wienerwald* home, 1–7 February 1943, 3 March 1943, AA, 4.1.0/82467182.
93  BIK, Ulrike Z., interviewed by Michaela Tasotti, 3 November 2021, Wiener Neustadt, Transcript 17.
94  Menu for the *Wienerwald* home, 21–30 September 1943, n.d., AA, 4.1.0/82467262.
95  Schmitz-Köster, *"Deutsche Mutter, bist Du bereit ..."*, 150.
96  AA, 4.1.0/82448668.
97  Ebner to the Head of the Main Administration Department Wehner concerning the meal gong at the *Wienerwald* home, 9 August 1943, AA, 4.1.0/82463352.
98  Ibid.

Lang has graciously offered his office gong for this purpose. The gong is being sent to you separately".[99] He suggested that for the missing gong hammer "a makeshift substitute can certainly be found on site" and concluded with *"Heil Hitler!".*[100]

Babies' nutrition was regulated at least as strictly as mothers' in the *Lebensborn* homes. Breastfeeding was prioritised – a "duty" that, as ordered by Himmler himself, was to be fulfilled for at least six weeks for the benefit of the child.[101] All mothers were encouraged to breastfeed, as far as they were able to do so. The reason for this was the perceived direct correlation between the duration of breastfeeding and infant mortality. Ebner emphasised in a circular to the doctors in the homes that their medical skills could not "in the slightest" compete with the benefits that nature bestowed upon the infant through breast milk. Therefore, a reduction in the mortality rate, which had risen at the beginning of the war in *Lebensborn* homes, could only be achieved if women fulfilled their "maternal duties" towards their children.[102] The association would even cover the costs for unmarried women to extend their stay in the homes, so they did not have to stop breastfeeding prematurely to return to work.[103]

Mothers' willingness and ability to breastfeed were meticulously recorded. In the questionnaires compiled by the *Reichsführer-SS* for each "mother of a child" in a *Lebensborn* home, references were made to and notations were added for "breastfeeding willingness" and "breastfeeding ability", ideally "both very good". Further, in the section "Do mother and child require financial support from the SS," remarks can be found such as "No. Willingness to breastfeed: she breastfeeds effortlessly and fully, ability to breastfeed".[104] According to the *SS* questionnaires in the Pernitz registry office, 250 mothers in the *Wienerwald* home exhibited "good to excellent willingness to breastfeed", and only five displayed "poor" willingness. Of the women for whom this information is available, 205 were able to breastfeed, while 42, according to the questionnaire entries, were unable to do so.[105]

---

99  Head of the Main Administration Department Wehner to Trautmann concerning the meal gong at the *Wienerwald* home, 11 August 1913, AA, 4.1.0/82463353.

100 Ibid.

101 Lilienthal, *Der "Lebemsborn e. V."*, 65; Schmitz-Köster, *"Deutsche Mutter, bist du bereit ..."*, 229–30; Neumaier, *Das Lebensbornheim "Schwarzwald" in Nordrach*, 241–42.

102 Lilienthal, *Der "Lebemsborn e. V."*, 65.

103 Ibid.

104 Pernitz Registry Office, RF-Questionnaire, Rosa P., 1944. In the context of nutrition policy, a quantitative evaluation of the questionnaires on breastfeeding behaviour seemed particularly relevant for this paper. For more information also see the editorial of this volume.

105 BIK, Database *Lebensbornheim Wienerwald*. Thanks to Mag. Martin Sauerbrei-Almasy for the database queries.

If a mother had more than enough milk, she could express it and give it for a fee to the infant department for women with too little milk.[106] This "noble act of true neighbourly love" was proof that the mother "understood the meaning of the true *Volksgemeinschaft*", Harrer explained in her educational guide *The German Mother and Her First Child*, highlighting the ideological component of breastfeeding in the chapter on "breastfed children".[107] If a mother shirked her duty to breastfeed, this was considered, at least implicitly, a "betrayal of the *Volksgemeinschaft*", with potential consequences such as a negative internal assessment. This could lead to the withdrawal of all privileges, such as support in finding housing or employment and might mean that the woman was deemed unsuitable for future admission to a *Lebensborn* home.[108]

Apart from the nutritional and medical advantages of breastfeeding, the infants also benefited from physical closeness to and individual care from their mothers. Nappy changing and bathing also contributed to a closer bond between mother and child, which was not easy to foster. After all, new-borns spent most of their time in the "infant room" under strict rules and the watchful eyes of the nurses.[109] The mothers' daily routine was similarly strictly regimented.

## VI.  Everyday Life: Corseted in Diligence and Order

"'The child ennobles the mother' – so says the *Führer!* This nobility is expressed in the posture and actions of the expectant mother; it radiates from her proud, happy eyes as soon as the young mother holds her child, healthy and full of life, in her arms." According to a text on "mothers in the *Lebensborn* home," *Lebensborn* facilitated their "inner preparation for their forthcoming child, for which life outside does not allow them time or for which different circumstances do not afford them peace and quiet". As soon as the mother had settled into the home community, she was "cared for and protected". Furthermore, "the character of the home, the bright, beautiful and comfortable rooms, the care provided by the home's working community, the camaraderie of the other mothers, all foster a feeling of security and peace". The environment would soon become synonymous with 'home' in the traditional sense – at least, that was the ideal.[110]

After this idyllic-sounding introduction, the text more or less subtly comes to the point – the contribution the mother was expected to make. "She familiarises herself with the regulated daily routine of the home and joins the ranks of those

---

106  Neumaier, *Das Lebensbornheim "Schwarzwal" in Nordrach*, 242.
107  Harrer, *Die deutsche Mutter und ihr erstes Kind*, 136.
108  Neumaier, *Das Lebensbornheim "Schwarzwald" in Nordrach*, 242.
109  Schmitz-Köster, *"Deutsche Mutter, bist du bereit …"*, 230.
110  "Mütter im Lebensbornheim", n.d., AA, 4.1.0/82453148.

who toil and labour for this home and maintain its comfort and order". This meant specifically that "the cleanliness which is maintained and is prevalent in every *Lebensborn* home – the orderliness of the house, kitchen, laundry room, medical rooms, maternity and infant rooms and the kindergarten, the floors. and basements – requires many diligent hands. The mother joins in here, and soon she becomes a skilful, diligent housewife in the various areas of her duties". There were "supporting courses offered by the *Reichsmütterdienst*, which are harmoniously incorporated into the overall work plan of the house [...] – in short, covering everything that a housewife and mother needs".[111]

The text also touches upon the ideological training programme, without naming it explicitly: "Mothers are involved in the organisation of community evenings. Variety shows and musical performances by mothers alternate with lectures of both a serious and cheerful nature. These unique social gatherings within the *Lebensborn* homes give rise to moments of inner reflection."[112] Following this reference to the attractive leisure programme, there is another description of the duties of the women residing at the home: "Thus, the mothers' days are filled with activities that contribute to shaping the life of *Lebensborn* homes as exemplary in terms of external cleanliness and an internal spirit of community and camaraderie".[113]

In a *Lebensborn* home, the day was ruled by the clock – with fixed meal times and prescribed breastfeeding, bathing and sleeping times "irrespective of personal needs".[114] In addition to attending organised courses, women were assigned easy tasks in the kitchen and house.[115] They did not need to worry about the children themselves – breastfeeding, changing nappies and bathing was done under the supervision of a ward sister. The new-borns spent most of their time in the "infant room", where nurses cared for them. The older children from six months of age slept, played, and ate under the supervision of nursery teachers or nurses in the kindergarten – again with specific rules, such as communal potty-training, which is regarded as highly controversial these days.[116]

Unsurprisingly, conflicts arose time and again in the homes, where dozens of women in exceptional circumstances were accommodated in close quarters shortly before or after childbirth. On the one hand, there was often rivalry between single and married women, with the latter seeing themselves as the "elite" due to their *SS* husbands and demanding preferential treatment, such as being accommodated in single rooms. For ideological reasons, *Lebensborn* made at-

---

111 Ibid.
112 Ibid.
113 Ibid.
114 Schmitz-Köster, *"Deutsche Mutter, bist du bereit ..."*, 257.
115 Lilienthal, *Der "Lebensborn e.V."*, 65–6.
116 Schmitz-Köster, *"Deutsche Mutter, bist du bereit ..."*, 229.

tempts to prevent this as far as possible and to strengthen the community spirit in the home. After all, all women, whether married or single, were supposed to be – or at least to appear – equal, which was reflected in their clothing, the way they were addressed, and their tasks in the Lebensborn.[117] Therefore, the *Reichsführer-SS*'s questionnaires not only evaluated their qualities as housewives, but also their attitude towards the house community in some cases in great detail and quite critically: "She was unpleasant and disruptive due to her 'egoism' and grumbling", for example.[118]

On the other hand, the mothers themselves also complained about the staff at the home and the healthcare provided, sometimes using surprisingly candid language. For example, one mother protested against impersonal and inconsiderate treatment by pointing out that the women in the *Lebensborn* home were not "birthing machines". Another mother defied a doctor's order by stating, "I'm not in Dachau here".[119] However, violations of home rules and criticism sometimes resulted in severe consequences, as is demonstrated by the case of two women who danced a waltz one evening in the day room of the *Wienerwald* home, thus breaking the wartime dance prohibition. They were turned on so severely that one of them refused the position she was offered as a caretaker in the home and left.[120]

The rigorous way violations of the rules were addressed within the SS is illustrated by the following example. In the *Wienerwald* home, the senior nurse reported to Ebner that a mother had allegedly complained that "the doctors are too cheeky towards the married women".[121] From today's perspective, this second-hand statement would likely fall under the category of "gossip". However, in the totalitarian system of the National Socialist state and within the structures of the SS, this led to the interrogation of several SS men who were only peripherally involved. The possibility of the Gestapo interrogating Mrs. P. was considered, but *SS-Standartenführer* Pflaum "refrained [from doing so] for the time being because I believe she might make a statement on this matter of her own accord".[122] However, "immediate disciplinary action" should be taken against "SS comrade P.," the husband.[123] Eventually, it emerged that the statement had been made by *SS-Rottenführer* Max B., who had visited his wife in the *Lebensborn* home *Wie-*

---

117  Ibid, 208.
118  Pernitz Registry Office, RF-Questionnaire Margarete B., 1944.
119  Lilienthal, *Der "Lebensborn e.V."*, 68.
120  Schmitz-Köster, *"Deutsche Mutter, bist du bereit ..."*, 210.
121  Letter from Pflaum to Ebner about a complaint from the *Wienerwald* home, 6 August 1939, AA, 82457122.
122  Report to Pflaum on disciplinary case P., 13 November 1939, AA, 82457124.
123  Letter from Pflaum to Ebner about a complaint from the *Wienerwald* home, 6 August 1939, AA, 82457122.

*nerwald.* He thought "he remembered [...] that *SS-Oberscharführer* S. had told him, 'the doctors here in the home are making advances towards the married women and the children are not being cared for'".[124]

Subsequently, B. was interrogated by the *90th SS-Standarte* and *SS-Oberscharführer* S. was interrogated by his service unit.[125] The consequence was harsh: B. was to be expelled from the *SS* because he had proven himself to be "unworthy of the *SS*" through his behaviour. Two decisive reasons were given for this: "B. is solely and exclusively responsible for the serious slander about the home's doctors. In a cowardly manner, he tried to shift the blame onto Mrs. P., or his comrade S." This was "a degradation of an institution of the *Reichsführer-SS* and a serious violation of the honour of an impeccable *SS* doctor, an innocent *SS* comrade and the wife of an *SS-Führer*".[126]

## VII.   Conclusion

Everyday life in the allegedly "exclusively charitable and benevolent" *Lebensborn* association was deeply imbued with the ideology of National Socialist "racial policy". Everything was done to support "racially and hereditarily valuable expecting mothers, who, after careful examination of their own family and the family of the progenitor, were assumed to give birth to equally valuable children". The explicit objective of the "exclusively charitable and benevolent" association was to care for these children and their mothers, as stated in the initially cited statutes.[127] The attention and privileges bestowed upon these mothers were based on the assessment that they fell on the right side of so-called "positive eugenics".[128] The ideology of "good blood" permeated all areas of the *Lebensborn*, including the *Wienerwald* home – from the choice of first names, name-giving ceremonies, and the celebration of other festivities to training provided to mothers in line with the National Socialist worldview, and even extending to dietary choices and daily routines, which emphasised diligence and order. The child was always front and centre, considered to be the "nobility of the future". Yet, these children were often saddled with a challenging legacy to carry forward.

---

124  Report to Pflaum on disciplinary case P., 13 November 1939, AA, 82457122.
125  Ibid.
126  Letter to Ebner on disciplinary case P., 16 December 1939, AA, 82457129.
127  *Verein Lebensborn e.V. in München, Broschüre Lebensborn eingetragener Verein.* Miesbach n.d., 8, NÖLA, Office of the Provincial Government of Lower Austria, Landesamt I/2, number 33/1975.
128  Schmitz-Köster, *"Deutsche Mutter, bist du bereit ..."*, 215.

Nadjeschda Stoffers / Lukas Schretter

# Student Nurses for *Lebensborn*. Daily Routines in the *Heim Wienerwald*, 1940–1945

## I.  Introduction

"I have once again been transferred to the infant ward, so now I have only weekdays off,"[1] wrote 17-year-old Marianne Leitner from the *Heim Wienerwald* to her mother in Klosterneuburg in a letter dated 15 April 1942.[2] The *Heim Wienerwald*, established in Feichtenbach in October 1938, was one of more than twenty maternity homes of the *Lebensborn* association, which was founded in 1935 by *Reichsführer SS* Heinrich Himmler to promote the birth of "hereditarily healthy" offspring. To boost the birth rate of the "racially" desired population share, pregnant unwed women who met the SS selection criteria were offered a discreet birthing option. In addition to unwed women, wives of members of the SS and the German police chose *Lebensborn* maternity homes to give birth to their children.[3] From late 1940 until the end of the war in 1945, Leitner completed her training to become an infant nurse, spending more than thirty months of her training in the *Heim Wienerwald*.

---

1  Letter from Marianne Leitner to her mother, 15 April 1942, lines 14–16, Box 147/4, NL 147/II Marianne Leitner, *Sammlung Frauennachlässe* (Collection of Collection of Women's Personal Papers; hereinafter SFN) at the Institute for History of the University of Vienna.
2  Marianne Leitner is referred to by her full name, other persons mentioned by Leitner are anonymised, following consultation with the SFN. Thanks are extended to Dr. Li Gerhalter (Head of SFN) for her support and provision of the bequest, and to *fernetzt – Verein zur Förderung junger Forschung zur Frauen- und Geschlechtergeschichte* (Association for Promoting Young Research on Women and Gender History), especially Pauline Bögner, for drawing the authors' attention to Leitner's bequest. The authors would also like to thank Otmar Binder for copy-editing the English version of this article. The article's realisation was supported by the Jubilee Fund of the Austrian National Bank, the Future Fund of the Republic of Austria, and the State of Lower Austria. Associated research was conducted at the Ludwig Boltzmann Institute for Research on Consequences of War, Graz – Vienna – Raabs (hereinafter BIK), in collaboration with the Institute of History of the University of Graz.
3  For ideological principles and goals of the *Lebensborn* association, see the editorial by Lukas Schretter and Barbara Stelzl-Marx in this volume.

This article on the staff of the *Heim Wienerwald* is largely based on the correspondence Leitner bequeathed to the *Sammlung Frauennachlässe* (Collection
of Women's Personal Papers, SFN) at the University of Vienna.[4] Among others,
the bequest consists in approximately 450 letters, including almost seventy of
Leitner's fully or partially preserved letters from the *Heim Wienerwald* to her
mother.

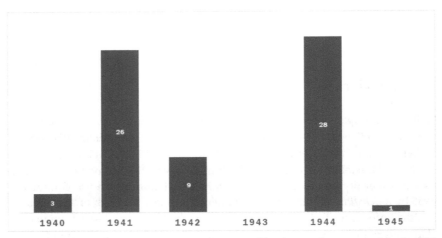

Letters of Marianne Leitner from the *Heim Wienerwald* to her mother preserved in the SFN

These letters provide insight into everyday life in the *Heim Wienerwald* and
reflect Leitner's horizon of experience. Historian Elissa Mailänder already engaged with Leitner's bequest in her gender history research, exploring lived
experiences of love, marriage, and sexuality among heterosexual, cis-gender,
non-Jewish, non-disabled German and Austrian men and women that constituted Hitler's *Volksgemeinschaft*.[5] Leitner's biography was also part of an exhibition titled *Fremde im Visier. Fotoalben aus dem Zweiten Weltkrieg* (Targeting
the Other: Photo Albums from World War II) at the *Österreichisches Volkskun-
demuseum* (Austrian Museum of Folk Life and Folk Art) in 2016/17.[6]

---

4  For more information see Li Gerhalter, "Geschichten und Voraussetzungen. Die Bestände der
   Sammlung Frauennachlässe am Institut für Geschichte der Universität Wien," *Unsere Heimat*
   81 (2010) 1: 27–41.
5  Elissa Mailänder, *Amour, Mariage, Sexualité. Une histoire intime du nazisme (1930–1950)*
   (Montrouge: Éditions du Seuil, 2021).
6  Petra Bopp, *Fremde im Visier. Fotoalben aus dem Zweiten Weltkrieg* (Bielefeld/Berlin: Kerber
   Verlag, 2009). The catalogue does not include information on Leitner as the exhibition only
   took place in Vienna several years after the catalogue's publication, and local modifications
   were not incorporated. Copies of the exhibition texts regarding Leitner are kept in the SFN, NL
   147/II.

Furthermore, this article includes the findings from an interview conducted with Hedwig Glattauer, neé Hartl, born in 1929.[7] Between 14 and 16 years of age, she was a student nurse in the *Heim Wienerwald*. How contemporary witnesses talk about National Socialism, what features in their stories and what is kept secret has been subjected since the end of the war to a process of steady change. This is shaped by nuances in the national commemorative discourse and by intrafamilial and milieu-specific ways of handing on memories from one generation to the next. As one of the few contemporary-witness interviews that could be conducted on the history of the *Heim Wienerwald* in the 2020s, the interview with Hedwig Glattauer sheds light on the day-to-day life of a *Vorschülerin* (student nurse) and how she evaluated and processed her experience.[8] Interviews conducted with descendants of the women who gave birth in the *Heim Wienerwald* between 1938 and 1945 seldom address the home's staff – unless their mothers had been employed there postpartum.[9]

Additionally, this article is based on the files kept in the Arolsen Archives as well as on TV documentaries about the history of the *Heim Wienerwald*, in which the employees are the subject of discussion.[10] The research body on the structure, ideology, and function of *NS-Schwestern* as well as on midwifery under National Socialism has expanded since the turn of the millennium.[11] Studies specifically

---

7 For this article, Hedwig Glattauer consented to the use of her full name and is referred to by her married name, i.e. the name she had at the time of the interview. The authors have opted for this in order to refer to the retrospective background of the memories cited.

8 Hedwig Glattauer, interviewed by Lukas Schretter, 109 minutes, 28 October 2021, interview in possession of BIK.

9 Between 2021 and 2022, interviews were conducted with thirty-four individuals who were born in the *Heim Wienerwald* between 1938 and 1945. See Lukas Schretter and Nadjeschda Stoffers, "Ambivalent but Not Indifferent: Interview Narratives of *Lebensborn* Children from the Wienerwald Maternity Home, 1938–1945," in *Childhood during War and Genocide: Agency, Survival, and Representation*, edited by Joanna Beate Michlic, Yuliya von Saal, and Anna Ullrich (Göttingen: Wallstein, 2024), 283–96. (European Holocaust Studies 5).

10 *Geheimsache Lebensborn*. Film. Austria. Directed by Beate Thalberg. 42 min., Vienna, ORF 2003 (CultFilm). Other documentaries related to the *Heim Wienerwald* include: *Lebensborn – die vergessenen Opfer*. Film. Austria. Directed by Robert Altenburger and Andreas Novak. 53 min., Vienna, Menschen und Mächte, ORF 2019. *Kinder für das Vaterland: Das Schicksal der Lebensborn-Kinder*. Film. Austria. Directed by Christoph Bendas. News Magazine Thema, Vienna, ORF2, 5 December 2016. *Die "Auserwählten" – das Schicksal der Lebensborn-Kinder*. Film. Austria. Directed by Christoph Bendas. 11 min., Vienna News Magazine Thema, ORF2, 21 April 2021.

11 Susan Benedict and Linda Shields (eds.), *Nurses and Midwives in Nazi Germany. The "Euthanasia Programs"* (New York: Routledge, 2014); Bund Deutscher Hebammen e.V. (ed.), *Zwischen Bevormundung und beruflicher Autonomie. Die Geschichte des Bundes Deutscher Hebammen e.V.* (Karlsruhe: Bund Deutscher Hebammen, 2006); Gregor Dill, *Nationalsozialistische Säuglingspflege. Eine frühe Erziehung zum Massenmenschen* (Stuttgart: Enke, 1999), esp. 65–81; Wolfgang Uwe Eckart, *Medizin in der NS-Diktatur. Ideologie, Praxis, Folgen* (Wien – Köln – Weimar: Böhlau, 2012), esp. 204–14; Antje Kehrbach and Monika Tschernko, *Zur*

referencing the staff of the *Lebensborn* homes have been conducted by researchers such as Georg Lilienthal, Dorothee Schmitz-Köster, Dorothee Neumaier, Anna Bräsel, Thomas Bryant, and Volker Koop.[12] Mention should also be made of PhD dissertations and Master theses, such as those by Elisabeth Märker, Katja Aumayr, and Corinna Fürstaller.[13]

---

*Rolle der Berufsorganisation der Hebammen im Nationalsozialismus. Stellungnahme des Bundes Deutscher Hebammen e.V.* (Karlsruhe: Bund Deutscher Hebammen, 2002); Sophie Ledebur, "Zur Geschichte der Hebammen in Wien während der NS-Zeit," in *Im Dienste der Volksgesundheit. Frauen – Gesundheitswesen – Nationalsozialismus,* edited by Ingrid Arias (Wien: Verlagshaus der Ärzte, 2006), 141–76; Wiebke Lisner, "'A Birth is Nothing out of the Ordinary Here…' Mothers, Midwives and the Private Sphere in the 'Reichsgau Wartheland', 1939–1945," in *Private Life and Privacy in Nazi Germany,* edited by Elizabeth Harvey, Johannes Hürter, Maiken Umbach, and Andreas Wirsching (Cambridge: Cambridge University Press, 2019), 304–30; Wiebke Lisner, "Geburtshilfe im Kontext von Gemeinschafts- und Rassenpolitik. Hebammen als weibliche Expertinnen im 'Reichsgau Warteland' 1939–1945," in *Der Ort der "Volksgemeinschaft" in der deutschen Gesellschaftsgeschichte,* edited by Detlef Schmiechen-Ackermann, Marlis Buchholz, Bianca Roitsch, and Christiane Schröder (Paderborn: Ferdinand Schöningh Verlag, 2018), 311–23. (Studien zu Konstruktion, gesellschaftlicher Wirkungsmacht und Erinnerung 7); Wiebke Lisner, *"Hüterinnen der Nation." Hebammen im Nationalsozialismus* (Frankfurt/Main – New York: Campus, 2006), esp. 313–24; Wiebke Lisner, "Mutter der Mütter – Mütter des Volkes? Hebammen im Nationalsozialismus," in *Sie waren dabei. Mitläuferinnen, Nutznießerinnen, Täterinnen im Nationalsozialismus,* edited by Marita Krauss (Göttingen: Wallstein, 2008), 42–61; Wiebke Lisner, "'Neue Hebammen' für den 'Neuen Staat'? Hebammenausbildung im Nationalsozialismus," in *Rheinische Hebammengeschichte im Kontext,* edited by Daniel Schäfer (Kassel: Kassel University Press, 2010), 225–50. (Kölner Beiträge zur Geschichte der Ethik und Medizin 1); Anja Katharina Peters, *Der Geist von Alt-Rehse. Die Hebammenkurse an der Reichsärzteschule 1935–1941* (Frankfurt am Main: Mabuse-Verlag, 2005); Anja Katharina Peters, *Nanna Conti. Eine Biographie der Reichshebammenführerin* (Berlin: Lit, 2018). (Schriftenreihe der Stipendiatinnen und Stipendiaten der Friedrich Ebert Stiftung 50); Fariba Sauer-Forooghi, *Emma Rauschenbach (1870–1946). Ein Leben im Dienste des deutschen Hebammenwesens* (Aachen: Shaker, 2004); Julia Schwarzenberger, *Hebammen im Nationalsozialismus* (Linz: Trauner, 2008). (Linzer Schriften zur Frauenforschung 37); Kirsten Tiedemann, *Hebammen im Dritten Reich. Über die Standesorganisation für Hebammen und ihre Berufspolitik* (Frankfurt/Main: Mabuse, 2001).

12  Thomas Bryant, *Himmlers Kinder. Zur Geschichte der SS-Organisation "Lebensborn e.V." 1935–1945* (Wiesbaden: marixverlag, 2011); Anna Bräsel, "Das Lebensborn-Heim Hochland in Steinhöring," in *Kinder für den "Führer". Der Lebensborn in München,* edited by Angelika Baumann and Andreas Heusler (München: Franz Schiermeier, 2013), 96–108, esp. 98–100; Volker Koop, *"Dem Führer ein Kind schenken." Die SS-Organisation Lebensborn e.V.* (Wien – Köln – Weimar: Böhlau, 2007), esp. 95–129; Dorothee Neumaier, *Das Lebensbornheim "Schwarzwald" in Nordrach* (Baden-Baden: Tectum, 2017); Dorothee Neumaier, *Dr. Hildegard Feith. Ärztin im Lebensbornkinderheim "Sonnenwiese".* Forschungsbericht deposit_hagen 2019, DOI:10.18445/20190805-113757-0, accessed on 10 September 2023); Georg Lilienthal, *Der "Lebensborn e.V.". Ein Instrument nationalsozialistischer Rassenpolitik,* 2nd. ed. (Frankfurt/Main: Fischer Taschenbuch, 2008), esp. 60–63; Dorothee Schmitz-Köster, *"Deutsche Mutter, bist du bereit…" Alltag im Lebensborn,* 2nd. ed. (Berlin: Aufbau, 2011), esp. 105–47.

13  Katja Aumayr, "Der Lebensborn e.V. zwischen Mythos und Realität. Ideologie, Organisation und Nachwirkungen," Master Thesis, University of Linz, 2023, esp. 54–58; Corinna Fürstaller, "Lebensbornheime in Österreich," Diploma Thesis, University of Vienna, 2010, esp. 58–62;

## II.    Into the *Lebensborn*: Arriving at the *Heim Wienerwald*

Marianne Leitner was born in Klosterneuburg in Lower Austria on 11 June 1924. Her father, a technician at the Austrian *Siemens-Schuckert Werke*, died on 17 March 1927. She was brought up by her mother, a civil servant at the *Elektrisches Werk* in Klosterneuburg.[14] Leitner was an only child, which, according to Mailänder, explains the close relationship documented in the letters between mother and daughter.[15] From autumn of 1930, Leitner attended a co-educational primary school[16] and spent four years at the *Bundes-Real- und Obergymnasium* in Klosterneuburg.[17] On 13 June 1938, three months after the so-called *Anschluss*, she joined the *Bund Deutscher Mädel*.[18] In September of the same year, at the age of 14, she wrote to the *Landesschulrat Niederdonau* to be admitted to the one-year household school of the *Frauenbildungsanstalt Judenau*, with the intention of becoming a gardener.[19] After successfully completing her school education,[20] she worked in *Landdienst* from September 1939 to February 1940.[21] A farmer in Kleinrötz/Harmannsdorf confirmed in September 1940 that her employment was terminated by mutual consent.[22]

In early December 1940, Leitner received a directive

"to i m m e d i a t e l y [emphasis in original] report to the SS Mothers' and Infants' Home 'Lebensborn e.V.', Heim Wienerwald, near Pernitz, Post Ortmann, Wiener-Neustadt district, and to present herself to the head nurse, Else Schwartmann."[23]

---

Elisabeth Märker, "'Rassisch wertvoll.' Die positive Eugenik: Ihre Handhabung am Beispiel des Lebensbornvereins im 'Heim Alpenland' und 'Heim Wienerwald'", PhD diss., University of Innsbruck, 1999, esp. 375–87.

14  Application by Leitner to the *Landesschulrat Niederdonau in Wien*, stamped 19 September 1938, SFN, NL 147/II, Box 147/2.

15  Mailänder, *Amour*, 152.

16  Klosterneuburg Primary School Report, 11 July 1931, SFN, NL 147/II, Box 147/2.

17  Klosterneuburg High School Report, academic year 1936/37, SFN, NL 147/II, Box 147/2.

18  Confirmation of entry to the *Bund Deutscher Mädel in der Hitlerjugend*, 30 June 1938, SFN, NL 147/II, Box 147/3.

19  Application to the *Landesschulrat Niederdonau in Wien*, stamped 19 September 1938, SFN, NL 147/II, Box 147/2.

20  Certificate from the *Berufs- und Haushaltungsschule der Frauenbildungsanstalt in Judenau*, academic year 1938/1939, SFN, NL 147/II, Box 147/2.

21  Letter from the *Gemeindeverwaltung des Reichsgaues Wien, Personalamt, Abteilung 2* to Leitner's mother, 1 November 1940, SFN, NL 147/II, Box 147/2.

22  Declaration dated 20 September 1940, SFN, NL 147/II, Box 147/3. According to Elissa Mailänder, Leitner arrived at a midwifery school in the *Heim Wienerwald*, run by *Lebensborn* in the summer of 1940, see Mailänder, *Amour*, 152.

23  Conscription from the *Gauleitung Niederdonau, Abteilung III Wohlfahrtspflege und Jugendhilfe*, 12 December 1940. "You will be employed there as a student nurse, receiving a monthly pocket money of RM 10, board, and lodging. You will not receive any uniform as an intern. You need about three weeks of laundry, sturdy shoes, and your other private clothes."

Leitner complied with this request. In her first letter from the *Heim Wienerwald*
to her mother, the 16-year-old reported on her arrival:

> "I bought a ticket to Pernitz and happily arrived there. To my horror, I realised this was
> not the designated maternity home and that the actual place was 1½ hours away in
> Feichtenbach."[24]

Consequently, she took "the next train back [to Ortmann] and trotted merrily on
for an hour with the suitcase. At the end of the day, I was where I needed to be."[25]
Most maternity homes of the *Lebensborn* association were situated in remote
areas, far from major cities. The distance of eighty kilometres from Klosterneuburg via Vienna's *Südbahnhof* to the *Heim Wienerwald* meant effectively
a one-day journey.[26]
Almost three years after Marianne Leitner's first arrival, in the autumn of
1943, Hedwig Glattauer started working as a student nurse in the *Heim Wienerwald*. Until then, Glattauer had lived with her parents in Pressbaum near
Vienna. At the age of 13, she and two of her classmates were recruited by the
*Nationalsozialistische Volkswohlfahrt* (National Socialist People's Welfare Organisation, *NSV*). She said she had never heard of *Lebensborn* before but accepted the offer because she hoped to work in a children's home and thought the
nursing training with *NSV* would be a way to achieve her career goals:

> "When [the head nurse] came into the class, she did not say that it had anything to do
> with the SS. She only said that it was a home for mothers and infants. [...] There was no
> mention of the SS. I would not have been able to imagine anything regarding the SS."[27]

After preparatory training in Baden near Vienna during the summer of 1943, she
celebrated her 14th birthday that autumn in the *Heim Wienerwald*.[28] If her position at *Lebensborn* had not been terminated at the end of the Second World War
in 1945, Glattauer said, she would probably have completed her nurse training in
Feichtenbach.[29]
    Both Marianne Leitner[30] and Hedwig Glattauer[31] reported that they were put
up in double rooms in the attic of the *Heim Wienerwald*. The facility's amenities

---

    For work, Waschkleider (Dirndl) [sic!] are recommended. Bring: food stamps, tax card,
    workbook, and employee insurance card," SFN, NL 147/II, Box 147/3.
24  Letter dated 00 December 1940, lines 6–10, SFN, NL 147/II, Box 147/4. Since this letter does
    not specify the exact date, it is only possible to provide the month and the year.
25  Ibid., lines 11–14.
26  Ibid., lines 3–6 and 15–20.
27  BIK, Glattauer, interview, 56.
28  Ibid., 4–5.
29  Ibid., 21.
30  Letter dated 00 December 1940, lines 20–23, SFN, NL 147/II, Box 147/4.
31  BIK, Glattauer, interview, 24–25.

seemed noteworthy to both of them, as there was "central heating throughout."[32] Marianne Leitner expressed her appreciation of the hygienic arrangements, the comfort of the institution, and the varied, generous meal plan.[33] Hedwig Glattauer had been used to a lower standard of living: "The room was rather nice, and we had running water, which was new to me because we did not have that at home."[34] On their days off, breakfast was served in their rooms.[35]

## III.    Running the *Lebensborn:* The Staff of the *Heim Wienerwald*

### 3.1    The Home Management

In every *Lebensborn* home, including the *Heim Wienerwald*, a (male)[36] SS doctor held the highest authority.[37] The director of a *Lebensborn* maternity home was subordinate only to the *Lebensborn* board and the central administration, which was based in Berlin from 1936 and relocated to Munich in 1938. Before the war, practicing paediatricians from the vicinity of the homes were detailed to assist the home directors. They performed health checks on the children every four weeks and advised the nursing staff accordingly. Every month, clinical reports from the maternity homes were evaluated by a gynaecologist. When infant mortality rates in the homes rose in early 1940, four additional consulting physicians were appointed. They were subordinated to Ebner and inspected the *Lebensborn* homes twice a year.[38]

The duties of a *Lebensborn* home's director included making themselves available to pregnant women and mothers "as counsellors for their needs at all times."[39] He was expected to engage with the home community, "occasionally

---

32 Letter dated 00 December 1940, line 41. As the war progressed, there was a shortage of heating material: "All [residential] rooms are unheated, only in the wards and in the day room it is warm. But that is what a bed is for." Letter dated 12 February 1942, lines 37–42, SFN, NL 147/II, Box 147/4.
33 Letter dated 16 January 1941, lines 34–42, SFN, NL 147/II, Box 147/4.
34 BIK, Glattauer, interview, 24.
35 Ibid., 25.
36 In almost every *Lebensborn* home, a male doctor was also the home's director. Exceptions were the *Heim Sonnenwiese* in Kohren-Salis, which was run by a female doctor, see Neumaier, *Dr. Hildegard Feith*, and the *Heim Friesland*, where this position was vacant resp., a pregnant doctor took over the medical care temporarily, Schmitz-Köster, *"Deutsche Mutter"*, 106–08.
37 For an organisational chart of the *Lebensborn* homes see *Dienstanweisung*, n. d. [1938], AA, 4.1.0/8209800, Ref. 82448188.
38 Lilienthal, *Der "Lebensborn e.V."*, 60–61.
39 *Dienstanweisung für die Ärzte des Lebensborn*, 18 September 1943, AA, 4.1.0/8210800, Ref. 82450403.

spending evenings with the mothers in the common room."[40] Only in emergencies did he act in his capacity as a physician. According to an order of 1938, the director "represents the home to the outside world and bears ultimate responsibility for everything that happens in the home."[41] All staff were expected to obey his orders. Hiring and firing decisions were the responsibility of the home's director in consultation with *Lebensborn*'s headquarters. Access to *Lebensborn* records was exclusively reserved to the director: "If the director of the home is also the civil registrar of his home, he is responsible for the proper keeping of the civil register books and lists."[42] He was also responsible for ideological training and the organisation of childcare courses.[43]

After the outbreak of the Second World War, when *Lebensborn* anticipated that more wives and fiancées of fallen *SS* members would seek shelter in its homes, Guntram Pflaum, member of the *Persönlicher Stab Reichsführer-SS*, *Stabsführer* in the *SS-Sippenamt* and, at the same time, managing director of the *Lebensborn* association from 1936 to 1940,[44] expressed a desire for all home directors "to look after these women <u>personally</u> [emphasis in original] in a comradely manner and to take care of them in every way."[45] In such cases, the director of a *Lebensborn* home had to prove that he was not only a physician, but also a *Seelenarzt*, a soul doctor, in line with Himmler's ideas.[46] From 1940 onwards, Himmler ordered the directors to spend four to five weeks at a large gynaecological clinic every one to two years in order to improve their knowledge of obstetrics.[47] Still, women filed several complaints, questioning the qualifications of the homes' directors.[48] Beyond the shortcomings in specific medical training, there were irregularities and

40  *Ärztliche Dienstanweisung für den Heimarzt*, 11 September 1939, AA, 4.1.0/8210800, Ref. 82450399.

41  *Dienstanweisung für die Heime des "Lebensborn" e.V.*, n. d., AA, 4.1.0/8209800, Ref. 82448179; *Dienstanweisung für die Heime des "Lebensborn" e.V.*, n. d., BA, NS 48/31.

42  Ibid.

43  Schmitz-Köster, *"Deutsche Mutter"*, 106. For a weekly training schedule, see Schmitz-Köster, *"Deutsche Mutter"*, 154–55. In addition to air-raid and first-aid courses as well as singing folk songs together, speeches by leading figures of the National Socialist Party, such as Hitler or Goebbels, were also listened to together on the radio. A "political weekly overview," presented by a staff member, is also mentioned.

44  Ernst Klee, *Das Personenlexikon. Wer war was vor und nach 1945* (Hamburg: Nikol Verlagsgesellschaft, 2016), 459.

45  *Sonderanordnung*, 7 November 1939, AA, 4.1.0/8210000, Ref. 82448597.

46  Ibid.

47  Letter from Ebner to Stöckel requesting to send one of his doctors to Stöckel's hospital in Berlin, 20 May 1940, AA, 4.1.0/8210000, Ref. 82448619.

48  Complaints were to be directed to Himmler, who intended to read these personally. Letter from Himmler to the management of *Lebensborn*, AA, 4.1.0/8210200, Ref. 82448914, and AA, 4.1.0/8209900, Ref. 82448301. For complaints by *Lebensborn* mothers against the home directors and staff, see also Bryant, *Himmlers Kinder*, 215–32.

accidents, such as an infant who reportedly died from burnings caused by an electric pad malfunction, while his mother was still in childbed.[49]

Student nurses in the *Heim Wienerwald* had hardly any contact with its director. Hedwig Glattauer recalled: "We have only seen him. They are unapproachable! Especially in their SS uniform! We were nothing to them."[50] SS men who belonged to a *Lebensborn* home had to observe a specific dress code. In 1939, Himmler decreed that with the SS service uniform, "regardless of whether the honour sword or dagger is worn, a waist belt, shoulder strap and/or sash must be put on. This applies also in case a coat is worn. No buckling over when trousers are worn."[51]

From November 1938 to 1941, the position of director in the *Heim Wienerwald* was held by SS *Unterscharführer* Karl Sernetz, a physician from Styria. He lived in the home with his wife from 1939 onwards. Prior to taking up his duties in the *Heim Wienerwald*, he was called to the *Lebensborn* home in Steinhöring in October 1938 for instruction and training.[52] In the *Heim Wienerwald*, he received a monthly salary of RM 700.[53] Later he worked in the *Gersthof* clinic in Vienna.[54]

SS *Obersturmführer* Norbert Schwab, a dentist also from Styria, took over from Sernetz and remained director until mid-1944. Before coming to Feichtenbach, he had been director of the *Heim Pommern* and *Heim Taunus*. Schwab moved to the *Heim Wienerwald* with his wife and their two children; two more children were born in Feichtenbach.[55] There were complaints that Schwab skimped on care for

---

49   Report from *SS-Oberführer* Pflaum to the *Reichsführung SS/Persönlicher Stab* from 13 June 1939, AA, 4.1.0/8210000, Ref. 82448561–82448569, and AA, 4.1.0/8213700, Ref. 82460864–82460881. The use of electric blankets was later prohibited by the *Lebensborn*. *Dienstanweisung für die Ärzte des Lebensborn*, AA, 4.1.0/8210800, Ref. 82450425.

50   BIK, Glattauer, interview, 22.

51   *SS-Dienstanzug*, 28 January 1939, AA, 4.1.0/8210000, Ref. 82448551.

52   *Besetzung der Stelle des Heimleiters von "Wienerwald"*, 11 October 1938, AA, 4.1.0/8212200, Ref. 82455074.

53   *Besetzung der Stelle des Heimleiters von "Wienerwald"*, letter from Ebner to Dermietzel, 3 October 1938, AA, 4.1.0/8210800, Ref. 82459618. Another applicant, Otto Dieter from Lausitz, was rejected because he showed a lack of interest in the *Lebensborn* movement. *Memorandum* by Ebner, 14 September 1938, AA, 4.1.0/8212200, Ref. 82455016. As a substitute for Sernetz, *Lebensborn* concluded a contract with Oskar Schmidt on 1 January 1939, *Vertrag*, AA, 4.1.0/8210800, Ref. 82450624. On 15 May 1939, Otto Riedl was hired as a substitute for Karl Sernetz in the *Heim Wienerwald*, *Betr.: Stellvertretenden Heimleiter in Wienerwald*, AA, 4.1.0/8212200, Ref. 82455124.

54   Karl Sernetz, born on 11 December 1909, BA, R 9361-III/192969, and R 9361-III/556577.

55   Norbert Schwab, born on 4 December 1904, BA, R 9361-III/555836. In 2004, Judith Brandner conducted an interview with Getrude Schwab, Norbert Schwab's wife for a radio feature: *Lebensborn im Wienerwald. Ein Lungensanatorium als Gebäranstalt für arisches Leben*. Radio programme. Austria. Directed by Judith Brandner. 53 min., Vienna, Öl Hörbilder, 15 May 2004, see 08:35–12:39 min; 22:52–23:18 min; 35:22–36:39 min; and 48:35–48:45 min., <https://www.judithbrandner.at/radio/> (27 February 2024). From September 1943 to December 1943 "famulus" (intern) Paul John was working in the *Heim Wienerwald* as an

some mothers and favoured others.[56] Conflicts with staff were also recorded.[57] However, Hedwig Glattauer recalled that she had found him quite amiable: "Well, I thought he was very nice, although I did not have much to do with him."[58] Marianne Leitner's letters, in which the home directors are only mentioned in passing, reveal her reservation towards him: when Schwab was seen off by the home community with a dancing event at Easter 1944, she was "asked by the doctor [to dance], I declined at first, but then I had to and it went relatively well."[59]

On 16 April 1944, August Hagemeier, formerly director of the *Heim Pommern*, took over from Schwab and served until the end of the war in 1945.[60] Leitner reported in July 1944 that she preferred receiving medical treatment in Klosterneuburg during her holidays rather than being examined by the director. This refers to an evident power imbalance between the mostly female staff and the older male supervisors of the *Lebensborn* homes.[61] In some cases this even led to abuse: at the *Heim Friesland* nurse Helga S. reported lewd advances by the home's administrator.[62]

The director of a *Lebensborn* home supervised the home physician (where he did not fill this position himself), head nurse, administrator, and secretary. The administrator of the home was in charge of "the entire agricultural and gardening operations, the entire technical and manual area, making purchases on the instructions of the head nurse, the maintenance of the buildings, including the control of mechanical equipment."[63] The administrator was appointed independently of the director. According to Glattauer, the administrator stayed on when Hagemeier replaced Schwab.[64] In official matters he reported to the director of the home, in matters of house rules, administration of finances, correspondence, records, and statistics to the head nurse. The secretary therefore had access to confidential information and was bound to strict confidentiality.[65]

---

obstetrician. *Famuli, Lebensborn-Personalabteilung*, 29 November 1943, AA, 4.1.0/8210800, Ref. 82450675.

56 Letters from Schwab to Ebner concerning the report of the *Reichssicherheitshauptamt* from 14 April 1943, and 23 April 1943, AA, 4.1.0/8209700, Ref. 82448940. See also letter from the *SS-Standartenführer und Amtschef im Persönlichen Stab* of Himmler to Schwab, June 1942, AA, 4.1.0/8211400, Ref. 82452096. Besides being director of the *Heim Wienerwald* Schwab also worked as theatre doctor at Vienna's *Burgtheater*, for which he was criticised by Ebner. Letter from Ebner to Schwab, 24 June 1942, AA, 4.1.0/8212300, Ref. 82455335.

57 *Memorandum* by Ebner, 28 January 1843, AA, 4.1.0/8212300, Ref. 82455340.

58 BIK, Glattauer, interview, 20.

59 Letter dated 10 April 1944, lines 28–33, SFN, NL 147/II, Box 147/4.

60 August Hagemeier, born on 6 November 1912, BA, R 9361-III/64289, and R 9361-III/528516.

61 Letter dated 24 July 1944, lines 10–14, SFN, NL 147/II, Box 147/4.

62 Schmitz-Köster, "*Deutsche Mutter*", 111.

63 *Dienstanweisung für die Heime des "Lebenborn" e.V.*, n.d., AA, 4.1.0/8209800, Ref. 82448182.

64 BIK, Glattauer, interview, 20.

65 *Dienstanweisung für die Heime des "Lebenborn" e.V.*, n. d., AA, 4.1.0/8209800, Ref. 82448187.

## 3.2     The Head Nurse

The head nurse was a member of the *NS-Schwesternschaft* (National Socialist Nursing Organisation, *NSS*). She was responsible for the internal administration of the *Lebensborn* home. According to an order of 1938, she was responsible for "matters of housekeeping and the employment of female staff."[66] While she was subordinate to the home's director in medical matters, all the nurses reported to her on domestic issues, as did the (female) chef, laundry staff, and household employees. The head nurse was responsible for assigning duties, allocating days off, and managing the nurses' holidays, in consultation with the director.[67] Her duties also included supervising the food supply and planning the weekly menus with the chef.[68] The order stipulated that "food orders should, as far as possible, be made in bulk to keep prices as low as possible."[69] In addition, after the winter of 1940/41, the head nurse was responsible for the distribution of coffee and had to report the home's coffee consumption to *Lebensborn* headquarters.[70] Furthermore, she was responsible for maintaining the linen stock, house furnishings, ensuring cleanliness in all rooms, and signing off on all household-related invoices.[71] On rare occasions, as in the *Heim Kurmark*, the head nurse was permitted to adopt "a child she had grown particularly fond of."[72]

In Marianne Leitner's bequest[73] and in Hedwig Glattauer's interview there are only two head nurses mentioned by name, Else Schwartmann[74] and a head nurse

---

66  Ibid., Ref. 82448181.
67  Ibid., Ref. 82448183.
68  Ibid., Ref. 82448181.
69  Ibid., Ref. 82448186.
70  Note regarding the meeting with the *Reichsführer-SS* on 1 January 1941, AA, 4.1.0/8209900, Ref. 82448332 and 82448333.
71  *Dienstanweisung für die Heime des "Lebensborn" e.V.*, n. d., AA, 4.1.0/48209800, Ref. 82448186.
72  *Memorandum* of the meeting with the *Reichsführer-SS* on 11 January 1941, and 13 January 1941, AA, 4.1.0/8209900, Ref. 82448333.
73  Conscription from the *Gauleitung Niederdonau, Abteilung III Wohlfahrtspflege und Jugendhilfe*, 12 December 1940, SFN, NL 147/II, Box 147/3.
74  Else Schwartmann was the head nurse in the *Heim Wienerwald* in December 1940, Conscription from the *Gauleitung Niederdonau, Abteilung III Wohlfahrtspflege und Jugendhilfe*, 12 December 1940, SFN, NL 147/II, Box 147/3. She also worked there in summer 1942, before moving to Norway, and from 1943 worked at other *Lebensborn* facilities. Ebner to Schwartmann, 17 September 1942, AA, 4.1.0/8209700, Ref. 82447947. Schwartmann also gave birth to a son in 1942 in a *Lebensborn* home in Bergen, Norway. According to Schmitz-Köster, it is likely that she later accompanied a transport of Norwegian children to Germany where she worked at *Heim Friesland* and shifted from working as a Brown Nurse to working as a Red Cross Nurse, Schmitz-Köster, *"Deutsche Mutter"*, 119. After the end of the war, Schwartmann continued working in Hohehorst, ibid., 81 and 396.

by the name of Gerda.[75] Records also mention other head nurses such as Anna Dickel, who apparently worked in the *Heim Wienerwald* in May 1944, perhaps on an interim basis.[76] Leitner's and Glattauer's accounts attest to the strict discipline the head nurses imposed on their subordinates and to the respect the staff had for them.

In the letters to her mother, Marianne Leitner always mentioned the head nurses in their function, never by name, highlighting the distance between employees and their superiors. For instance, she wrote in an early letter that "today we have to have coffee with the head nurse at 1/2 4 h."[77] It is evident that she considered this invitation from Else Schwartmann as an obligation rather than as a casual gathering. Recreational activities outside the home, described by Leitner as *Gefolgschaftsausflug* ("allegiance" trip), are also likely to have been the exception rather than the rule.[78] Such outings included, for example, watching movies at the nearby cinema in Pernitz[79] and going for a swim together in the town of Bad Vöslau.[80] In their spare time, the head nurses were more likely to socialise with the home's management staff and selected members of the *NSS*. "Yesterday, our head nurse, the two administrators, and three nurses made a trip to the Schneeberg. They returned today, somewhat exhausted,"[81] Leitner wrote in 1944.

Hedwig Glattauer recalled that head nurse Gerda was strict with her subordinates. She remembered that when she accidentally broke a vase during cleaning, she was told by the head nurse to learn how to handle a broom properly. "I did not know how to tidy up," she recalled, "I only learned that there. At home, it was always my elder sister who did this."[82] Glattauer suspected that the vase

---

75  The surname of the head nurse Gerda was not mentioned by Marianne Leitner and Hedwig Glattauer and could not be determined beyond doubt. Leitner mentioned the mobility of the staff including head nurse Gerda: "Our head nurse together with several nurses and midwives are leaving for an SS home in Holland," letter dated 17 May 1944, lines 33–35, SFN, NL 147/II, Box 147/4. A few letters later, the reason of the journey was made evident, when Leitner wrote to her mother: "Today our head nurse left us because she is going to run a Lebensborn home in Holland and on 1.V. ⌍ [sic!] five nurses and a midwife will follow," letter dated 23 May 1944, lines 13–19, SFN, NL 147/II, Box 147/4. This could be a reference to the *Heim Gelderland* in Nijmegen, which, however, never went on stream. Lilienthal, *Der "Lebensborn e.V."*, 179–82.

76  *Schwesternstandsmeldung* from 2 May 1944, AA, 4.1.0/8210400, Ref. 82449688.

77  Letter dated 25 December 1940, line 11–13, SFN, NL 147/II, Box 147/4. Another mention of such gatherings can be found in the letter dated 28 December 1941, line 26–28, SFN, NL 147/II, Box 147/4.

78  Letter dated 17 July 1944, line 7, SFN, NL 147/II, Box 147/4.

79  Ibid., lines 6–15.

80  Letter dated 22 August 1941, lines 17–21, SFN, NL 147/II, Box 147/4.

81  Letter dated 31 August 1944, lines 35–40, SFN, NL 147/II, Box 147/4.

82  BIK, Glattauer, interview, 13. Hedwig Glattauer also recounted that the same head nurse informed her that her older brother had fallen at the front. Upon hearing the news, she suppressed her emotions and did not cry. She herself put down her reaction to how the news was delivered to her: the head nurse told her that her brother had fallen for Hitler and the

might have been valuable, possibly dating back to the *Wienerwald* lung san-atorium, led by two Jewish physicians from 1904 until its "Aryanisation" in spring 1938.[83]


## 3.3   The Nursing Staff

In *Lebensborn* maternity homes, apart from the head nurse, staff included postnatal nurses, midwives, infant and toddler nurses, and student nurses. Ac-cording to the home's statutes of 1938, they reported to the home's director on all matters concerning the health care of the mothers and children. For all other matters, the head nurse was their supervisor.[84] While all employees of *Lebensborn* homes were expected to "perform their duties to the best of their abilities, [...] fostering a spirit of camaraderie amongst themselves to collectively contribute to the well-being of the mothers and children entrusted to the home,"[85] there was little contact among employees from different hierarchical levels. As Hedwig Glattauer noted, "it was all very segmented. The nurses, student nurses, oper-ators, and cleaning women all kept themselves to themselves. During work, we occasionally interacted a little, but not much."[86] In her letters, Marianne Leitner distinguished between management, particularly the head nurse, and the nursing staff and other employees, with the latter receiving only passing mention.

*Lebensborn* had an agreement with the *NSV* for the provision of nursing staff in its maternity homes. At first, the *NSV* committed to providing *NS Schwestern* for all *Lebensborn* homes.[87] However, due to the *NSV*'s inability to allocate a sufficient number of trained nurses, in addition to these so-called Brown Nurses,

---

fatherland. However, after her brother's death, she was granted time to spend with her family in Pressbaum. BIK, Glattauer, interview, 12–13 and 39.

83  On the history of the lung sanatorium *Wienerwald* and the expropriation of the two doctors in 1938, see Hiltraud Ast, *Feichtenbach, eine Tallandschaft im Niederösterreichischen Schnee-berggebiet*, published by *Marktgemeinde Pernitz* (Wien: Brüder Hollinek, 1994), 62–77. Hilde Ernstbrunner, former staff member in the lung sanatorium Wienerwald as well as in the *Heim Wienerwald*, recalled the takeover of the building in 1938 in an interview conducted by Beate Thalberg: "[When I was [working in the lung sanatorium], there were two floors full of people. They were there until the Germans came. Then they left, they all drove away. The next day they [the National Socialists] took them [the patients] all away." *Geheimsache Lebensborn*, 13:37–13:54. Next to Hilde Ernstbrunner, Walburga Kremr, and Edith Baley, also former staff members in the *Heim Wienerwald*, briefly spoke about their work for *Lebensborn* in this documentary.

84  *Dienstanweisung für die Heime des "Lebensborn" e.V.*, n. d., AA, 4.1.0/8209800, Ref. 82448183.

85  Ibid., Ref. 82448188.

86  BIK, Glattauer, interview, 56.

87  Birgit Breiding, *Die Braunen Schwestern: Ideologie – Struktur – Funktion einer nationalso-zialistischen Elite* (Stuttgart: Steiner 1998), 266–78. (Beiträge zur Wirtschafts- und Sozialge-schichte 85).

nurses of the *Reichsbund der Freien Schwestern und Pflegerinnen* (Reich Association of Free Nurses) – also referred to as Blue Nurses – were hired.[88] Over the years, the ratio between Brown and Blue Nurses shifted.[89] For instance, in April 1944 in the *Heim Wienerwald*, out of a total of twenty nurses, fifteen were identified as *NS Schwestern* and five as Blue Nurses.[90]

Although *Lebensborn* preferred *NS Schwestern* to Blue Nurses because of their reliable National Socialist ideological orientation, the former did not always live up to the association's expectations. Some were too young and inexperienced, others left *Lebensborn* once they had completed their training to work in other sectors of the *NSV*. *NS Schwestern* had to resign if they became pregnant and were not yet married. Some of them probably "still see something immoral in extramarital motherhood,"[91] as Ebner noted. He also lamented that some *NS Schwestern* lacked the right attitude towards the mothers. A major conflict emerged in February 1940 when ten *NS Schwestern* from the *Heim Wienerwald* complained to Ebner: the home director, Karl Sernetz, and the head nurse had imposed travel restrictions on some nurses after inspecting their private rooms.[92] Correspondence has also survived between Ebner and a nurse named Anna Werling, who refused to travel from the *Heim Wienerwald* to Dresden for a postnatal care training course.[93] According to Schmitz-Köster's research on the *Heim Friesland*, it was the nursing staff who gave rise to most conflicts and disturbances within a *Lebensborn* home.[94] In the search for suitable staff, *Lebensborn* intended to establish their own midwifery and nursing schools. Himmler planned for the first course to commence in 1942 to distinguish *Lebensborn*'s work from the *NSV*.[95] However, these training facilities of *Lebensborn* homes never materialised.[96]

---

88 Lilienthal, *Der "Lebensborn e.V."*, 61.

89 According to Schmitz-Köster, only Blue Nurses worked at the *Heim Friesland* in Hohehorst initially. However, after Ebner's intervention in 1939, the number of Blue Nurses was reduced to one third of the nursing staff. Schmitz-Köster, *"Deutsche Mutter"*, 128–29. She also indicates that the majority of Brown Nurses set great store by the principles of obedience and subordination. Ibid., 131. Thomas Bryant estimates that in 1940, 93.7% of the *Lebensborn*'s nurses were Brown Nurses. See Bryant, *Himmlers Kinder*, 201.

90 *Schwesternstandsmeldung und Schwesternstatistik für den Monat April 1944*, AA, 4.1.0/ 82449685, Ref. 8210400. In the same month, Brown Nurses were in an overwhelming majority in twelve more *Lebensborn* homes. The thirteen listed homes employed 137 Brown Nurses and only eighteen Blue Nurses – five of them in the *Heim Wienerwald*, and none in the *Heim Alpenland*, *Heim Friesland*, *Heim Hochland*, and *Heim Moselland*.

91 Ebner, *Vertrauliche Denkschrift über die Schaffung einer eigenen Lebensborn-Schwesternschaft*, 8 October 1940, AA, 4.1.0/8210600, Ref. 82450018.

92 Ebner to Sernetz, *Raumkontrolle*, 20 February 1940, AA, 4.1.0/8210700, Ref. 82450257.

93 Ebner to Werling, *Fortbildungskurs*, 25 May 1939, AA, 4.1.0/8211800, Ref. 82453723.

94 Schmitz-Köster, *"Deutsche Mutter"*, 131.

95 *Säuglingsschwestern-Schulen*, 29 December 1941, AA, 4.1.0/8210600, Ref. 82450063.

In each *Lebensborn* home, a midwife was responsible for delivering children and caring for them after birth. She was also in charge of the disinfection of medical instruments, managing bandages and laundry, and ensuring the cleanliness and sterility of the operating and birthing rooms. Her working hours depended upon the number of births. In addition to deliveries, she worked in the infant and postnatal departments as directed by the head nurse.[97] She frequently examined expectant mothers, prepared them for childbirth, and oversaw their postnatal recovery.[98] Typically, if there were no complications, only the midwife was present during childbirth.[99]

Infant nurses were in charge in the infant department, monitoring the infants' nutrition and reporting even the slightest disturbances or weight losses to the home's director. They were not permitted to unilaterally alter the infants' diets.[100] Following an incident in 1944, *Lebensborn* decreed that nurses were prohibited from hitting infants or pinching their noses to force them to swallow their food.[101] Infant nurses were furthermore instructed to "always personally persuade mothers to breastfeed their children themselves and not to stop doing so without good reason."[102] Feeding times were set at specific slots, and each mother was allotted forty-five minutes per session (6:00 a.m., 9:15 a.m., 12:45 p.m., 4:45 p.m., 8:45 p.m.). Under the guidance of the infant nurses, mothers participated in caring for the infants. However, the nurses had to ensure that no mother claimed privileges and strictly followed the guidelines.[103] From May 1942, *Lebensborn* aimed to have its maternity homes recognised as children's hospitals, allowing infant nurses to complete the second half of their training within the homes. This initiative – which never came to fruition – was expected to significantly ease the work in *Lebensborn* maternity homes.[104]

The nurses in charge of postnatal care were tasked with providing the best possible care to mothers after delivery and carefully cleaning the postnatal rooms. They had to ensure that the postnatal ward was not accessed unnecessarily; other women in a *Lebensborn* home were only allowed to visit

---

96 *SS-Obersturmführer* Brandt to *SS-Gruppenführer* Hilgenfeldt, *Ausbildung von Schwestern zum Zwecke des Lebensborns*, 27 October 1943, AA, 4.1.0/8210600, Ref. 82450192; also see Breiding, *Die Braunen Schwestern*, 271–72.

97 *Dienstanweisung für die Heime des "Lebensborn" e.V.*, n. d., AA, 4.1.0/8209800, Ref. 82448184.

98 For more information concerning the work of midwives in *Lebensborn* homes, see Lisner, *Hüterinnen der Nation*, 313–24; Schmitz-Köster, *"Deutsche Mutter"*, 123–27.

99 Schmitz-Köster, *"Deutsche Mutter"*, 124.

100 *Dienstanweisung für die Heime des "Lebensborn" e.V.*, n. d., AA, 4.1.0/8209800, Ref. 82448185.

101 *Rundschreiben*, 2 September 1944, AA, 4.1.0/8209600, Ref. 82447831, and 4.1.0/8210700, Ref. 82450288.

102 *Dienstanweisung für die Heime des "Lebensborn" e.V.*, n. d., AA, 4.1.0/8209800, Ref. 82448185.

103 Ibid.

104 Letter from *SS-Obersturmbannführer* Brandt to *Reichsgesundheitsführer SS-Gruppenführer* Conti, 23 May 1942, AA, 4.1.0/8210000, Ref. 82448708.

postnatal mothers in exceptional cases and with the director's explicit approval. Family visits during the postnatal period also required the director's consent.[105]

*Lebensborn*'s caregiving work was characterised by persistent staffing issues. After the outbreak of World War II, *Lebensborn* frequently complained of a lack of qualified doctors and nurses. In 1940, Himmler himself enquired if whether there were sufficient numbers of nurses in *Lebensborn* or if it was possible to "hire women willing to assist during the war. What options are available for such women? Could they possibly take an assistant nurse's exam?"[106] He also personally conveyed his interest in *Lebensborn* to the relevant staffing agencies to ensure that there was adequate staffing for the homes.[107] Female staff had to adhere to *SS* standards; for example, women working for *Lebensborn* were not allowed to wear lipstick or have painted nails. Such "misconduct", prevalent in society, could only be countered through propaganda and strict regulations within the *SS*, argued *SS-Hauptsturmführer* Lang, the head of *Lebensborn*'s personnel department, in a 1941 letter to Ebner.[108]

*Lebensborn* mothers were also recruited as staff. From 1938, when *Lebensborn*'s growing demand for skilled workers such as typists, nurses, kindergarten teachers, and laundresses could not be met any longer, the association hired single women who had given birth in its homes.[109] Mothers working in the maternity homes could only care for their own children during their free time. If they were found favouring their own children, they faced the risk of expulsion.[110] As the war progressed and there was a general labour shortage, mothers were increasingly employed at the *Lebensborn* headquarters in Munich.[111]

## 3.4    The Non-Medical Staff

The non-medical staff of the *Heim Wienerwald*, such as laundry personnel, seamstresses, and chambermaids, operated under the instructions of the head nurse.[112] The hiring and termination of household employees were executed by the institution's director in agreement with the head nurse.[113] Marianne Leitner

---

105 *Dienstanweisung für die Heime des "Lebensborn" e.V.*, n. d., AA, 4.1.0/8209800, Ref. 82448184.
106 *SS-Hauptsturmführer* Brandt to *Lebensborn*, 3 January 1940, AA, 4.1.0/8210000, Ref. 82448603.
107 Lilienthal, *Der "Lebensborn e.V."*, 61.
108 *Betrifft: Anmalen der Damen in der SS-Dienststelle*, 30 December 1941, AA, 4.1.0/8209900, Ref. 82448348.
109 Lilienthal, *Der "Lebensborn e.V."*, 69; this was also the case for several mothers in the *Heim Wienerwald*.
110 *Allgemeine Anordnung, Nr. 147*, 30 April 1939, 4.1.0/8210500, Ref. 82449989.
111 Lilienthal, *Der "Lebensborn e.V."*, 69.
112 *Dienstanweisung für die Heime des "Lebensborn" e.V.*, n. d., AA, 4.1.0/8209800, Ref. 82448186.
113 Ibid.

casually mentioned to her mother various employees she encountered during her time in the *Heim Wienerwald*.[114] This included administrative staff, such as the (former) gardener[115] and his wife,[116] the "Schöffir"[117] or chauffeur,[118] the mechanic,[119] the administrator,[120] the head chef, her staff, and the laundresses.[121]

From 1943 to 1945, the period of Hedwig Glattauer's training at the institution, many of the staff hailed from the *Altreich*. Whereas the high-ranking (medical) staff had come from "abroad", employees in the lower hierarchical tier, like the kitchen staff, were recruited from the immediate vicinity.[122] Female cleaning staff, according to her, ranked below the trainee nurses in the institution's hierarchy.[123]

Although not specifically documented for the *Heim Wienerwald*, *Lebensborn* staff also included "foreign workers," meaning civilian foreign forced laborers, prisoners of war (POWs), and inmates from concentration camps. In 1941, the *Heim Wienerwald* employed POWs.[124] For the *Heim Friesland*, one "foreign worker" is documented.[125] Between the summer of 1942 and the end of the war, at

---

114  Leitner frequently wrote about her colleagues and superiors, especially about (changing) head nurses, for example in letters from 25 December 1940, lines 4–6; 25 December 1940, lines 11–13; 28 December 1941, lines 26–28; 11 August 1941, lines 7–9; 23 October 1941, lines 19–22; 19 April 1944, lines 42–46; 17 May 1944, lines 33–35; 23 May 1944, lines 13–19; 10 October 1944, lines 14–18. She also wrote about several midwives, see letters from 4 December 1941, lines 12–20; 17 May 1944, lines 33–35; 23 May 1944, line 18; 17 June 1944, lines 6–15; 31 August 1944, lines 35–40. The home's director has been mentioned in letters from 10 October 1943, line 51; 12 November 1944, lines 3–9, also referred to as the "doctor" in letters from 2 April 1943 [stamped 4 April 1944], lines 14 and 45; 17 June 1944, line 12; 24 July 1944, lines 13–14; 31 August 1944, line 44–46. The doctor "with wife and children [and] his sister" was mentioned in a letter dated 2 April 1943 [stamped 4 April 1944], lines 45–46, SFN, NL 147/II, Box 147/4. In 1939, a year before Leitner's arrival in the *Heim Wienerwald*, besides the doctor, the office staff, ten sisters, and ten student nurses, there were 15 people employed in "house and kitchen," five representatives of the *Frauenhilfsdienst*, five male staff members and four helpers as well as one person from the *Mütterschule*. See *Personal der Heime des "Lebensborn e.V."*, 1 October 1939, AA, 4.1.0/82449663, Ref. 8210400.

115  The gardener, according to Leitner, was at the Eastern Front in April that year. Letter dated 2 April 1943 [stamped 4 April 1944], lines 45–49. SFN, NL 147/II, Box 147/4.

116  Ibid., line 42 resp. 51, SFN, NL 147/II, Box 147/4.

117  Ibid., line 49, SFN, NL 147/II, Box 147/4.

118  Letter dated 2 May 1944, line 37, SFN, NL 147/II, Box 147/4.

119  Letter dated 2 April 1943 [stamped 4 April 1944], line 49, SFN, NL 147/II, Box 147/4.

120  Letter dated 2 May 1944, line 36, SFN, NL 147/II, Box 147/4.

121  Letter dated 2 April 1943 [stamped 4 April 1944], lines 47–48, SFN, NL 147/II, Box 147/4.

122  BIK, Glattauer, interview, 24.

123  Ibid., 19 and 21.

124  *SS Untersturmführer* Ernst Ragaller wrote regarding renovations in the *Heim Wienerwald*: "The prisoners in the camp [sic!] seem to be doing well; I was told that they are working diligently." *Reisebericht des SS-Untersturmführers Ragaller in das Heim "Ostmark" in Pernitz*, 20 October 1941, AA, 4.1.0/8211300, Ref. 82452054. For further information on Ragaller see Lilienthal, *Der "Lebensborn e.V."*, 109, 120–21, and 172.

125  Schmitz-Köster, *"Deutsche Mutter"*, 366–67.

least forty female and up to fourty-two male inmates from the *Ravensbrück* and *Dachau* concentration camps performed forced labour for *Lebensborn* at its Munich headquarters and at the *Heim Moselland* in Bofferdingen, the *Heim Franken* in Ansbach, the *Heim Hochland* in Steinhöring, and the *Heim Taunus* in Wiesbaden.[126]

## IV.     Inside the *Lebensborn*: Everyday Work and Daily Routine

### 4.1     Marianne Leitner, 1940–1942

Marianne Leitner took over a variety of roles in different training phases in the *Heim Wienerwald*. Immediately after her arrival she was assigned to the maternity ward. However, due to her tender age she was redirected to kitchen duties on her very first day.[127] A few weeks later, on 9 January 1941, she expressed contentment with another change in her assignment, noting:

> "I have been in the infant ward since 31 December, in the milk kitchen for a provisional 14 days, to be precise. My duty starts early at 1/2 7 h, which means I get up at 6 h every day. I then work until 1/2 1 h or 1 h. I am then off duty until 1/2 5 h, after which I go back to work and finish by 6 / 1/2 7 h It is really great."[128]

By August of the same year, she was delegated by the head nurse to perform kitchen duties for ten days.[129] Soon after she took on a temporary role in the infant ward.[130] By October 1941, she was transferred to another ward.[131]

In the autumn of 1941, Leitner informed the head nurse of her intention to become an infant care nurse and on 17 November 1941, she described the bustling activity in the ward to her mother: "Three births on Saturday, two on Sunday, two on Monday, and one on Tuesday. It is easy to imagine that we are kept rather busy."[132] In fact, two births per day were higher than the long-term

---

126 Sabine Schalm, "KZ-Häftlinge für den Lebensborn" in *Kinder für den "Führer"*, 132–36; Christl Wickert, "Ravenbrücker KZ-Häftlinge als Zwangsarbeiterinnen beim Lebensborn (1943-1945). Befunde zu einem eher vergessenen Kapitel der Zwangsarbeitergeschichte," *Zeitschrift für Geschichte* 62 (2014) 12: 1013–32.
127 Letter dated 00 December 1940, lines 15–20, SFN, NL 147/II, Box 147/4.
128 Letter dated 9 January 1941, lines 14–21, SFN, NL 147/II, Box 147/4.
129 Letter dated 11 August 1941, lines 7–10, SFN, NL 147/II, Box 147/4.
130 Letter dated 22 August 1941, lines 13–15, SFN, NL 147/II, Box 147/4.
131 Letter dated 23 October 1941, line 6, SFN, NL 147/II, Box 147/4. The activities undertaken on the *Stockwerk* and which ward was referred to by that name are not specified in the letters.
132 Letter dated 17 November 1941, lines 26–32, SFN, NL 147/II, Box 147/4. See also letter dated 23 October 1941, lines 19–22, SFN, NL 147/II, Box 147/4.

average. Between autumn 1938 and April 1945, the *Heim Wienerwald* witnessed the birth of approximately 1,350 children, averaging out to four births a week.[133] Over the next few years, Leitner continued her training as an infant care nurse. In her letters she often remarked on the considerable workload.[134] Occasionally she provided specific details of her duties, as in February 1942 when she mentioned assisting in a minor surgical procedure.[135] However, her responsibilities, until her transfer to Cologne in the spring of 1942 were not confined to nursing training alone.[136] She was also assigned menial chores by the head nurse.[137]

In her correspondence, Leitner placed significant emphasis on the nutritional situation in the *Heim Wienerwald*. Particularly in the initial weeks and months, she praised the food provisions, sending her mother detailed accounts of the meals. It is likely that she had not enjoyed such a healthy diet at her mother's home in Klosterneuburg.[138]

"Just imagine, on Tuesday we had pork schnitzel, large as toilet lids and 1 mm [sic!] thick. On Saturday, we had lung stew and bread dumplings, and today we had minced meat. As you can see, we are not lacking meat. Tuesday, Thursday, and Sunday are meat days; on the other days we are served vegetable, flour-based, and cold spread dishes. Every evening, there is tea."[139]

---

133 For further information, see the article by Lukas Schretter, Martin Sauerbrey-Almasy, and Barbara Stelzl-Marx in this volume.

134 Letter dated 24 November 1941, lines 3–4, SFN, NL 147/II, Box 147/4.

135 Letter dated 4 February 1942, lines 26–27, SFN, NL 147/II, Box 147/4.

136 Leitner's last letter prior to her departure from the *Heim Wienerwald* is dated 22 March 1942. The first letter from Cologne was sent on 2 April 1942. See the notes by Elissa Mailänder in the SFN, NL 147/II, Box 147/4 resp. Mailänder, *Amour*, 169. In Cologne, Leitner worked at the Lindenburg Children's Hospital, run by the NSV since 1935, see Mailänder, *Amour*, 169. The residential address was Wittgensteinerstraße 14. See the sender address in the SFN, NL 147/II, Box 147/4. According to Mailänder, Leitner described her training period in Cologne in letters to her mother as pleasant. She mentioned ideological trainings, for instance, when she asked her mother to send the family copy of *Mein Kampf* to Cologne. She praised the "camaraderie" among colleagues. After the clinic was evacuated in the summer of 1943 due to ongoing Allied air raids, Leitner, as per Mailänder, was an intern in an eye clinic in Maribor (then Marburg an der Drau, modern-day Slovenia) in autumn and winter 1943, see Mailänder, *Amour*, 171–72. For the history of the Lindenburg Children's Hospital in Cologne, see the article by Nicola Wenge cited by Mailänder: Nicola Wenge, "Kölner Kliniken in der NS-Zeit. Zur tödlichen Dynamik im lokalen Gesundheitswesen," in *Kölner Krankenhausgeschichten. Am Anfang war Napoleon...*, edited by Monika Frank and Friedrich Moll (Köln: Verlag des Kölnischen Stadtmuseums, 2006), 546–69, esp. 547–48. The SFN also keeps letters from Leitner to her mother stamped in Friedau (present-day Ormož, in northeastern modern-day Slovenia).

137 Letter dated 4 February 1941, lines 35–53, SFN, NL 147/II, Box 147/4.

138 For instance, letter dated 9 January 1941, lines 41–43, SFN, NL 147/II, Box 147/4.

139 Letter dated 16 January 1941, lines 34–42, SFN, NL 147/II, Box 147/4. Schmitz-Köster also refers to a relatively abundant diet plan in the *Lebensborn* homes, including "a lot of vegetables and [...] meat three to four times a week." Schmitz-Köster, *"Deutsche Mutter"*, 150.

Leitner also took pride in her weight gain, mentioning it repeatedly and always in a positive context.[140] Due to the abundant supplies at the home, there were times she would save food items to send to her mother by post, including her "cake voucher,"[141] and oranges.[142] However, as the war wore on, the staff at the home learned from external workers about the growing shortage of food coupons, with the intimation that the overall food situation outside the home was deteriorating. This disparity between her personal experiences at the home and what she heard prompted Leitner to ask her mother if the reports were true.[143]

## 4.2    Hedwig Glattauer, 1943–1945

Similar to Marianne Leitner's account, Hedwig Glattauer noted that the allocation of trainees to their respective tasks was done on a rotational basis.[144] Initially, she worked in the kitchen, located in the building's basement. Her workday began at 5 o'clock in the morning.[145] Her tasks included washing dishes, handling milk deliveries, and stoking the kitchen stove. Her supervisor was responsible for the kitchen staff,[146] enforced harsh discipline,[147] and was described as "very distant and strict,"[148] with Glattauer recalling, that "we always made ourselves small when she came."[149]

After several weeks, she moved from the kitchen to the laundry room, and later she served as a waitress in the dining hall. She was also employed as a cleaner on the ground floor, in the maternity ward on the first floor – which she disliked because of its persistent unpleasant smell[150] – and in the infant ward on the second floor. "We did stints in all the departments, always under supervision."[151]

---

140  Letter dated 30 September 1941, lines 27–28, SFN, NL 147/II, Box 147/4.
141  Letter dated 22 December 1941, lines 12–13; letter dated 20 January 1942, lines 26–29; letter dated 15 March 1942, lines 28–29, SFN, NL 147/II, Box 147/4. The *Kuchenkarte* (cake voucher) seems to have been a food ration card, a mechanism for collecting/distributing specific food items, in this case, cakes.
142  Letter dated 14 January 1942, lines 61–65, SFN, NL 147/II, Box 147/4.
143  Letter dated 22 February 1942, lines 33–37, SFN, NL 147/II, Box 147/4.
144  BIK, Glattauer, interview, 8.
145  Work in the kitchen inevitably began earlier than that of the nurses, who typically began their duties at 6 a.m. or 7 p.m. According to the official guidelines, either nurses or assistants were scheduled for the evening shift from 7 p.m. to 10 p.m., ensuring they had their time off during the morning hours. A dedicated nurse was allocated for the night shift from 8 p.m. to 8 a.m. After a four-week duration, another nurse would replace her. *Dienstanweisung für die Heime des "Lebensborn" e.V.*, n. d., AA, 4.1.0/8209800, Ref. 82448183.
146  *Dienstanweisung für die Heime des "Lebensborn" e.V.*, n. d., AA, 4.1.0/8209800, Ref. 82448186.
147  BIK, Glattauer, interview, 9.
148  Ibid., 8.
149  Ibid., 9.
150  Ibid., 24.

Shortly before the end of the war, the head nurse assigned her to the home's nursery, situated in an adjacent part of the building. For roughly two months leading up to the evacuation of the facility, she was involved in childcare. According to the 1938 service directive, as a nurse for older children (starting from one year of age) she reported directly to the home's director or the head nurse rather than to the infant-care nurse.[152] Most of the children under her care were those of staff members and the home's director.[153] She found this role particularly satisfying, as it aligned most closely with her professional aspirations at the time. "We could truly work with the children. We dressed them and went for walks with them."[154]

Glattauer recalled that she had minimal interaction with the women who were about to give birth or had just delivered in the home. One exception was her role as a waitress serving the *Lebensborn* mothers in the dining room, where the dining table was arranged in a horseshoe shape. According to Glattauer, both trainees and staff would stand in the room as the mothers took their meals. The staff dined separately at a smaller table within the same space at different times.[155] Student nurses were not permitted to enter the rooms of these mothers, not even for cleaning duties. Glattauer recounted: "The [mothers] were kept quite secluded."[156] Apart from cleaning tasks in the infant section, she had no contact with the infants either.

## 4.3   Marianne Leitner, 1944–1945

Marianne Leitner returned to the *Heim Wienerwald* in April 1944, resuming her position as an infant nurse.[157] In her first letter stamped by the Ortmann post office, she informed her mother about the demanding work routine:

"There is plenty of work, with over 80 children and not as many mothers. Today, I was responsible, alongside another nurse, for two rooms housing 14 children. I rose early at 1/2 6 h (a practice I foresee continuing) and, aside from a mere two-hour break, worked until 1/2 8 h – a full 12-hour shift constantly on my feet. Needless to say, I am exhausted today."[158]

---

151  Ibid., 9.

152  *Dienstanweisung für die Heime des "Lebensborn" e.V.*, n. d., AA, 4.1.0/8209800, Ref. 82448183.

153  BIK, Glattauer, interview, 32.

154  Ibid., 31.

155  Ibid., 10.

156  Ibid., 23.

157  According to *Lebensborn* documents, Leitner was once again in the *Heim Wienerwald* since 1 April 1944. *Schwesternaufstellung*, 3 May 1944, AA, 4.1.0/8210400, Ref. 82449681. This was confirmed by the letters sent by Leiter from the post office in Ortmann at the beginning of April 1944, see SFN, NL 147/II, Box 147/4.

158  Letter dated 2 April 1943 [stamped 4 April 1944], lines 70–80, SFN, NL 147/II, Box 147/4.

However, it seems Leitner felt comfortable again within the community. Three months later, she updated her mother saying, "I have settled in well and have my own room again, with only five children, which makes the work enjoyable."[159] Only a week later, she was moved to a breastfeeding room with eight to eleven mothers.[160] According to Leitner, there was still

> "a lot to do, and one must be careful not to make a mistake as they [the supervisors] watch closely. The upside is, when the mothers leave, they occasionally give me gifts. Just yesterday, I received a pair of new stockings, on Wednesday two handkerchiefs and 5 Reichsmark."[161]

Apart from such descriptions of her job demands other aspects of work were mentioned only in passing. For instance, during sunny days, the infants in their cribs were taken to the balconies by the nurses.[162] By winter 1944, she noted that the older children were out on their sledges around the home.[163]

The provisioning situation changed drastically between 1944 and 1945 due to the war, contrasting sharply with the period from 1940 to 1942. During her initial years of training in the *Heim Wienerwald*, Leitner merely asked her mother to send everyday items, as there was no need for extra food, with plenty available on-site.[164]

From 1944 onwards, however, she repeatedly asked her mother for food parcels, for specific dishes to be prepared when she visited her in Klosterneu-burg[165] or to bring everyday items[166] and food[167] during visits to the *Heim Wie-*

---

159  Letter dated 4 July 1944, lines 13–16, SFN, NL 147/II, Box 147/4.

160  Letter dated 21 July 1944, lines 18–21, SFN, NL 147/II, Box 147/4. Spatially separate nursing rooms are also reported from other *Lebensborn* homes. Margarete Dörr, *Durchkommen und Überleben. Frauenerfahrungen in der Kriegs- und Nachkriegszeit* (Frankfurt/Main: Campus Verlag, 1998), 172.

161  Letter dated 21 July 1944, lines 21–33, SFN, NL 147/II, Box 147/4.

162  Letter dated 2 April 1943 [stamped 4 April 1944], line 31–32, SFN, NL 147/II, Box 147/4.

163  Letter dated 12 November 1944, lines 17–21, SFN, NL 147/II, Box 147/4.

164  Topics such as alarm clocks and toothpaste, letter dated 00 December 1940, lines 31 and 45; letter dated 14 January 1942, lines 91–94; money, letter dated 18 December 1940, line 5; clothing, shoes, cameras, shampoo, and writing paper, letter dated 16 January 1941, lines 12–16 and 25–27; letter dated 24 March 1941, lines 21–23; letter dated 2 April 1941, lines 60–63; letter dated 29 May 1941, line 28–29; letter dated 22 August 1941, lines 17–21; letter dated 23 October 1941, lines 23–25; letter dated 24 November 1941, lines 11–14; letter dated 4 December 1941, lines 24–27; letter dated 15 March 1942, lines 10–17; letter dated 15 April 1942, line 29, letter dated 16 April 1942, lines 12–16; wool and sweets, letter dated 11 August 1941, line 16–17; letter dated 16 September 1941, lines 11–13; letter dated 18 September 1941, lines 27–31; letter dated 12 February 1942, lines 3–7 and 62–65; and toiletries, letter dated 22 February 1942, lines 43–53; letter dated 22 March 1942, lines 34–36 are mentioned, SFN, NL 147/II, Box 147/4.

165  "May I affectionately remind you that elderberry compote is one of my favourite dishes? Thursday's menu, a bowl of elderberry, and for Friday, dumplings, or noodles with cu-

*nerwald.*[168] Upon returning to Feichtenbach, she commented, "the food here is good, but it pales in comparison to Friedau. I feel hungrier than I ever did at home. I often wish I had what I had at home."[169] Her joy was palpable when, in summer 1944, a mother gifted her a "large piece of raw smoked bacon."[170]

Not only in the *Heim Wienerwald*, but also in the Pernitz community, supplies were dwindling. In winter 1944, she complained about the poor shopping options:

> "I doubt anything is available; last week in W[iene]r Neustadt I had a tough time. I was tasked to buy stockings and a nursing bra for a mother. I had to visit fourteen shops before securing the items. Nothing else was available."[171]

Besides her daytime duties, from mid-1944 Leitner occasionally had night shifts from 8 p.m. to 8 a.m.[172] After a four-week cycle, another nurse would take over.[173] Even during her initial week of this schedule, she told her mother daytime visits were possible as the night watch "was not too demanding."[174] By October 1944, Leitner noted the strain of these shifts, saying she had become "too lazy to write," and her only leisure activity was reading.[175]

---

cumber salad. Of course, if you have something different, it will not be turned down." Letter dated 31 August 1944, lines 8–16, SFN, NL 147/II, Box 147/4.

166 Topics such as clothing, letter dated 26 April 1944, lines 3–25; letter dated 2 May 1944, lines 12–14; letter dated 18 May 1944, line 19–20; letter dated 23 May 1944, lines 41–48; letter dated 6 October 1944, lines 44–49; toiletries, letter dated 17 May 1944, lines 23–26; letter dated 23 May 1944, lines 4–9; knitting utensils, letter dated 1 June 1944, lines 7–16; letter dated 8 June 1944, lines 67–70; letter dated 10 October 1944, lines 56–64; and writing paper or stamps, letter dated 17 July 1944, lines 45–47), are mentioned, SFN, NL 147/II, Box 147/4.

167 Letter dated 2 April 1943 [stamped 4 April 1944] lines 19–22; letter dated 10 April 1944, lines 3–7; letter dated 2 May 1944, lines 12–18; letter dated 23 May 1944, lines 59–60; letter dated 10 October 1944, lines 80–82; letter dated 9 December 1944, lines 3–9, SFN, NL 147/II, Box 147/4.

168 Family visits to the home's staff were strictly regulated. See *Abschrift eines Schreibens von Heinrich Himmler an die Geschäftsführung des Lebensborn*, 31 July 1939, AA, 4.1.0/8209900, Ref. 82448300; *Erlaubnis für Besuche der NS-Schwestern in den "Lebensborn"-Heimen*, 31 October 1939, AA, 4.1.0/8210700, Ref. 82450247. Some letters indicate that Marianne Leitner's mother probably stayed at the "Mandlinghof" in Feichtenbach, letter dated 29 May 1941, lines 6–9; letter dated 23 October 1941, lines 17–19; letter dated 10 April 1944, lines 13 and 35–36, SFN, NL 147/II, Box 147/4. From 1944 onwards, this seems to change: Marianne Leitner asked her mother to sit "in her room" and wait for her, letter dated 26 April 1944, lines 22–23, or explicitly offered: "You can sleep in my room," letter dated 18 May 1944, lines 73–74, SFN, NL 147/II, Box 147/4.

169 Letter dated 2 April 1943 [stamped 4 April 1944], lines 22–26, SFN, NL 147/II, Box 147/4.

170 Letter dated 24 July 1944, lines 22–25, SFN, NL 147/II, Box 147/4.

171 Letter dated 9 December 1944, lines 17–26, SFN, NL 147/II, Box 147/4.

172 Letter dated 18 May 1944, lines 13–15, SFN, NL 147/II, Box 147/4.

173 *Dienstanweisung für die Heime des "Lebensborn" e.V.*, n. d., AA, 4.1.0/8209800, Ref. 82448183.

174 Letter dated 23 May 1944, lines 56–59, SFN, NL 147/II, Box 147/4.

175 Letter dated 10 June 1944, lines 4–8, SFN, NL 147/II, Box 147/4.

Around the time she was appointed as a night nurse in the *Heim Wienerwald*, she applied for a transfer to a *Lebensborn* home in Norway. Disappointedly, she wrote to her mother in May 1944 that this seemed unlikely,

> "because they only requested one of us [nurses], despite both of us applying simultaneously. It seems the senior of us two is given priority, and she will be leaving as soon as her paperwork is ready. [...] Her journey is by plane from Berlin to Oslo. You are probably relieved, but I am heartbroken! I was looking forward to the trip, especially the flight and visiting Norway. Now I will likely have to spend the winter here."[176]

Staff mobility within the more than twenty maternity and children's homes in the German Reich and occupied territories was common.[177] While her senior colleague travelled to Norway in October 1944,[178] the home's director August Hagemeier chose Leitner from several nurses to take a child from the *Heim Wienerwald* to its mother in Bavaria – a task Leitner deemed both a responsibility and an honour.[179]

## V. Beyond the Everyday: Home Community Festivities

Everyday routines in the *Heim Wienerwald* were frequently punctuated by celebrations. Hedwig Glattauer summarised that "they celebrated everything."[180] In addition to Easter,[181] the home community celebrated Christmas and – in accordance with National Socialist ideology – the Yule Festival. Glattauer recalled crafting sessions in the lead-up to Yule, and the baking of cookies.[182] A Yule tree was also present, "decorated almost solely with apples and gingerbread."[183] To this day, she keeps a place card from the Yule Festival, inscribed with "Hedi" in her own handwriting.[184]

---

176 Letter dated 5 May 1944, lines 26–31, and 35–44, SFN, NL 147/II, Box 147/4.
177 Personnel often came from the *Heim Friesland* in Hohehorst to the *Heim Wienerwald*. Notable staff includes head nurse Else Schwartmann and Hildegard S., who gave birth to children fathered by one of the administrators of the *Heim Friesland*, Otto Bachschneider. Worth mentioning is also *SS Untersturmführer* Walter Decker, the administrator of the *Heim Friesland*, who came to the *Heim Wienerwald* in the spring of 1944. Schmitz-Köster, *"Deutsche Mutter"*, 112–14, and 145–46.
178 Letter dated 28 October 1944, lines 15–18, SFN, NL 147/II, Box 147/4.
179 Letters dated 10 October 1944, lines 42–51; 12 November 1944, lines 3–9, SFN, NL 147/II, Box 147/4.
180 BIK, Glattauer, interview, 15.
181 Letter dated 10 April 1944, lines 26–29, SFN, NL 147/II, Box 147/4.
182 BIK, Glattauer, interview, 54.
183 Ibid., 59.
184 Ibid., 15.

In a 1940 post-Yule letter to her mother, Marianne Leitner referred to "Christmas parcels."[185] The following year, however, she wrote that

"on 21 Dec, we have the Yule celebration, where we are also performing 'Goldmarie and Pechmarie.' This time, I have a minor role again. Christmas gifts will be on 24 Dec."[186]

Moreover, Leitner informed her mother that all mothers and senior staff from *Lebensborn* received a "ceramic plate adorned with the SS insignia,"[187] whereas the student nurses were each given three handkerchiefs, which they had to hem themselves.[188]

Not only did the qualified nurses and student nurses receive gifts from *Lebensborn*, but they also received presents from the *NSS*. At a tea party hosted by head nurse Else Schwartmann, the elder nurses received Christmas gifts which consisted of more than double their monthly salary and two pairs of stockings.[189] Furthermore, members of the staff in the *Heim Wienerwald* were randomly assigned a person to whom they gave a gift.[190] Other Christmas preparations in Advent 1944 included making and hanging an Advent wreath, as well as jointly constructing a "Christmas pyramid made of apples and fir branches."[191]

Leitner's letters also mention celebrations for *Heim Wienerwald* employees' birthdays.[192] Mention is also made of Adolf Hitler's birthday on 20 April, and the farewell party for the home's director Schwab in April 1944, where a "colourful evening with folk dances and the like"[193] was organised. Another "colourful evening" took place on 1 May 1944, with traditional dances performed in regional costumes.[194] However, when the home's director Schwab permitted staff and

---

185  Letter dated 28 December 1941, lines 18–26, SFN, NL 147/II, Box 147/4.

186  Letter dated 17 November 1941, lines 51–55, SFN, NL 147/II, Box 147/4. The same play had been rehearsed in the home the previous year. Letter dated 18 December 1940, lines 26–28, SFN, NL 147/II, Box 147/4.

187  Letter dated 25 December 1940, lines 6–9, SFN, NL 147/II, Box 147/4. Also, see the description of the *Julteller* which the interviewees at the *Heim Friesland* received for the Yule celebration in Schmitz-Köster, *"Deutsche Mutter"*, 164.

188  Letter dated 25 December 1940, lines 9–11, SFN, NL 147/II, Box 147/4.

189  Ibid., lines 15–16.

190  These included, for instance, a bookshelf, or a bottle of schnapps. Letter dated 9 December 1944, lines 29–33, SFN, NL 147/II, Box 147/4. Both medical and non-medical staff participated in this custom.

191  Letter dated 4 December 1944, lines 15–20, SFN, NL 147/II, Box 147/4.

192  "They forgot about my birthday here, they remembered only in the kitchen, so we could celebrate with black tea and cake just half an hour before midnight. Part of me is glad no one knew, as here you are sung to on such occasions." Letter dated 13 June 1944, lines 9–17, SFN, NL 147/II, Box 147/4.

193  Letter dated 19 April 1944, lines 34–40, SFN, NL 147/II, Box 147/4.

194  Letter dated 26 April 1944, lines 4–8, SFN, NL 147/II, Box 147/4. "On 1 May we had a 'jolly evening,' which left nothing to be desired. Us nurses performed folk dances and the spokespersons played the tale of the princess and the swineherd. The court ladies were

some *Lebensborn* mothers to dress up and dance on Carnival Tuesday in 1941, he had to justify this spontaneous, "wholly improvised small event"[195] to Ebner. Another "highlight" of the home's regular activities were the naming ceremonies, where newborns deemed "hereditarily valuable" were to be formally inducted into the SS *Sippengemeinschaft.*[196]

According to Mailänder, Leitner's letters portray an image of a workplace where "a very positive atmosphere prevailed, marked by camaraderie and social commitment."[197] Yet, Mailänder emphasises, given the daily life in the *Heim Wienerwald*, it is hard to believe that Leitner was not aware of the transfer of children classified as "hereditarily inferior" to the *Wiener Städtische Fürsorge-Anstalt "Am Spiegelgrund."*[198] Decades later, Hedwig Glattauer stressed that children born in the home were well-treated and were neither "neglected"[199] nor "abandoned."[200] She claims she was unaware of the murder of certain children as part of the National Socialist child "euthanasia" programme: "It was all a secret. You were not told anything."[201] She emphasised the limited responsibility she had as a student nurse. In addition, the *Germanisierung* ("germanisation") of children by *Lebensborn* was mentioned neither in Leitner's letters nor in the interview with Glattauer.[202]

## VI.   Around the Home: Recreational Activities

By the end of 1940, after working in the home for roughly three weeks, Leitner already felt integrated into a collective "us" of the student nurses. Her letters suggest that she quickly forged strong relationships and contacts.[203] For instance,

---

dressed very sweetly with sheets as a kind of crinoline." Letter dated 2 May 1944, lines 21–29, SFN, NL 147/II, Box 147/4.

195  *Schulungsbericht für Monat Februar 1941*, 10 March 1941, AA, 4.1.0/8211900, Ref. 82454087.
196  For naming ceremonies in *Heim Wienerwald*, see the article by Barbara Stelzl-Marx in this volume.
197  Mailänder, *Amour*, 155.
198  Ibid. For the murder of children born in the *Heim Wienerwald* as part of the National Socialist child "euthanasia" programme, see the article by Sabine Nachbaur in this volume.
199  BIK, Glattauer, interview, 22.
200  Ibid., 32.
201  Ibid., 61.
202  In one letter, Leitner casually mentioned a friend of hers, who was "on transports of Baltic children." Letter dated 16 October 1944, lines 27–29, SFN, NL 147/II, Box 147/4. However, this friend, who had completed a *Fürsorgerinnenschule* in Vienna, does not seem to have worked for *Lebensborn*. For more information on the *Lebensborn* "germanisation" programme, see Ines Hopfer, *Geraubte Kindheit. Die gewaltsame Eindeutschung von polnischen Kindern in der NS-Zeit* (Wien – Köln – Weimar: Böhlau, 2010).
203  Mailänder, *Amour*, 155.

she made plans to swap food[204] with another newcomer.[205] A few weeks later, the 16-year-old wrote to her mother about another friend:

> "On Sunday, I had the day off, and with my best mate Erika, who is from Sudetenland, I went to Waxeneck, a popular skiing destination for the Viennese. We were the subject of amusement for skiers because we had no skis. We turned around and slid down the steep slope, which was great fun. By the time we returned [to the home], our feet were soaking wet, so we had to change immediately."[206]

Each entry and exit of the student nurses through the main door of the *Heim Wienerwald* was logged by the doorman.[207] The *Waxeneck*, a plateau about a kilometre away from the home with a refuge established in 1919, was a favourite getaway for staff.[208] Breaks during working hours, set by the head nurse for all nursing staff,[209] could also be spent in their digs.[210] Apart from these two friends she made in the *Heim Wienerwald*,[211] Leitner mentioned several more, with whom she went looking for lily of the valley,[212] swapped her day off,[213] or went hiking:

> "Last Sunday, Resi and I went to Waxeneck, where we had some cake and fruit juice. The snow was knee-deep, and there was not a snow rose in sight. There was a narrow path, but if you slid off it, you would find yourself knee-deep in snow. On our way down, we fell a few times, which made us laugh uncontrollably."[214]

In the summer, the young staff would often head to Bad Vöslau for swimming,[215] try their hand at making ice cream,[216] or go berry picking.[217] After returning from

---

204 "Last week, we received approximately 100 g of bean coffee, as we only brew ordinary coffee in the institution. Thus, Elisabeth and I decided that one month I would send both our rations home, and the following month we would do it the other way round." Letter dated 25 December 1940, lines 29–34, SFN, NL 147/II, Box 147/4.

205 Letter dated 00 December 1940, lines 31–35, SFN, NL 147/II, Box 147/4.

206 Letter dated 16 January 1941, lines 43–53, SFN, NL 147/II, Box 147/4.

207 BIK, Glattauer, interview, 57.

208 Letter dated 26 April 1944, lines 26–34, SFN, NL 147/II, Box 147/4.

209 *Dienstanweisung für die Heime des "Lebensborn" e.V.*, n. d., AA, 4.1.0/8209800, Ref. 82448183.

210 BIK, Glattauer, interview, 54.

211 Activities with Erika are also mentioned in subsequent letters, for example, in letter dated 20 August 1944, lines 49–53. This probably refers to *NS-Schwester* Erika N., AA, 4.1.0/8210400, Ref. 82449681.

212 Letter dated 29 May 1941, lines 30–33, SFN, NL 147/II, Box 147/4.

213 Letter dated 4 December 1941, lines 7–15, SFN, NL 147/II, Box 147/4.

214 Letter dated 4 February 1942, lines 27–38, SFN, NL 147/II, Box 147/4. In addition, other friends are mentioned, e.g. Josefine in the letter dated 19 April 1944, lines 5–8, SFN, NL 147/II, Box 147/4, probably referring to *NS-Schwester* Josefine R., AA, 4.1.0/8210400, Ref. 82449681; Annemarie in letter dated 26 April 1944, lines 29–34, SFN, NL 147/II, Box 147/4, probably referring to *NS-Schwester* Annemarie P., AA, 4.1.0/8210400, Ref. 82449674; and Irma in the letter dated 13 June 1944, line 34, SFN, NL 147/II, Box 147/4.

215 Letter dated 20 August 1944, lines 49–53, SFN, NL 147/II, Box 147/4.

216 Letter dated 8 June 1944, lines 49–53, SFN, NL 147/II, Box 147/4.

Klosterneuburg to the home, Leitner would drop in on a colleague to catch up on the latest gossip and events of the day.[218] Her letters to her mother, detailing her leisure activities with colleagues, were consistently informal.

Another popular pastime for the staff was going to the cinema in Pernitz.[219] In the extant letters from the *Heim Wienerwald,* there are eleven mentions of jointly watching movies such as *Jud Süß,*[220] *…reitet für Deutschland,*[221] *13 Stühle,*[222] *6 Tage Heimaturlaub,*[223] and *Schrammeln.*[224] Starring leading actors such as Hans Moser and Heinz Rühmann, these movies combined ideological propaganda and popular entertainment.[225]

Another activity shared by the student nurses and qualified nurses was writing letters to "unknown soldiers" on the frontline. Particularly during her first months in the *Heim Wienerwald,* Leitner displayed considerable uncertainty about what such letters should contain:

"Can you believe it? Elisabeth [a female friend and colleague in the *Heim Wienerwald*] is writing to Niki [a male friend from Klosterneuburg], an unknown soldier. But do not tell Aunt Anna [probably Niki's mother]. We have been sitting with these letters for two evenings, trying to make them sound grand, but they turn out quite silly. My own 'unknown' has not yet replied."[226]

In addition to writing letters, student nurses and qualified nurses collaborated with colleagues to prepare *Liebesgaben* ("love gifts"),[227] such as knitted garments.[228] At times Leitner asked her mother to send cigarettes and alcohol to

---

217 Letter dated 17 July 1944, lines 15–20, SFN, NL 147/II, Box 147/4.
218 Letter dated 28 October 1944, lines 8–15, SFN, NL 147/II, Box 147/4.
219 Letter dated 16 January 1941, lines 56–61, SFN, NL 147/II, Box 147/4.
220 Letter dated 7 February 1941, lines 23–26, SFN, NL 147/II, Box 147/4.
221 Letter dated 22 August 1941, lines 36–38, SFN, NL 147/II, Box 147/4.
222 Letter dated 14 January 1942, lines 70–73, SFN, NL 147/II, Box 147/4.
223 Letter dated 22 March 1942, lines 14–17, SFN, NL 147/II, Box 147/4.
224 Letter dated 28 October 1944, lines 29–32, SFN, NL 147/II, Box 147/4.
225 For more information regarding National Socialist cinema in today's Austria see, e.g., Wolfgang Pensold, *Die Geschichte des Kinos in Österreich. Ein Spiel mit Licht und Schatten* (Wien: Böhlau, 2024), esp. 192–218; Klaus Christian Vögl, *Angeschlossen und gleichgeschaltet. Kino in Österreich 1938–1945* (Wien – Köln – Weimar: Böhlau, 2018).
226 Letter dated 7 February 1941, lines 5–13, SFN, NL 147/II, Box 147/4.
227 Regarding World War I, Christa Hämmerle defines *Liebesgaben* as encompassing everything "donated, collected, sent, and distributed that was useful for or required by the soldiers to aid their combat readiness, but also for their families, including tobacco, pastry, sweets, clothing, sewing kits, soap, candles, pencils, etc." Christa Hämmerle, *Heimat/Front: Gender Histories of World War I in Austria-Hungary* (Wien – Köln – Weimar: Böhlau, 2014), esp. 119–27, here: 122–23.
228 "We also need to knit for the soldiers. Firstly, I lack a clothing card and secondly, money. So, I'm unravelling socks I've recently knitted as they are too small for a man and will knit mittens instead." Letter dated 28 December 1941, lines 44–53, SFN, NL 147/II, Box 147/4.

include them in these packages.[229] Sometimes she also asked her to prepare a parcel for a soldier.[230] Besides cigarettes, clothing and alcohol, stationery and lighters were dispatched from the *Heim Wienerwald* to the frontlines.[231]

## VII.    Leaving the *Lebensborn:* Evacuation and the End of the War

Throughout the war from autumn 1944 to April 1945, Hedwig Glattauer recollected that the *Heim Wienerwald* remained largely shielded from the ravages of the war:

> "It felt like an island. Like a remote island. You could not feel the war there. Not at all. We never even saw any aircraft, despite the bombing of Wiener Neustadt."[232]

She mentioned a singular air raid alarm just before the war's culmination, during which she took shelter in the cellar alongside the children in her care.[233] "Otherwise, it was so peaceful […] as if there had never been a war at all. I assume those outside the facility must surely have felt the war more acutely?"[234]

In her correspondence, Marianne Leitner also mentioned the war only sporadically. She wrote to her mother about the reassignment of acquaintances at the front lines, which she came to know about through letters.[235] She also described in some detail occasional trips outside the facility when the home's staff encountered a guard accompanying prisoners on beer-procuring errands.[236] Rumours, such as about the bombing raids on the *Minoritenkirche*, the *Michaelerkirche*, and the Vienna *Riesenrad*,[237] coupled with the uncertainty stemming from the seclusion of the facility, prompted Leitner to enquire from her mother about the situation in major cities and industrial installations targeted by the Allies. She

---

229  Letters dated 2 April 1941, line 35; 20 August 1941, lines 15–17; 30 September 1941, lines 30–33; and 12 February 1942, lines 29–32, SFN, NL 147/II, Box 147/4.
230  Letter dated 22 August 1941, lines 6–10, SFN, NL 147/II, Box 147/4.
231  Letter dated 14 January 1942, lines 21–37, SFN, NL 147/II, Box 147/4.
232  BIK, Glattauer, interview, 55.
233  Ibid., 29.
234  Ibid., 55.
235  Leitner regularly relayed to her mother information she received through letters from a friend and soldier named Willi, detailing his whereabouts, be it in Bielitz, the South of France, or the Eastern Front. Furthermore, the death of her friend Niki – the one, to whom her friend and colleague Elisabeth had been writing as "unknown soldier" – on the frontlines in September 1941 is briefly mentioned in one of the letters: "P.S. Just received the sad news this evening that Niki has fallen. I could not believe it, but now it is true." Letter dated 30 September 1941, lines 40–43, SFN, NL 147/II, Box 147/4.
236  Letter dated 17 November 1941, lines 13–18, SFN, NL 147/II, Box 147/4. No further details about "the prisoners" and the "guard" are mentioned in the letters.
237  Letter dated 18 May 1944, lines 55–58, SFN, NL 147/II, Box 147/4.

remarked in a tone of resignation that "one rarely gets accurate information here, which forces one to rely on exaggerated tales."[238]

In stark contrast to Hedwig Glattauer's account, Marianne Leitner wrote about witnessing several air raids from close quarters starting from June 1944. She even observed an aerial assault on Wiener Neustadt from a safe distance.[239] The restrained tone in which she described these alarms and raids suggests she was possibly aiming at reassuring her mother, emphasizing the composure she and the home's administration maintained during these perilous times. This sentiment can be inferred from a letter excerpt dated late August 1944:

> "Regrettably, we had another alarm, this time on a Sunday, which saw us taking shelter in the cellar for 2½ hours. Nonetheless, we were pleased to have made full use of the otherwise beautiful days, particularly as the weather is now deteriorating."[240]

During early summer 1944, the night shifts in the infant ward, to which Leitner was regularly assigned,[241] were uneventful: "The night shifts are rather pleasant; so far, we have not had to retreat to the basement."[242] However, by the autumn of that year, air raids seem to have become a frequent occurrence in the daily routine of the home. An air strike in early October 1944 posed an immediate threat. Leitner wrote to her mother in distress that

> "two planes flew very low [...] releasing their incendiary canisters right above our facility. Whether their poor aim was intentional or not, none hit the building directly. One landed on the dining room balcony, but fires erupted everywhere. One fire was found smouldering in the meadow behind the building, near the coal pile, in front of the rear entrance. An inspection team that visited in the afternoon counted around four hundred canisters dispersed around the facility, with approximately forty being duds. This time, we got away with a scare. In Muggendorf, near Pernitz, reportedly 35 explosive bombs were dropped. Guests from Vienna, visiting the mothers, indicate that the situation there is dire."[243]

This extract from the latter lacks the light and reassuring tone in which attacks were previously described. The change is probably due to the shock of the recent raid and its immediate aftermath. Leitner's assumptions about the situation in the cities were based on information about the bombing of major cities such as Vienna and Wiener Neustadt. Some of this information was provided to the home staff by visitors of resident *Lebensborn* mothers. As the war neared its end,

---

238  Ibid., lines 58–62.
239  Letter dated 8 June 1944, lines 12–36, SFN, NL 147/II, Box 147/4.
240  Letter dated 31 August 1944, lines 26–32, SFN, NL 147/II, Box 147/4.
241  Letters dated 8 June 1944, lines 37–38; 13 June 1944, lines 17–20; 8 August 1944, lines 24–30, SFN, NL 147/II, Box 147/4.
242  Ibid, lines 47–49.
243  Letter dated 10 October 1944, lines 18–41, SFN, NL 147/II, Box 147/4.

it became increasingly difficult for staff to get extended leave. Leitner wrote to her mother that the head nurse was trying to keep all staff on site. This was to prevent the start of work shifts from being delayed or cancelled due to travel disruptions caused by alarms and bombings.[244]

In April 1945, the *Heim Wienerwald* was evacuated in anticipation of the imminent occupation by Soviet forces.[245] Hedwig Glattauer recalled that

"suddenly, they announced our evacuation. 'Quickly pack your belongings!' They had waited for as long as feasible. But by then, the Russians were already at the border. Trouble was truly brewing."[246]

While the remaining *Lebensborn* mothers and some of the staff were evacuated to the *Lebensborn* headquarters at the *Heim Hochland* in Steinhöring, according to Glattauer, the student nurses were sent back to their families:

"They instructed us to 'Pack everything! Take only the essentials! [sic!]' I had a small suitcase. I packed only what was absolutely necessary and left behind many items. Then a bus arrived, and we were taken to Neulengbach. There was a monastery there, I believe in Altlengbach. For the journey, they provided us with a large schnitzel sandwich. Already seated on the bus, I felt unwell during the trip. [laughs] It was dreadful."[247]

Marianne Leitner, however, was evacuated to the *Heim Hochland* in Steinhöring, where *Lebensborn* consolidated the remaining staff and "residents," including the children.

"[In April 1945], 20 of us from a children's home, along with 40 infants and toddlers, travelled there [to Steinhöring] over six days. We were accompanied by a stork that brought us three-fold increase in our number during that period."[248]

In the transition period between April and May 1945, shortly before the arrival of US American forces, a significant portion of the *Heim Hochland*'s staff left, some due to a planned evacuation on 29 April 1945, others on their own initiative.

---

244 Ibid., lines 7–18.
245 A list from 31 March 1945 exists, detailing the nursing staff in the *Heim Wienerwald*. Leitner is one of the six nurses listed. *Schwesternmeldung*, 12 April 1945, AA, 4.1.0/82449700, Ref. 8210400. Hilde Ernstbrunner also remembered the end of the *Heim Wienerwald* in the film of Beate Thalberg: "They did not even let me [fetch] my workbook. [...] As it was, they threw everything into the heater. [sic!] The books, everything was thrown into the heater. And they said to us: 'You can go home,'" *Geheimsache Lebensborn*, 38:24–38:36.
246 BIK, Glattauer, interview, 28–29.
247 Ibid., 28.
248 Photo album with written entries, which seem to have been added at a later date, see SFN, NL 147/II, Box 147/7a. Therefore, Marianne Leitner's notes give different numbers to those of the Catholic Youth Welfare of Steinhöring, which only assigned 18 of the 162 children, who were at Steinhöring when U.S. forces arrived, to the *Heim Wienerwald*. See Oswald, *Den Opfern verpflichtet*, 53. See also a list of all children present when the U.S. forces arrived, AA, 4.1.2/81796213, Ref. 8321126.

Ebner and the head nurse chose to remain at the home.[249] There were reports of the local civilian population looting supplies at that stage.[250] Simultaneously, the few remaining *Lebensborn* staff members attempted to destroy evidence of the association's activities by burning documents. Notably, Steinhöring not only held the records of the *Heim Hochland* but also nearly all the documents from the association's Munich headquarters.[251] Leitner noted:

> "We managed to secure as much as possible. All records were destroyed, uniforms and brown outfits were burnt, and pictures and slogans were removed. Essentially, every measure was taken to portray the home as an ordinary mother and child institution. All the male members left, presumably for the mountains, with only the chief leader remaining as the head doctor."[252]

Historian Anna Bräsel references the local clergyman, Ludwig Köppl, suggesting that additional records were also destroyed by the "outraged local villagers."[253] In early May 1945, the *Heim Hochland* home was eventually occupied by US troops:[254]

> "They finally arrived. One tank after another drew up. Shots were fired outside the home, possibly to gauge if there was any resistance. They [the soldiers] then entered and rigorously searched every room. While some seemed approachable, others appeared quite menacing. [...] The boss [probably Ebner] was taken away but, miraculously, was spared execution. Threats of execution were made towards us and even the children. Whether this was merely an intimidation tactic or genuine remains uncertain. In any case, our state of being under supervision intensified. For a few days, our assistant physician managed the facility alone until a new doctor arrived, a German. Initially, due

---

249  Oswald, *Den Opfern verpflichtet*, 54, and Bräsel, *Leitung und Mitarbeiter des Lebensborn*, 112. In a 1990 interview with the *Süddeutsche Zeitung*, the then Catholic parish priest of Steinhöring, Ludwig Köppl, stated that some nurses committed suicide at the *Heim Hochland* prior to the arrival of the Allied soldiers. See also Volker Koop, *"Dem Führer ein Kind schenken"*, 213.

250  A partially preserved report detailing Leitner's experiences towards the end of the war can be found in her bequest. It seems to have been written retrospectively: "Annemarie brought up the idea of escaping. Toni agreed, and on the evening of 1 May, they left. The timing was fortunate as we were going into the supply barracks to get fabrics that the *Oberführer* [Ebner] had made available to us. The commotion because of the disappearance of the four nurses was overshadowed by other unsettling events and experiences. The local populace stormed the barracks, looting everything that was not nailed down, and even that." Undated report by Marianne Leitner, lines 32–38, SFN, NL 147/II, Box 147/2.

251  Oswald, *Den Opfern verpflichtet*, 55, and Bräsel, *Lebensborn-Heim Hochland*, 106.

252  Undated report by Marianne Leitner, lines 38–49, SFN, NL 147/II, Box 147/2.

253  Former *Lebensborn* employees, in post-war interrogation protocols, stated that the remaining documents had been handed over to American troops and claimed that these troops subsequently destroyed them. Bräsel, *Lebensborn-Heim Hochland*, 106.

254  While Volker Koop and Anna Bräsel date the takeover to 2 May 1945 (see Koop, *"Dem Führer ein Kind schenken"*, 213, and Bräsel, *Lebensborn-Heim Hochland*, 106), Rudolf Oswald specifies 3 May 1945 (see Oswald, *Den Opfern verpflichtet*, 54).

to his American uniform, we mistook him for an American. The misconception was soon clarified. To complicate matters, there was a scarlet fever outbreak, which led to a prolonged quarantine."[255]

Leitner believed that in the period following the arrival of the U.S. troops, leaving the home would have been unwise because "American soldiers were everywhere, and the barracks were occupied by Russians."[256] The home was now a "children's home, paediatric hospital, and maternity ward," where demobilised soldiers and civilians passed through.[257]

On 25 May 1945, Munich's Mayor Karl Scharnagl entrusted the management of the children's and mother's home to the Catholic Caritas Association of the Archdiocese of Munich-Freising, which in turn assigned this task to the aforementioned clergyman Ludwig Köppl.[258] Leitner wrote about the subsequent daily work and the poor condition of the children, attributing it to the arduous escape and adverse weather. She did not perceive the presence of the American soldiers as liberation but instead, after the defeat of the German Reich, noted: Only the onset of spring seemed "to commence its unstoppable triumphant march, unhindered by any nation's fate."[259]

Marianne Leitner returned to her mother in Klosterneuburg in September 1945.[260] In Vienna, she eventually secured a position as a paediatric and infant nurse.[261] Her bequest comprised photo albums showcasing numerous gatherings with former colleagues and acquaintances whom she had met during her training.[262]

After the end of the war, when Vienna was threatened with famine, Hedwig Glattauer recalled spending a year in Hollabrunn in a children's aid pro-

---

255  Undated report by Marianne Leitner, lines 49–82, SFN, NL 147/II, Box 147/2. Leitner's account aligns with research findings by Rudolf Oswald: following the arrest of Ebner, the vacant position was filled with a young physician by the name of Kleinle, who, as a member of the *Wehrmacht*, had been taken captive by the Allies. Oswald, *Den Opfern verpflichtet*, 72.
256  Undated report by Marianne Leitner, lines 84–86, SFN, NL 147/II, Box 147/2.
257  Ibid., lines 95–100.
258  Bräsel, *Lebensborn-Heim Hochland*, 107; Oswald, *Den Opfern verpflichtet*, 72–73.
259  Undated report by Marianne Leitner, lines 120–122, SFN, NL 147/II, Box 147/2.
260  Notes by Marianne Leitner in a photo album, n. d., SFN, NL 147/II, Box 147/2.
261  Letter of thanks for 25 years of service by Viennese councillor Hans Bock in 1970, SFN, NL 147/II, Box 147/2. In 1945 Leitner joined the *Österreichicher Gewerbschaftsbund* (Austrian Trade Union Confederation, *ÖGB*), see certificate to commemorate 40 years of *ÖGB* membership in 1985, SFN, NL 147/II, Box 147/2. Later she supported the SOS Children's Village, see certificate to commemorate 35 years of sponsorship for the SOS Children's Village, n. d., SFN, NL 147/II, Box 147/2, and the Austrian Tourist Club, see certificate of the Austrian Tourist Club, Section Klosterneuburg, to commemorate 25 years of membership in 2002, SFN, NL 147/II, Box 147/2.
262  SFN, NL 147/II, Box 147/2.

gramme.[263] At the age of 17, she returned to Vienna and continued her training at the *Rudolfinerhaus*.[264] Four years later, she met Kurt Glattauer, who had survived the Holocaust as a so-called *Mischling*; his Jewish father and stepmother had been murdered in Theresienstadt.[265] Hedwig and Kurt Glattauer married in 1953.[266] Hedwig Glattauer then changed employers, as the *Rudolfinerhaus* did not accept married nurses. She worked for the city of Vienna until giving birth to her first child.[267]

## VIII. Conclusion

As a student nurse and young infant nurse, Marianne Leitner was not involved in decision-making processes of the *Heim Wienerwald* leadership. Consequently, her letters reflect less on the overall history of *Lebensborn* or the *Heim Wienerwald*, and more on the perceptions and professional ambitions of a young woman within the National Socialist system. Starting her education in the National Socialist health sector at age 16, she witnessed the war's end in 1945 at the age of 20 as a then fully trained *NS-Säuglingsschwester*. Her letters give insight into the hierarchical structures, roles, and functions within the home and how they were gendered, shaping both daily life and leisure time in the isolation of the home. Much like Marianne Leitner, Hedwig Glattauer was separated from her family for the first time as a nearly 14-year-old student nurse in the *Heim Wienerwald*. The training probably represented not only an opportunity for her to achieve her professional goals but may also have been seen by her parents as their daughter moving to what was perceived as a secure environment.

The sources cited in this article were created in different contexts: the documents from Marianne Leitner's bequest were largely written between 1940 and 1945, while the interview with Hedwig Glattauer was conducted in 2021. Nevertheless, in both narratives a picture emerges where the *Heim Wienerwald* was

---

263 BIK, Glattauer, interview 41–42.
264 Ibid., 42–43.
265 Ibid., 35–36. See also Michaela Raggam-Blesch, "Überleben nach den großen Deportationen. 'Mischehefamilien' in Wien," in *Letzte Orte. Die Wiener Sammellager und die Deportationen 1941/42*, edited by Dieter J. Hecht, Michaela Raggam-Blesch, and Heidemarie Uhl (Wien: Mandelbaum, 2019), 150–69, esp. 161–62; Michaela Raggam-Blesch, "Alltag unter prekärem Schutz. Mischlinge und Geltungsjuden im NS-Regime in Wien," *zeitgeschichte* 43 (2016) 5, 292–307, esp. 294; Michaela Raggam-Blesch "Nachbarn, Freund*innen, Fremde. Kontakte von 'Mischehefamilien' im jüdischen und nicht-jüdischen Umfeld in der Zeit des NS-Regimes in Wien," in *Außerordentliches. Festschrift für Albert Lichtblau*, edited by Regina Thumser-Wöhs, Martina Gugglberger, Birgit Kirchmayr, Grazia Prontera, and Thomas Spielbüchler (Wien – Köln – Weimar: Böhlau, 2019), 271–85, esp. 274–75.
266 Email from Hedwig Glattauer's son to Lukas Schretter, 20 October 2020.
267 BIK, Glattauer, interview, 43.

perceived by student nurses as a comfortable place for training and work, largely insulated from the impact of war and equipped with ample provisions and a decent living standard. Both women were young when they started working in the home and presumably integrated themselves quickly into the community. In the interview, Glattauer was able to recall few details of the daily routine in retrospect and emphasised that the children born in the home were treated well. However, she underlined that she could only recount the experiences of "a 14-year-old,"[268] had had little responsibility, and compared her role to a "smally cog in a large machine."[269] In contrast, Leitner's correspondence with her mother includes her daily work in the *Heim Wienerwald*, detailing the various tasks and roles as a student nurse and infant nurse. She writes about the internal hierarchy of the home staff, ceremonial occasions, her leisure activities, desires, daily experiences, and impressions. Both Leitner's letters and Glattauer's interview do not reveal that the main purpose of the *Heim Wienerwald* was to prevent abortions by "Aryan" mothers and to increase the birth rate of the "racially desirable" population, i. e. that *Lebensborn* was an instrument of National Socialist racial and population policy.[270] They did not mention, or mentioned only in passing, ideological training, lectures, and further education that took place in the *Heim Wienerwald* as in all other *Lebensborn* homes.

Based on her research on the *Heim Friesland*, Dorothee Schmitz-Köster concludes that there was no such thing as a typical *Lebensborn* employee profile. It rather consisted in "a mix of true believers and pragmatists, of the grateful and the compliant, of those without reservations and those who believed they were in the right place, a place for the 'chosen.'"[271] All appeared to have only encountered or recognised the ostensibly positive aspects of *Lebensborn*. This aligns with the findings of the present study. In addition, the sources presented here provide new insights into the hitherto little researched last days of the *Heim Wienerwald* before, during, and after the so-called evacuation of the home's residents from Feichtenbach to Steinhöring.

---

268  Ibid., 62.
269  Ibid., 19.
270  Lilienthal, *Der "Lebensborn e. V."*.
271  Schmitz-Köster, *"Deutsche Mutter"*, 147.

Sabine Nachbaur

# "Undesirables" among the *Lebensborn* children. The *Heim Wienerwald* and the National Socialist child "euthanasia" program

## I.   Introduction

On 8 April 1942, the director of the *Lebensborn* maternity home *Wienerwald*, Norbert Schwab, sent what was one of several reports on Brigitte Schmidt, a "mentally retarded child" at the *Heim Wienerwald*, to his superior, the head of healthcare at the *Lebensborn* headquarters, Gregor Ebner. He informed Ebner that the child was "to be transferred at the earliest possible date to Vienna's *Städtische Fürsorgeanstalt 'Am Spiegelgrund'*", an institution that was "active also with a view to eradication".[1] This letter is the only known document to emerge from *Lebensborn* so far that refers directly to the National Socialist child murder program, euphemistically referred to as "euthanasia".[2]

---

1   *SS-Obersturmführer* and Director of the Maternity Home Wienerwald Dr. Schwab to the Head of Healthcare at the Lebensborn e.V., *SS-Oberführer* Dr. med. Gregor Ebner, 8 April 1942, Arolsen Archives (hereinafter: AA), 4.1.0/8211200, Ref. 82451649. The research for this paper, in connection with the projects "'Lebensborn-Heim Wienerwald': Tabu und Projektion" and "Geboren im Lebensbornheim Wienerwald. Sammlung, Dokumentation und Aufbereitung lebensgeschichtlicher Interviews", was enabled by the Jubilee Fund of the Austrian National Bank, the Future Fund of the Republic of Austria, and the Province of Lower Austria. The research was carried out at the Ludwig Boltzmann Institute for Research on Consequences of War, Graz – Vienna – Raabs, in cooperation with the Institute of History at the University of Graz.

2   First cited by Georg Lilienthal, *Der "Lebensborn e.V.". Ein Instrument nationalsozialistischer Rassenpolitik.* 2nd ed. (Frankfurt am Main: Fischer, 2008), 102–03. The document on Brigitte Schmidt is also part of a discussion on the role of paediatrician Hans Asperger in the National Socialists' child "euthanasia program": Herwig Czech, "Hans Asperger und der Nationalsozialismus: Konturen einer Kontroverse," in *Monatsschrift Kinderheilkunde* 168 (2020) 3: 163–75, here 171; Werner Maleczek, "Was wusste Asperger von den Morden am 'Spiegelgrund'? Entgegnung auf Herwig Czech," in *Monatsschrift für Kinderheilkunde* 169 (2021) 9: 860–61, here 861. See also Herwig Czech, *Erfassung, Selektion und "Ausmerze". Das Wiener Gesundheitsamt und die Umsetzung der nationalsozialistischen "Erbgesundheitspolitik" 1938 bis 1945. Forschungen und Beiträge zur Wiener Stadtgeschichte* (Wien: Deuticke, 2003), 114. On Hans Asperger more generally see: Herwig Czech, Hans Asperger, National Socialism and "race hygiene" in Nazi-era Vienna. Molecular Autism 9 (2018), 1–43.

In the maternity homes of the *SS* association *Lebensborn*, founded in 1935 by Heinrich Himmler as a population-policy instrument to boost the birth rate of "racially valuable" children, unmarried women who met the *SS*'s racist "selection criteria" and wifes of members of the *SS* and the police were to give birth in a caring environment.[3] The *Heim Wienerwald* in Pernitz/Lower Austria was one of the largest maternity homes of the *Lebensborn*, where an estimated 1350 children were born.[4] It is needless to say that the *Lebensborn* materntiy homes' express purpose – to produce a new "elite" as defined by the standards of the *SS* – could not prevent some children from being born with mental or physical disabilities or from falling seriously ill shortly after birth. A medical directive dated 4 March 1940 mandated all *Lebensborn* homes, the *Lebensborn* management and the headquarters of the association in line with a decree issued by the *Reichsministerium des Innern* (Reich Ministry of the Interior)[5] to report to the local health authority any newborns who were "suspect" of being "afflicted with [...] pathologies", such as "imbecility or mongolism", "microcephaly", "hydrocephaly", "malformations" and "paralyses, including Little's disease".[6]

In his standard work on *Lebensborn*, Georg Lilienthal mentions diseased *Lebensborn* children.[7] Similarly, Dorothee Schmitz-Köster follows up clues to children born in *Lebensborn* homes who almost certainly fell victim to the Na-

---

3 See *Satzung des Lebensborn e.V.* (Statutes of the registered association *Lebensborn*), cited in Lilienthal, *Der "Lebensborn e.V."*, 43: "[The mission of Lebensborn includes] providing accommodation and care for racially and genetically valuable single mothers, who after a careful examination by the Rasse- und Siedlungshauptamt-SS of their own family and of the genitor's family may be expected to give birth to equally valuable offspring." See also Niederösterreichisches Landesarchiv (Provincial Archive of Lower Austria; NÖLA), Office of the Provincial Government of Lower Austria, Landesamt I/2, Zahl 33/1975, *Verein Lebensborn e.V. in München, Broschüre Lebensborn eingetragener Verein*. Miesbach o.J., 8. See also *Satzung des Vereins "Lebensborn" e.V.*, 24 December 1937, AA, 4.1.0/8209800, Ref. 82448142.

4 For more information see the article of Lukas Schretter, Martin Sauerbrey-Almasy and Barbara Stelzl-Marx in this volume.

5 Copy of strictly confidential decree issued by the *Reichsministerium für Inneres* on the mandatory notification of malformed etc. newborns, Deutsche Digitale Bibliothek, IV b 3088/39, 18 August 1939, online at https://www.deutsche-digitale-bibliothek.de/item/5QV5YFMEB2JHJNQPOUEMDLVIJZWFW723 (6 July 2023).

6 Medical directive No. 41 on the mandatory notification of malformed newborns, 4 March 1940, AA, 4.1.0/8211500, Ref. 82452482. Little's disease is an obsolete term for infantile cerebral palsy, also known as cerebral poliomyelitis, broadly speaking, a cerebral movement disorder.

7 See esp. Georg Lilienthal, *Der "Lebensborn e.V."*; see also Georg Lilienthal, "Der 'Lebensborn e.V.'. Förderung 'wertvollen' Lebens als Kontrast zur Vernichtung 'lebensunwerten' Lebens," in *Psychiatrie im Nationalsozialismus. Ein Tagungsbericht des Landeswohlfahrtsverbandes Hessen*. Kassel 1989, 45–56; Georg Lilienthal, "Der 'Lebensborn e.V.' und seine Folgen," in *Verschwiegene Opfer der SS. Lebensborn-Kinder erzählen ihr Leben*, edited by Astrid Eggers and Elke Sauer (Leipzig: Engelsdorfer Verlag, 2015), 217–27.

tional Socialist child "euthanasia" program.[8] A research report by Dorothee Neumaier on the medical director of the *Lebensborn Kinderheim Sonnenwiese* in Kohren-Salis, Hildegard Feith, mentions children who were transferred from the from the children's home to the *Landesanstalt* Großschweidnitz in Saxony, where they were almost certainly murdered in the context of the National Socialist child "euthanasia" program.[9] Among others, cases of sickness and death in the *Heim Wienerwald* are dealt with in Corinna Fürstaller's diploma thesis.[10] The *Dokumentationsarchiv des österreichischen Widerstandes* (Documentation Archive of Austrian Resistance; DÖW), especially Herwig Czech[11] and Wolfgang Neugebauer,[12] Matthias Dahl[13] and Brigitte Riegele[14] have published above all relevant

---

8  See esp. Dorothee Schmitz-Köster, "'*Deutsche Mutter, bist du bereit...*'. *Der Lebensborn und seine Kinder*", 2nd ed. (Berlin: Aufbau TB, 2011), 108 and 124; Dorothee Schmitz-Köster and Tristan Vankann, *Lebenslang Lebensborn. Die Wunschkinder der SS und was aus ihnen wurde* (München: Piper Verlag, 2012). Most recently: Dorothee Schmitz-Köster, *Unbrauchbare Väter. Über Muster-Männer, Seitenspringer und flüchtende Erzeuger im Lebensborn* (Göttingen: Wallstein, 2022).

9  See Dorothee Neumaier, *Dr. Hildegard Feith: Ärztin im Lebensbornkinderheim "Sonnenwiese"*. Hagen 2019. FernUniversität in Hagen, online at: https://ub-deposit.fernuni-hagen.de/receive/mir_mods_00001541 (21 April 2023).

10  Corinna Fürstaller, "Lebensbornheime in Österreich", unpublished diploma thesis, University of Graz, 2010. For a medical perspective on complications, deaths and illnesses in an obstetric context at the *Lebensborn* homes and the activities of *Lebensborn* physicians see Clara Hullmeine, "Das Lebensborn-Projekt als Teil der nationalsozialistischen Geburtenförderung – eine Auswertung der geburtshilflichen Ergebnisdaten der deutschen Lebensbornheime im 'III. Reich',", unpublished doctoral dissertation, Medizinische Fakultät Charité – Universitätsmedizin Berlin, 2019; Matthias David and Andreas D. Ebert, "Medizin im Nationalsozialismus. Der nationalsozialistische 'Lebensborn e.V'. – Anmerkungen zur Rolle der beratenden Gynäkologen", *Geburtshilfe und Frauenheilkunde* 73 (2019) 3: 211–12.

11  Furthermore see esp. Herwig Czech, *Erfassung, Selektion und "Ausmerze". Das Wiener Gesundheitsamt und die Umsetzung der nationalsozialistischen "Erbgesundheitspolitik" 1938 bis 1945* (Wien: Deuticke, 2003); Herwig Czech, "Zuträger der Vernichtung? Die Wiener Universitäts-Kinderklinik und die NS- Kindereuthanasieanstalt 'Am Spiegelgrund',", in *Festschrift 100 Jahre Universitätsklinik für Kinder- und Jugendheilkunde*, edited by Arnold Pollak (Wien: Univ.-Klinik für Kinder- und Jugendheilkunde, 2011), 23–54; Herwig Czech, "Der Spiegelgrund-Komplex. Kinderheilkunde, Heilpädagogik, Psychiatrie und Jugendfürsorge im Nationalsozialismus," *ÖZG* 25 (2014) 1/2: 194–219.

12  See esp. *NS-Euthanasie in Wien*, edited by Eberhard Gabriel and Wolfgang Neugebauer (Vienna: Böhlau Verlag, 2000); Wolfgang Neugebauer, Herwig Czech and Peter Schwarz, "Die Aufarbeitung der NS- Medizinverbrechen und der Beitrag des DÖW," in *Bewahren. Erforschen. Vermitteln*, edited by Dokumentationsarchiv des österreichischen Widerstandes (Wien: Dokumentationsarchiv des österreichischen Widerstands, 2008), 109–23; most recently Herwig Czech, Wolfgang Neugebauer, Peter Schwarz, *Der Krieg gegen die "Minderwertigen": Zur Geschichte der NS-Medizin in Wien*. Katalog zur Dauerausstellung der Gedenkstätte Steinhof im Otto Wagner-Spital. (Vienna: DÖW, 2018).

13  Matthias Dahl, *Endstation Spiegelgrund. Die Tötung behinderter Kinder während des Nationalsozialismus am Beispiel einer Kinderfachabteilung in Wien, 1940 bis 1945* (Vienna: Erasmus, 1998); Matthias Dahl, "Die Tötung behinderter Kinder in der Anstalt 'Am Spie-

works on the National Socialist child "euthanasia" program[15] in the *Ostmark*/the *Alpen- und Donau-Reichsgaue*.

This paper focuses on Brigitte Schmidt, who was murdered in the context of the National Socialist child "euthanasia" program. Furthermore, it casts light on the questions whether other children born at the *Heim Wienerwald* received comparable diagnoses and what consequences those in power at the home and in the association as well as the parents drew from this situation. To this end, various source materials were consulted. The files at the *Standesamt Pernitz II* (Registry Office Pernitz II) contain references to children born at the *Heim Wienerwald*, who died during birth or shortly thereafter or who were diagnosed with physical or mental disabilities.[16] Especially relevant is Ebner's correspondence on medical topics, particularly as regards children's diseases. This correspondence is accessible in the Arolsen Archives. From February 1938 until March 1942 Ebner was an executive board member of *Lebensborn*. From 1937 until 1945 he was also the (medical) director of *Heim Hochland* in Steinhöring near Munich, where as well the association's headquarters were located. Given that he was head of healthcare of *Lebensborn*, a position he held from March 1940, the directors of the *Lebensborn* homes were obliged to report to him on occurrences at the institutions

gelgrund' 1940 bis 1945," in *NS-Euthanasie in Wien*, edited by Eberhard Gabriel and Wolfgang Neugebauer (Wien: Böhlau, 2000), 75–92.

14  On documents relevant to the *Spiegelgrund* held by the Wiener Stadt- und Landesarchiv (Municipal and Provincial Archives of Vienna; WStLA), see Brigitte Riegele, "Kindereuthanasie in Wien 1940–1945. Krankengeschichten als Zeugen," in *Die ermordeten Kinder vom Spiegelgrund. Gedenkdokumentation für die Opfer der NS-Kindereuthanasie in Wien*, edited by Waltraud Häupl (Köln: Böhlau, 2015), 25–43.

15  On the National Socialist child "euthanasia" program in general, see esp. Ernst Klee, *"Euthanasie" im Dritten Reich. Die "Vernichtung lebensunwerten Lebens"* (Frankfurt am Main: Fischer Taschenbuch, 2010; Udo Benzenhöfer, "NS-'Kindereuthanasie': 'Ohne jede moralische Skrupel'," *Deutsches Ärzteblatt* 97 (2000) 42, A 2766–72; Ernst Klee and Willi Dreßen, "Nationalsozialistische Gesundheits- und Rassenpolitik. 'Lebensunwertes Leben', Sterilisation und 'Euthanasie'," in *Sozialisation und Traumatisierung. Kinder in der Zeit des Nationalsozialismus*, edited by Ute Benz and Wolfgang Benz. 3rd ed. (Frankfurt am Main: Fischer, 1998), 103–116; on the extent different professions were involved, see i.a. Wiebke Lisner, *"Hüterinnen der Nation". Hebammen im Nationalsozialismus* (Frankfurt am Main – New York: Campus, 2006); Lothar Pelz, "Kinderärzte im Netz der 'NS-Kindereuthanasie' am Beispiel der 'Kinderfachabteilung' Görden," *Monatsschrift Kinderheilkunde* 151 (2003): 1027–32. On the National Socialist "euthanasia" in general, see esp. Ernst Klee, *Auschwitz, die NS-Medizin und ihre Opfer*. 7th ed. (Frankfurt am Main: Fischer, 2001); Hans-Walter Schmuhl, *Rassenhygiene, Nationalsozialismus, Euthanasie. Von der Verhütung zur Vernichtung "lebensunwerten Lebens", 1890–1945* (Göttingen: Vandenhoeck & Ruprecht, 1987). (Kritische Studien zur Geschichtswissenschaft 75).

16  Gemeinde Pernitz, Registry Office Pernitz II. Office Pernitz II. In his report on the *Heim Wienerwald* from 2001, Knotzinger refers to children who were born with disabilities. He argues that there was no evidence of children being killed. See Günther Knotzinger, "Das SS-Heim 'Wienerwald' und die Geschichte des Hauses von 1904 bis zur Gegenwart," unpublished manuscript, Feichtenbach, 2001, 37–38.

they were responsible for, such as specific illnesses, the outbreak and progression of infectious diseases and measures to contain them, such as vaccinations, the closure of the homes for visitors and/or the isolation of individual mothers or children, transfers to hospitals, and deaths. The latter were the subject of a monthly report sent to Himmler. Statistics concerning individual homes and the association as a whole have come down to us. The source material for the years 1939 to 1943 is plentiful; for the years 1944 to 1945 only little is extant.[17]

What has also been taken into consideration is relevant material in the *Wiener Stadt- und Landesarchiv* (Municipal and Provincial Archives of Vienna) regarding the *Spiegelgrund*[18] and Dorothee Schmitz-Köster's private collection, which she bequeathed to the Arolsen Archives in 2021.[19] Information on the fathers of *Lebensborn* children may be gleaned from personnel files at the *Bundesarchiv* (German Federal Archives) in Berlin-Lichterfelde,[20] provided they were members of the SS or had left their footprint in SS files for other reasons. For the research on the victims of the National Socialist child "euthanasia" program at *Heim Wienerwald*, the holdings of the *Bezirkshauptmannschaft* (District Governate) Wiener Neustadt-Land would have been of crucial significance, as it should have been reported to the health authority of that district when children with disabilities were born. These files went up in flames in 1945.[21]

---

17  AA, DE ITS 4.1 Lebensborn, for information on the holdings see the website of the Arolsen Archives online at: https://collections.arolsen-archives.org/de/search/topic/4-1?s=Lebensborn (7. July 2023).

18  WStLA, M.Abt. 209, 1.3.2.209.10, Wiener Städtische Nervenklinik für Kinder ("Am Spiegelgrund").

19  AA, collection Schmitz-Köster. Additional research was carried out in the holdings of the *Wiener Universitätskinderklinik* at the WStLA, the archives of the *Lern- und Gedenkort Schloss Hartheim* and the NÖLA/collection *Heil und Pflegeanstalt Gugging*. Patient files relevant to the topic of this paper in the keeping of the *Deutsches-Rotes-Kreuz-Kinderspital* (*DRK-Kinderspital*), Vienna's *Wilhelminenspital* and the *Kinderklinik der Stadt Wien–Glanzing* could not be retrieved. Requests for information directed to memorials for the victims of the National Socialist "euthanasia" or relevant archives have so far failed to yield any new results. For further research on the National Socialist' "decentralised" child "euthanasia", the body of coroner's reports held at the WStLA is relevant. This, however, does not apply to the cases under investigation in this paper. See the following researched volumes: WStLA, M.Abt. 212, BGA 19, 1.3.2.212.119.B1.1–3 and BGA 13/14 1.3.2.212.113.B1.1–3.

20  Bundesarchiv Berin-Lichterfelde (Barch), R 9361-II.

21  Information provided by the NÖLA to the author, 1 April 2021.

## II. "An organisation for the killing of mentally retarded or congenitally physically malformed children"[22] – The National Socialist Child "Euthanasia" Program

From 1932, the National Socialists had been planning the murder of individuals with congenital physical and/or mental disabilities in accordance with the principles of "racial hygiene". The aim was to upgrade the "race" by "destroying lives unworthy of living". The *Gesetz zur Verhütung erbkranken Nachwuchses* (Law for the Prevention of Genetically Diseased Offspring) of 1933 and the forced abortions and sterilisations for which it provided a legal basis were steps towards the systematic killing of people with disabilities from 1939 onwards, again euphemistically referred to as "euthanasia".[23]

The strictly confidential decree issued by the *Reichsministerium des Innern*, on the *"Meldepflicht von missgestalteten usw. Neugeborenen"*[24] (Mandatory Notification of Malformed etc. Newborns), dated 18 August 1939, provided the basis for the registration and the murder of children in the context of the National Socialist child "euthanasia" program. As opposed to the *"Aktion T4"* (Operation T4), the killing of children was not terminated officially in 1941.[25] The child murder program was continued until 1945 in the wards of public health care institutions, above all by withholding food and the prescription of lethal medication.[26] In the Reich, there were at least 37 "special children's wards" ("*Kinderfachabteilungen*"), such as Großschweidnitz in Saxony and the *Spiegelgrund* in Vienna.[27] Founded in Berlin as a front organisation of the *Kanzlei des Führers*, the *Reichsausschuß für die wissenschaftliche Erfassung erb- und anlagebedingter schwerer Leiden* (Reich Committee for the Scientific Registration of Serious Hereditary and Congenital Diseases, hereinafter: *Reichsausschuss*) and its activities in providing expert opinions held sway over the life and death of the

---

22 Viktor Brack on the *Reichsausschuß für die wissenschaftliche Erfassung erb- und anlagebedingter schwerer Leiden* (Reich Committee for the Scientific Registration of Serious Hereditary and Congenital Diseases, hereinafter: *Reichsausschuss*) cited in Klee, "Euthanasie", 333.

23 Klee, Dreßen, "Nationalsozialistische Gesundheits- und Rassenpolitik," 103–11. For continuities between the murder of patients and the systematic mass murder in National Socialist extermination camps, see most recently *"Euthanasie" und Holocaust. Kontinuitäten, Kausalitäten, Parallelitäten*, edited by Jörg Osterloh and Jan Erik Schulte (Paderborn: Brill Schöningh, 2021). (Schriftenreihe der Gedenkstätte Hadamar 1).

24 Czech, *Erfassung*, 109.

25 In spite of the formal termination of the *"Aktion T4"* in 1941, people with disabilities continued to be murdered in the context of a "decentralised euthanasia", esp. by neglect and lethal medication. See Benzenhöfer, "NS-'Kindereuthanasie'", A 2772.

26 Klee, Dreßen, "Nationalsozialistische Gesundheits- und Rassenpolitik", 111.

27 Dahl, "Tötung", 3; Czech, "Der Spiegelgrund-Komplex," 195; Riegele, "Kindereuthanasie," 28. The precise number of "special children's wards" has not been established.

children that were brought to its notice.[28] This enabled the perpetrators, above all the responsible medical doctors, to shirk responsibility for the murder of their patients. However, the formulations used by the doctors in their reports usually anticipated the decision by the *Reichsauschuss*.[29] In all probability, 5,000 to 10,000 children were murdered in the context of the National Socialist child "euthanasia" program; estimates of the total number are much higher, as many children were also murdered in the "*Aktion T4*" and locally, outside the "special children's wards" by medication or malnutrition.[30]

## III.   The *Spiegelgrund*

One of the first killing centres of the National Socialist child "euthanasia" program was the "special children's ward" *Am Spiegelgrund*. It had only been preceded by a "special children's ward" at the *Landesanstalt* Görden in Brandenburg.[31] In 1942, the *Wiener Städtische Jugendfürsorgeanstalt Am Spiegelgrund* (Vienna's Municipal Youth Welfare Institution Am Spiegelgrund), which had been founded as part of the *Heil- und Pflegeanstalt Am Steinhof* in July 1940, had its name changed to *Heilpädagogische Klinik der Stadt Wien Am Spiegelgrund* (Therapeutic Pedagogical Clinic of the City of Vienna *Am Spiegelgrund*). The "special children's ward" was at that stage an integral part of the welfare institute. In the autumn of 1942, two pavilions, 15 and 17, were hived off from the *Jugendfürsorgeanstalt* and established as a separate institution, called *Wiener städtische Nervenklinik für Kinder* (Vienna's Municipal Nerve Clinic for Children). Its alleged purpose was the "admission of cases [at the behest] of the *Reichsausschuß für die wissenschaftliche Erfassung erb- und anlagebedingter schwerer Leiden* and of moronic, ineducable minors".[32] The "*Säuglingsabteilung*" (infant unit) in Pavilion 15, known internally as "*Reichsausschuss* unit", was the main venue for the murders in the context of the National Socialist child "euthanasia" program.[33]

The majority of children admitted to this "*Kleinkinder- und Säuglingsstation*" (infant and toddler ward) whose medical records have been preserved were from

---

28  On the *Reichsausschuss* and registration, see Klee, "Euthanasie," 334–35.
29  Czech, *Erfassung*, 104 and 106; Czech, "Der Spiegelgrund-Komplex," 195; Riegele, "Kinder-euthanasie," 28 and 35.
30  Cf. Klee, "Euthanasie," 336–39; Pelz, "Kinderärzte," 1027.
31  Czech, "Der Spiegelgrund-Komplex," 196.
32  Riegele, "Kindereuthanasie," 31. In this article the term *Spiegelgrund* (in italics) is used for the "special children's ward" of the *Wiener Städtische Jugendfürsorgeanstalt Am Spiegelgrund* or, as it was called after 1942, the *Wiener Städtische Nervenklinik für Kinder*.
33  Czech, "Der Spiegelgrund-Komplex," 196–97, and Riegele, "Kindereuthanasie," 19 and 29.

Vienna and Lower Austria.[34] Health authorities played a key role in the registration of the victims: They reported the children to the *Reichsausschuss*. At the *Spiegelgrund* these notifications were not passed on until after admission to the "special children's ward".[35]

In Pavilion 15, the children were murdered predominantly through the administration of an overdose of barbiturates. As the medication was not logged in the medical records, resulting infections were mentioned to create the impression of a "natural" cause of death. Some children were subjected to risky medical examinations to find evidence of organic cerebral diseases or out of scientific curiosity – at a stage when they would already have been extremely weak from malnourishment or hypothermia.[36] "Children capable of laughing and playing games were turned into apathetic basket cases and then killed" – this is Riegele commenting on the *Spiegelgrund*.[37] Czech characterises the *Spiegelgrund* as a "death zone at the hub of a widely ramified system of public, party-directed and private welfare institutions".[38] Part of this "administrative network"[39] of the National Socialist child "euthanasia" program were therefore not only welfare offices and other institutions devoted to youth and general welfare, but also the *Heim Wienerwald*.[40]

---

34  Riegele, "Kindereuthanasie," 35; the exact catchment area of *Am Spiegelgrund* is unknown. Czech, *Erfassung*, 113.
35  Czech, *Erfassung*, 110–11.
36  Dahl, "Tötung," 16–17; Riegele, "Kindereuthanasie," 39–42; for the "treatment" – tantamount almost certainly to the killing – of the children in the "special children's ward", see i.a. Klee, "Euthanasie," 340. The way the children were murdered was similar in all "special children's wards". As for the putative clinical diagnostics, some institutions such as the *Spiegelgrund*, set greater store by it than others. This was probably to do with research activities that were pursued there; see Benzenhöfer, "NS-'Kindereuthanasie'," A 2771. For medical research carried out on victims of the National Socialist child "euhanasia" program, see i.a. Klee, "Euthanasie," 366–85. For the *Spiegelgrund*, see i.a. Czech, "Der Spiegelgrund-Komplex," 203–12.
37  Riegele, "Kindereuthanasie," 41.
38  Czech, *Erfassung*, 110–11.
39  Pelz, "Kinderärzte," 1031.
40  See also the mention of the *Heim Wienerwald* in Brigitte Schmidt's ID document. Aufnahmsprotokoll (admission protocol), 29 April 1942, WStLA, M.Abt. 209.10., Wiener Städtische Nervenklinik für Kinder ("Am Spiegelgrund"), B1.

## IV.    The *Lebensborn* and the National Socialist "Euthanasia" in the *Ostmark*/the *Alpen- und Donau-Reichsgaue*

Even though there was no formal link connecting the *Lebensborn* and the National Socialist child "euthanasia" program,[41] the initially cited quote – "active with a view to eradication" – shows that this SS association was in some way complicit in the murder of children in the context of the child "euthanasia" program.

The *Lebensborn* applied the SS's racist "selection criteria" to the pregnant women who sought admission to a *Lebensborn* maternity home as well as to the children born in the homes. Children born physically or mentally sick or with disabilities were registered in several *Lebensborn* homes as were cases of children falling seriously ill after birth.[42] If children did not conform to its preconceived ideas, the *Lebensborn* management reacted by dismissing both mother and child from the home. The association distanced itself from children who opposed its actual pronatalist objectives. The guardianship the *Lebensborn* and sometimes even Himmler himself took on for children was revoked. Children with allegedly serious physical or mental disabilities "had lost the right to exist" and "were handed over to special institutions by the *Lebensborn* management".[43] In some cases an adoption proved life-saving, in others mothers may have left the home with their children in time. There may even have been those who survived their committal to a "special children's ward".[44]

As a consultant at the *Rasse- und Siedlungshauptamt* (Race and Settlement Main Office; *RuSHA*) the head of healthcare and executive board member Ebner stated his views on how to deal with "congenital diseases" quite clearly. In reply to Wolfgang W.'s question of whether the "mental illness" of his wife Walburga might be alleviated by having her transferred from the *Heil- und Pflegeanstalt* Gabersee to a "private clinic", Ebner stated:

---

41  See also Schmitz-Köster, *"Deutsche Mutter"*, 247.

42  For children murdered in the *Landesanstalt* Großschweidnitz in Saxony, see Neumaier, *Dr. Hildegard Feith*. For suspected victims of the National Socialist child "euthanasia" program, see, among others, individual cases in Lilienthal, *Der "Lebensborn e.V."*, 102–03; Lilienthal, *"'Der Lebensborn e.V.' und seine Folgen,"* 221; Lilienthal, *"Der 'Lebensborn e.V.'. Förderung"*, 51–52. For *Heim Friesland*, see Schmitz-Köster, *"Deutsche Mutter"*, 243 and 246. In *Heim Pommern*, the number of children born with physical or mental disabilities was statistically recorded. See Schmitz-Köster, *"Deutsche Mutter"*, 125.

43  Quotation: Lilienthal, *Der "Lebensborn e.V.,"* 102. Among others, one child from *Heim Harz* was murdered, ibid., 95; Schmitz-Köster, *Unbrauchbare Väter*, 129. For an example from *Heim Pommern*, see Lilienthal, *"Der 'Lebensborn e.V.'. Förderung"*, 52. See also Lilienthal, *"'Der Lebensborn e.V.' und seine Folgen,"* 221.

44  For the example of adoption see Schmitz-Köster, *Unbrauchbare Väter*, 130.

"As a National Socialist my view is that in cases of congenital diseases that are incurable according to a medical assessment only those financial means are to be expended that are absolutely necessary [...] It is, however, necessary to inform these relatives of the actually existing possibilities of a cure to prevent unnecessary expenditure of a financial kind being made, which would result in these means being withdrawn from [the healthcare of] healthy people."[45]

According to this correspondence, Walburga W. was transferred on 17 January 1941 to the *Heil- und Pflegeanstalt* Niedernhart/Linz an der Donau.[46] She was murdered at the *Tötungsanstalt* (extermination centre) Hartheim.[47]

## V. Biographies of Children That Failed to Match the SS Ideal

In a radio interview, Helga S., born in the *Heim Wienerwald* in 1943, mentioned that her mother, who was a secretary at the home between 1943 and 1945, was aware of a child who "was sent to the *Spiegelgrund*, for observation, as they said". The child "was having problems". It had probably "been different somehow from most children". She did not know whether these differences "were only physical, but in all probably they also affected [the child's] behaviour". It was unknown "what happened further down the line but one could guess it".[48]

The following three life stories or, more accurately, the three medical histories of children born in the *Heim Wienerwald* are based on a handful of data drawn from different documents, above all from medical records. The cited examination results and diagnoses are essential for research on their life stories, where medical terminology rubs shoulders with expressions from everyday speech and

---

45  Letter from Dr. Ebner to Herr Ludwig Ramlmayr, lawyer, 14 January 1941, 4, AA, 4.1.0/ 8213200, Ref. 82459175 to 82459178.

46  Letter from Ludwig Ramlmayr, lawyer, to *SS-Oberführer* Ebner, 25 January 1941, AA, 4.1.0/ 8213200, Ref. 82459180.

47  See Memo from the Documentation Centre Hartheim, 22 November 2021. According to this memo Walburga W. had been transferred from the Heil- und Pflegeanstalt Garbersee on its dissolution on 17 January 1941 to the Heil- und Pflegeanstalt Eglfing-Haar before she was murdered in Hartheim. For more information on the different stations Walburga W. has been transferred to and if Niedernhart was one of them further research needs to be done. For the *Tötungsanstalt* Hartheim, see e.g. *Tötungsanstalt Hartheim. Oberösterreich in der Zeit des Nationalsozialismus*, vol. 3., edited by Brigitte Kepplinger, Gerhart Marckhgott and Hartmut Reese, 3rd ed. (Linz: Oberösterreichisches Landesarchiv/Lern- und Gedenkort Schloss Hartheim, 2013).

48  *Geboren im Nazi-Entbindungsheim Wienerwald*. Radio programme Ö1, "Moment – Leben heute", 19 January 2023, Director: Jonathan Scheucher, 12:49.240–14:43.520, here 14:33.520–14:43.520.

terms heavily imbued with ideology.[49] They therefore need to be subjected to extensive textual criticism. Extant files concerning the parents also provide information on the children's lives but the source material on the mothers is rather thin. Files on fathers who were members of the SS and/or the *Wehrmacht* or who left a footprint in SS files for some other reason offer comparatively more information. These three life stories are exemplary for children whose life was viewed as "unworthy of living" (*lebensunwertes Leben*) by the National Socialist regime. Their "purpose is to recreate from fragments of human lives a picture that aims to restore a semblance of their identity to these human beings".[50]

### 5.1     "[...] with a smile that has repeatedly been noticeable over several weeks"[51]

Brigitte Schmidt was born in August 1941 at the *Heim Wienerwald*. Unwed at that time, her mother, Gerda Schmidt, was twenty years old when she gave birth to her daughter. Brigitte's father, Gustav L., was a mechanical engineer by trade. As an *SS-Unterscharführer* he was in Vienna in 1941.[52] Shortly after the birth of Brigitte at the *Heim Wienerwald* he and Gerda H. – not to be confused with Gerda Schmidt – married in Hamburg in early September 1941.[53]

On 4 November 1941 – Brigitte Schmidt was almost three months old and still in the home – the director of *Heim Wienerwald*, Schwab, informed Ebner that the child was displaying symptoms of "Little's disease". Visiting paediatrician Erich Gasser suggested, according to Schwab, that this was a case of "something like a small cerebral focus [of the disease]" and advised subjecting the child to further observation: "I believe the child should now be admitted to a special ward [*Fachabteilung*] to enable a precise neurological diagnosis".[54] Gasser's sugges-

---

49 Ulrich Müller and Corinna Wachsmann, "Krankenakten als Lebensgeschichten," in *Die nationalsozialistische "Euthanasie"-Aktion "T4" und ihre Opfer. Geschichte und ethische Konsequenzen für die Gegenwart*, edited by Petra Fuchs, Wolfgang U. Eckart, Christoph Mundt, Maike Rotzoll, Paul Richter and Gerrit Hohendorf (Paderborn – München– Wien –Zurich: Ferdinand Schöningh, 2010), 189–99, here 193 and 197.
50 Ibid., 199.
51 *SS-Obersturmführer und Heimleiter* Dr. Schwab to the Head of Healthcare at the Lebensborn e.V., *SS-Oberführer* Dr.med Ebner, 6 February 1942, AA, 4.1.0/8213200, Ref. 82459715.
52 See *RuSHA* questionnaire, Barch, R 9361-III/123225, fol. 2984. Note the sender on the following document: Registered mail, Gustav L., *SS-Unterscharführer*, 3.Kp.A.Abt.Div.Wiking, Wien 87, *SS-Kaserne* to *Rasse- und Siedlungshauptamt* SS, Berlin, dated 19 June 1941, Barch, R 9361-III/123225, fol. 3062. Note also the request in this letter for permission of his marriage to Gerda H. to be granted: "Furthermore, I would ask for my request to be approved of asap as my unit may be given marching orders any day now and I intend to get married beforehand."
53 Copy of the marriage certificate, Barch, R 9361-III/123225, fol. 3048.
54 Letter from *SS-Obersturmführer und Heimleiter* Dr. Schwab to the Head of Healthcare at the Lebensborn eV. *SS-Oberführer* Dr. Ebner, 4 November 1941, AA, 4.1.0/8213300, Ref. 82459713.

tion that Brigitte's health might improve – she had reacted to people around her "with a smile that has repeatedly been noticeable over several weeks"– should not blind us to the fact that judgement had already been passed on the child.[55] On 9 February 1942, Ebner wrote to Schwab that he thought it "expedient if you had the child transferred to a special ward [*Fachabteilung*] when the oppportunity arises so that we are no longer in doubt about a diagnosis".[56] The acknowledgement of paternity by Gustav L. is documented one month later.[57] The ensuing notification of the state authorities would in any case have ended the secrecy of paternity, as *Lebensborn* did not take on guardianship of children with physical or mental disabilities.[58]

On 29 April 1942 eight-months-old Brigitte Schmidt was transferred from the *Heim Wienerwald* to the *Spiegelgrund*.[59] In Schwab's letter to Ebner, the writer referred to the real purpose of the *"Fachabteilung"*, to which Brigitte was to be transferred.[60] According to the death register, Brigitte died in Pavilion 15, the "special children's ward", a few months later, on 9 November 1942, aged one year and three months. "Mongolism and paralyses" and "pneumonia lobularis" are cited as the causes of death.[61]

The death of his daughter Brigitte and the pathologies she was diagnosed with had no negative repercussions on Gustav L.'s SS career. In a "genetic assessement" of Gustav L. issued in 1944, the *Staatliches Gesundheitsamt Flensburg* (Flensburg Health Authority) noted that "nothing has come to our notice that would incriminate him under health-related and genetic aspects".[62] In the same

---

55  Ibid.; also see Letter from *SS-Obersturmführer and Heimleiter* Dr. Schwab to the Head of Healthcare at the Lebensborn eV. *SS-Oberführer* Dr. Ebner, dated 6 February 1942, AA, 4.1.0/ 8213300, Ref. 82459715.

56  Letter from *SS-Oberführer* Dr. Ebner to the Director of the Heim Wienerwald, *SS-Obersturmführer* Dr. Schwab, 9 February 1942, AA, 4.1.0/8213300, Ref. 82459718.

57  Letter from the Head of Department Abteilung A2 to the *Heimstandesamt* Pernitz, 9 February 1942, Gemeinde Pernitz, Register Office Pernitz II, Brigitte Schmidt, 126/41. A letter dating to 6 February 1942 is extant from Gustav L.'s wife in Hamburg to the Head of the RuSHA, referring to her request for child allowance for her husband's "illegitimate child", Brigitte Schmidt. She was therefore aware of the child. See Barch, R 9361-III/123225, fol. 3054.

58  Schmitz-Köster, *"Deutsche Mutter"*, 198.

59  Czech, *Erfassung*, 114.

60  Letter from *SS-Obersturmführer und Heimleiter* Dr. Schwab to the Head of Healthcare at Lebensborn e.V. *SS-Oberführer* Dr. Gregor Ebner, 8 April 1942, AA, 4.1.0/8211200, Ref. 82451649.

61  Entry in the death register of the *Wiener Städtische Nervenklinik für Kinder* ("Am Spiegelgrund") 1940–1945, WStLA, 1.3.2.209.10. See also the extant notification of Brigitte Schmidt's death to the registry office: *Mitteilung des Standesamts 21, Wien-Penzing an das Standesamt Pernitz II*, 23 November 1942, Gemeinde Pernitz, Registry Office Pernitz II, Brigitte Schmidt, 126/41. The medical records of Brigitte Schmidt are not part of the WStLA's holdings on the *Wiener Städtische Nervenklinik für* Kinder (Am Spiegelgrund).

62  Letter from the *Reichsführer-SS Der Chef des RuS-Hauptamtes-SS Heiratsamt* to the *Staatliches Gesundheitsamt* Flensburg, 19 June 1944, Barch, R 9361-III/123225, fol. 3000.

year, 1944, Gustav L. again applied for a marriage permit after the death of Gerda H.. The bride-to-be was Hermenegilde D. from Graz. In the section dealing with the past of the applicant's family in the *RuSHA's* obligatory medical questionnaire, dated 25 June 1944, under the rubric "Children (including illegitimate ones) of the applicant" only one other, almost certainly illegitimate child, is listed, Werner, "three years old, *alive, healthy*".[63]


## 5.2   "Laughs the moment one engages its attention"[64]


Gerda M. had not yet married her later husband, Hans D., when she gave birth in the summer of 1941 to her first child, Klaus-Jürgen, at the *Heim Wienerwald*. The extant *Reichsführer-SS* questionnaire[65] notes that she fit in well with life at the home. She showed great love towards her child, intended to marry the father of her child, and met the "selection criteria of the SS racially, ideologically and characterwise".[66] Born in Katowice, she lived and worked as a nurse at the *Heil-und Pflegeanstalt* in Loben/Lublinitz (today Lubliniec), which had been annexed by the German Reich after the invasion of Poland.[67] In November 1941, Gerda M. married the father of her child, Hans D. in Loben/Lublinitz.[68] In line with an order issued by Himmler, Hans D. was not obliged to mention the child born out of wedlock in his application for a marriage permit. In addition, the couple had their wedding antedated.[69] In 1942, Hans D., who was working at that time as a camp doctor in the *Frontstammlager 368* near Warsaw in the *Generalgouvernement*

63 Medical Examination Questionnaire of the *RuSHA*, 25 June 1944, Barch, R 9361-III/123225, fol. 3002. The words in italics in the above quote are handwritten additions.

64 Medical records at the *Landes-Heil- und Pflegeanstalt* Leipzig-Dösen/Großschweidnitz, 10618, Sigune Imma D., n.d., AA, collection Schmitz-Köster. Quote: entry of 2 December 1943 at the *Heil- und Pflegeanstalt* Leipzig-Dösen.

65 Women who gave birth at one of the *Lebensborn* maternity homes and their children were assessed by the director of the home and the head nurse during their stay at the home. These assessments were included in the *Reichsführer-SS* questionnaire, which was destined for Himmler personally. See the paper by Lukas Schretter, Martin Sauerbrey-Almasy and Barbara Stelzl-Marx in this volume.

66 *Reichsführer-SS* questionnaire Gerda M., n.d., Gemeinde Pernitz, Registry Office Pernitz II, Klaus M., 101/1941.

67 Ibid. Bunzlau, today's Bolesławiec in Poland, was named as the place of residence of her son Klaus-Jürgen at a later stage. See Letter of discharge from the secretary of the Heim Ostmark to Lebensborn e.V. in Munich, 21 May 1942, Gemeinde Pernitz, Registry Office Pernitz II, Klaus M., 101/1941.

68 Letter from the Hauptabteilung A of Lebensborn e.V. to the Registry Office Pernitz II, 12 February 1942, Gemeinde Pernitz, Registry Office Pernitz II, Klaus M., 101/1941.

69 Letter from *SS-Standartenführer im Persönlichen Stab RFSS* Sollmann to Dr. D. *Sanitäts-Unteroffizier*, Lager Drachenbronn, 23 October 1941, Barch, R 9361-II/182002, fol. 1836; Schmitz-Köster, *Unbrauchbare Väter*, 105.

(General Governorate), applied in vain for a post as medical doctor and director of a *Lebensborn* facility.[70]

This application fitted in well with the CV Hans D. had compiled for the *SS*.[71] He had studied medicine at the University of Breslau (today Wrocław) until 1939. From 1934 until 1939 he had been a member of the *Sturmabteilung* (SA) in Breslau, from 1937 until 1940 medical doctor to the Hitler Youth.[72] From early 1940 he had worked in the psychiatric women's ward of the *Landesheil- und Pflegeanstalt Loben/Lublinitz*, where in all probability he met his later wife. No mass murders of adult patients in Loben of the kind that took place in 1939 in other psychiatric hospitals in Poland have yet come to light. The patients were probably murdered at the extermination centres of the "*Aktion T4*".[73] After Hans D. had been drafted to the *Wehrmacht* in February 1941, a "special children's ward" was installed at the *Landesheil- und Pflegeanstalt* Loben in the autumn of 1941.[74] Whether Hans D. was aware of the "euthanasia" murders committed there or whether he was even involved in them himself cannot be ascertained so far. His employment at the *Landesheil- und Pflegeanstalt Loben/Lublinitz* does not seem to have been terminated by the time he served in the *Wehrmacht*.[75]

Hans D. seems to have submitted his application for the post of doctor and director of a *Lebensborn* home when his wife was pregnant with the couple's second child. She gave birth to a girl, Sigune Imma, at the *Heim Wienerwald* in

---

70  Letter from *SS-Standartenführer im Persönlichen Stab RFSS* Sollmann to Dr. D. *Sanitäts-Unteroffizier*, Lager Drachenbronn, 23 October 1941, Barch, R 9361-II/182002, fol. 1836; Letter from *Reichsführer-SS, Persönlicher Stab* to the Head of the *SS-Hauptamt*, 31 [?] July 1942, Barch, R9361-II/182002, fol. 1842. It appears from the files that Hans D. was personally acquainted with the managing diector of the *Lebensborn*, Max Sollmann. His birth cohort (1915) was retained by the *Wehrmacht*, which meant that he could not be transferred to the *Waffen-SS*. His application was therefore given short shrift. Letter from the *Reichsführer-SS, Persönlicher Stab* to the "Lebensborn e.V." in Munich, dated 21 August 1942, Barch, R 9361-II/182002, fol. 1846. Having ended the war as a Soviet Prisoner of War, Hans D. continued his career after his release. He became a renowned university professor and highly acclaimed scientist. Schmitz-Köster puts Hans D. into the category of "*Zögerer und Zauderer*" (ditherers and procrastinators) among unmarried *Lebensborn* fathers. See Schmitz-Köster, *Unbrauchbare Väter*, 104–108.

71  Copy CV Hans D., n.d., Barch, R 9361-II/182002, fol. 1852.

72  Personalbogen Universität Greifswald Hans D., 3 June 1955, AA, collection Schmitz-Köster.

73  Kamila Uzarczyk, "Der Kinderfachabteilung vorzuschlagen. The selection and elimination of children at the Youth Psychiatric Clinic Loben (1941–45)," in *From Clinic to Concentration Camp. Reassessing Nazi Medical and Racial Research, 1933–1945*, edited by Paul Weindling (London: Routledge, 2017), 183–206, here 185. Transports of patients from the *Landesheil- und Pflegeanstalt* Loben in 1941 are on record. See ibid., 185.

74  Kamila Uzarczyk, "Der Kinderfachabteilung vorzuschlagen", 186.

75  Copy CV Hans D., n.d., Barch, R 9361-II/182002, fol. 1852.

January 1943.[76] Why Sigune Imma D.[77] was transferred on 5 March 1943 to the *Lebensborn* children's home *Sonnenwiese* in Kohren-Sahlis in Saxony cannot be inferred from the extant sources. It meant in any case that she remained in the care of *Lebensborn* and was not dismissed because of physical anomalies.[78] However, on 4 October 1943, the director of the *Heim Sonnenwiese* had Sigune Imma D. transferred to the University Children's Clinic Leipzig, which was at that time under the direction of Werner Catel.[79] She was diagnosed with "mongoloid imbecility with concurrent microhydrocephaly".[80] Ten days after the admission

---

76  Sigune Imma D. has left no traces in the files of the *Heim Wienerwald*, but her birth certificate states that she was born there. *Geburtsurkunde* Sigune Imma D., AA, collection Schmitz-Köster. See also: Schmitz-Köster, *Unbrauchbare Väter*, 106.

77  Although the children were victims of the National Socialist regime, their names – except Brigitte Schmidt's, which has already been published several times – are anonymized due to archival data protection regulations and/or research ethics considerations concerning relatives.

78  Schmitz-Köster proposes that the girl was transferred to *Heim Sonnenwiese* in Kohren-Sahlis thanks to the connections of her father. The author presumes that Sigunes's father Hans D. as a medical doctor knew about the reasons and consequences of her transfer. See Schmitz-Köster, *Unbrauchbare Väter*, 107. Hans D. was informed by Ebner of Sigune Imma's transfer to the *Landesheil- und Pflegeanstalt* Leipzig-Dösen; see Letter from *SS-Oberführer* Dr. Ebner to Dr. Feith-Butenschön, SS-Kinderheim Sonnenwiese, Kohren-Sahlis near Leipzig, 29 October 1943, AA, 4.1.0/8213400, Ref. 82459848. At the latest by the time, in 1941/42, resistance made itself felt against the mass killing of people with physical and mental disabilities. Thus, it may be presumed that the procedure was an open secret no longer confined to the "special children's wards"; see Pelz, "Kinderärzte", 1032. It could also have been the case that all this happened at the express wish of the mother, who accompanied her daughter to Kohren-Sahlis, see Schmitz-Köster, Vankann, *Lebenslang Lebensborn*, 306. For the admission to the *Heim Sonnenwiese*, see AA, collection Schmitz-Köster, Letter of the *Universitäts-Kinderklinik* Leipzig to the Reichsausschuß, dated 16 October 1943. The letter also confirms Pernitz as Sigune Imma's birth place.

79  Werner Catel was professor of paedriatics at the University of Leipzig during the National Socialist era. An expert active in the "*Aktion T4*", he was also at the forefront of the National Socialist child "euthanasia" program. In 1940 he installed a "special children's ward" in Leipzig-Dösen, see Ernst Klee, *Das Personenlexikon zum Dritten Reich. Wer war was vor und nach 1945* (Frankfurt am Main: Fischer 2003), 91.

80  Copy of the medical record of Sigune Imma D. compiled by the *Stadtkinderkrankenhaus* Leipzig, 16 October 1943, AA, 4.1.0/8213400, Ref. 82459846. Admission to the Children's Clinic "on behalf of the Reichsausschuss as a referral of the Staatliches Gesundheitsamt Borna and the SS-Kinderheim Sonnenwiese, Kohren, for observation. The child has been diagnosed as of 27 March 43 [...] as a 'mongolo imbecile' (mongoloide Idiotie)". Letter from the University Children's Clinic Leipzig to the *Reichsausschuss zur wissenschaftlichen Erfassung von erb- und anlagebedingten schweren Leiden*, 16 October 1943, AA, collection Schmitz-Köster. See also Report of the *Staatliches Gesundheitsamt* Borna, 27 March 1943 und letter from the *Reichsausschuß zur wissenschaftlichen Erfassung von erb- und anlagebedingten schweren Leiden* to the *Staatliches Gesundheitsamt* Borna, 14 May 1943, ibid., on the referral to the *Universitäts-Kinderklinik- und Poliklinik* Leipzig so that "the best care and a modern therapy [may] be applied to the extent possible". It is apparent from this report that no improvement or cure was expected. For more details on Sigune Imma D., see Schmitz-Köster, Vankann, *Lebenslang Lebensborn*, 305–12.

to the University Children's Clinic Leipzig and no more than two days after the compilation and the mailing of this diagnosis to the director of the *Lebensborn* children's home *Sonnenwiese*, Signe Imma D. was transferred again, this time "to the Landesanstalt Leipzig-Dösen in the context of the Reich Committee program for the Scientific Registration of Serious Hereditary and Congenital Diseases".[81] There she was described in the medical records as follows: "Lively little mongoloid, fidgets a great deal but cannot get up on her feet on her own. Laughs the moment one engages her attention. Engages with toys handed to [her]".[82] A few days later, on 7 December 1943, Signe Imma D. was transferred to the *Landesanstalt* Großschweidnitz, where her condition was initially described as "unchanged".[83] Within the next three weeks, her condition reputedly deteriorated due to a cold. On 23 December 1943, the director of the *Anstalt* Großschweidnitz wrote to Ebner that "according to a unanimous assessment made at the University Children's Clinic Leipzig and the special children's ward at Leipzig-Dösen [...] mongoloid imbecility [has been diagnosed] in the child. There is therefore no significant hope of improvement. As is typical of mongoloid imbeciles, this child is susceptible to mucous membrane infections and is suffering from bronchitis at present":[84] On 29 December 1943, Signe Imma D. died at the *Landesanstalt* Großschweidnitz, sharing this fate with hundreds of minors. The diagnosis, as has already been said, was "mongoloid imbecility"; the official cause of death was "bronchopneumonia".[85]

Signe Imma D. was denied the full period of observation conceded to other patients at the Großschweidnitz "special children's ward", where it lasted as a rule for six to eight weeks. Infections such as bronchopneumonia and pneumonia were deliberately induced by a combination of malnourishment, which weakened the immune system, and sedatives that further repressed protective bodily functions. The respiratory tract was particularly affected, leading to the development of the characteristic pneumonia. Ascribing death to a natural cause was designed to create a smoke screen for the systematic murder that was being

---

81  Letter from the *Stadtkinderkrankenhaus* Leipzig to Dr. Feith at the *Heim Sonnenwiese*, 16 October 1943, AA, 4.1.0/8213400, Ref. 82459846.

82  Medical records of the *Landes-Heil- und Pflegeanstalt* Leipzig-Dösen/Großschweidnitz, 10618, Signe Imma D., n.d., AA, collection Schmitz-Köster. The quote is drawn from an entry made on 2 December 1943 at the *Heil- und Pflegeanstalt* Leipzig-Dösen.

83  Medical records of the *Landes-Heil- und Pflegeanstalt* Leipzig-Dösen/Großschweidnitz, 10618, Signe Imma D., n.d., AA, collection Schmitz-Köster. After a bombing raid on Leipzig, the "special children's ward" of the *Landesanstalt* Leipzig-Dösen was relocated to Großschweidnitz on 7/8 December 1943, cf. Neumaier, *Dr. Hildegard Feith*, 21.

84  Letter from *Anstaltsdirektor* to the Head of Healthcare at "Lebensborn e.V." Steinhöring near Ebersberg/Oberbayern, 23 December 1943, AA, collection Schmitz-Köster.

85  Medical records of the *Landes-Heil- und Pflegeanstalt* Leipzig-Dösen/Großschweidnitz, 10618, Signe Imma D., n.d., AA, collection Schmitz-Köster.

committed at the "special children's ward".[86] Sigune Imma D.'s siblings – in late 1943 Gerda D. gave birth to another girl – were at first kept in the dark on the circumstances of her death. Only decades later did they learn where and how their sister had died.[87]

The diagnosis Sigune Imma D. was given was tantamount to a death sentence. That she was transferred to *Heim Sonnenwiese* in spite of it may well have had to do with her father's professional status and his personal connections. There is one other case where the correspondence between the children's clinic Leipzig and *Heim Sonnenwiese* points to efforts to keep individual children longer than usual in the "care" of welfare institutions: in November 1943, the children's clinic Leipzig enquired from the director of *Heim Sonnenwiese* "also on behalf of Herr Prof. Catel, who got to know you and the *Heim Sonnenwiese* in person on one occasion" whether the two-and-a-half-year-old, reputedly deaf-and-dumb child of a *Stabsarzt* killed in action could be admitted to the home for a year "for nurture and observation". The child's intellectual capacities were not in line with its age; even though it was having problems with the ingestion of food, its "general capacities and the state of its organs [were] so satisfactory" that "a final assessment [appeared] to require another year".[88] Ebner declined the request, arguing that "only racially and genetically unobjectionable children can be admitted to the homes".[89]

86  Neumaier, *Dr. Hildegard Feith*, 22. For the *Landesanstalt* Großschweidnitz, see i.a. Christoph Hanzig, "Von der provisorischen Unterbringung zur professionalisierten Ermordung. Kinder und Jugendliche während des Zweiten Weltkrieges in der Landesanstalt Großschweidnitz", in *Neues Lausitzisches Magazin*, vol. 140, edited by Präsidium der Oberlausitzischen Gesellschaft der Wissenschaften e. V. (Görlitz: Selbstverlag der Oberlausitzischen Gesellschaft der Wissenschaften e. V., 2018), 9–30; *"Euthanasie" in Großschweidnitz. Regionalisierter Krankenmord in Sachsen 1940–1945. Berichte des Arbeitskreises zur Erforschung der nationalsozialistischen "Euthanasie" und Zwangssterilisation, edited by* Dietmar Schulze and Maria Fiebrandt (Köln: Psychiatrie Verlag, 2016).

87  Schmitz-Köster, *Unbrauchbare Väter*, 107.

88  Letter from the *Universitäts-Kinder-Klinik und Poliklinik* in Leipzig, Dr. Hempel, to the *Kinderheim Sonnenwiese – Lebensborn* c/o Frau Dr. Feith, Kohren-Sahlis, 18 November 1943, AA, 4.1.0/8211200, Ref. 82451651.

89  Letter from *SS-Oberführer* Dr. Ebner to the *Universitäts-Kinderklinik und Poliklinik* in Leipzig c/o Herr Dr. med. Hempel and Frau Dr. med. Feith-Butenschön Kohren-Sahlis with the request to take note, 30 November 1943, AA, 4.1.0 /8211200, Ref. 82451653.

5.3    "[...] does therefore not fall under the remit of the Law for the Prevention of Congenitally Diseased Offspring"[90]

Leopoldine R. gave birth to her son Gerhard at the *Heim Wienerwald* in July 1939. Ludwig R., Leopoldine R.'s husband and the father of the child, a bakery assistant and member of the *Waffen-SS*, is on record as an *SS-Sturmmann* in July 1936.[91]

Both Leopoldine R. and her husband were arguably dyed-in-the-wool National Socialists. The questionnaires for their engagement and marriage note that she had been an "illegal" National Socialist during the time when the National Socialist Party was banned and that she had officially joined up on 1 September 1938.[92] In her CV she noted that she had had to give up her post as a domestic servant "because of political quarrels (the lady of the house was a Jew)".[93] Living in the vicinity of the *Heim Wienerwald* with her husband, she was admitted to the home only on the day she gave birth and left again after about two weeks, on 12 August 1939. Her son Gerhard, classified as "healthy", was discharged along with her.[94]

Several months later, Ludwig R. turned to the *Dienststelle SS-Oberabschnitt Donau* with a request for assistance. His son Gerhard had begun to show alarming symptoms, such as cries of pain and convulsions. An examination of the child by Franz Hamburger at the *Kinderklinik der Stadt Wien* (Children's Clinic of the City of Vienna) had led to the finding that the child's skullcap had a dent which might equally probably have been inflicted during birth or during pregnancy. The cranial bone was pressing down on a nerve, causing the child to display "characteristics of the mentally insane".[95] Ludwig R. had tried to have the child admitted to the children's clinic, but this had turned out to be impossible as a referral by the welfare doctor of the home municipality was needed. Fur-

---

90  Medical expert report, 22 November 1941, WStLA, 1.3.2.209.10 *Wiener Städtische Nervenklinik für Kinder* ("Am Spiegelgrund"), 1940–1945, Medical records of deceased children, Gerhard R., SK 230/41, 5.
91  *RuSHA* questionnaire, 30 August 1938, Barch, R 9361-III/168082, fol. 2022–2025, here fol. 2022; Gerhard R., list of *Heim* residents, Gemeinde Pernitz, Registry Office Pernitz II; Medical expert report, 22 November 1941, WStLA, 1.3.2.209.10 *Wiener Städtische Nervenklinik für Kinder* (Am Spiegelgrund), 1940–1945, Medical records of deceased children, Gerhard R., SK 230/41, 1. During Gerhard's sojourn at the *Spiegelgrund*, his father Ludwig R. was stationed at the *SS-Führerheim* Dachau.
92  Questionnaire, signed on 1 September 1938, Barch, R 9361-III/168082, fol. 2067 and Questionnaire, signed on 30 August 1938, Barch, R 9361-III/168082, fol. 2065. Application for engagement and marriage addressed to *Reichsführer-SS, Rasse- und Siedlungshauptamt*, 30 August 1938.
93  CV Leopoldine A., Barch, R 9361-III/168082, fol. 2045.
94  Gerhard R., list of *Heim* residents, Gemeinde Pernitz, Registry Office Pernitz II.
95  Copy of a letter from the Führer of the *SS-Oberabschnitt Donau* to Lebensborn e.V., 23 June 1941, AA, 4.1.0/8212600, Ref. 82456573.

thermore, the *Fürsorgeverband* Wiener Neustadt had objected to the child's transfer to a hospital in Vienna.[96] Ludwig R. was therefore turning to the *SS-Dienststelle* with the request that *Lebensborn* oversee further medical examinations of the child. He left it to *Lebensborn* "to take any and all decisions concerning the future welfare of the child".[97]

The *Stabsführer* of the *SS-Dienststelle Oberabschnitt Donau* not only described the case to the *Lebensborn* but also lodged a complaint on account of the lack of initiative on the part of the *Fürsorgeverband* Wiener Neustadt. It was intolerable "that a member of the SS who had received a marriage permit from the *Rasse- und Siedlungshauptamt-SS* should end up having to rear a mentally insane child".[98]

Having had his attention drawn to Ludwig R.'s request by the *SS-Dienststelle Oberabschnitt Donau*, Ebner asked home director Schwab to forward to him all files on Gerhard R. in the keeping of the *Heim Wienerwald*.[99] He informed the *Lebensborn* management that Gerhard R.'s mother, Leopoldine R., had complained as early as August 1940 "that the child had already exhibited serious mental deficiencies at the age of six months", "that this defect could almost certainly only have been inflicted at birth and that the home's doctor would inevitably have noticed it if he had cared to pay attention".[100] Ebner had at that time rejected the charge. Neither the doctor on duty in the *Heim Wienerwald* at the time in question, Karl Sernetz, nor the midwife were to blame for the child's state of health.[101] Ebner therefore rejected the request the child's father, Ludwig R., had addressed to the *SS-Dienststelle Oberabschnitt Donau*. It was not part of the mission of *Lebensborn* to make arrangement's for the child's examination or to decide what was to become of the child.[102]

The *SS-Dienststelle* refuted Ebner's argument that *Lebensborn* had no choice but to declare itself as "not in charge", as "according to its statutes" it allegedly cared "only for genetically valuable children"; by contrast, Gerhard R. was a "seriously mentally disturbed child."[103] The *SS-Dienststelle* cited Hamburger's medical report,[104] according to which Gerhard R.'s condition was "on no account

---

96 Ibid.
97 Ibid.
98 Ibid.
99 Letter from Gregor Ebner to the *Heimarzt Heim Wienerwald*, Norbert Schwab, 28 June 1941, AA, 4.1.0/8212600, Ref. 82456576.
100 Letter from Gregor Ebner to the Managing Director of "Lebensborn e.V.", *SS-Standartenführer* Sollmann, 1 July 1941, AA, 4.1.0/8212600, Ref. 82456582–82456583, 2.
101 Ibid.
102 Ibid.
103 Letter from Ebner to the Managing Director of "Lebensborn e.V", *SS-Standartenführer* Sollmann, 1 July 1941, AA, 4.1.0/8212600, Ref. 82456583, 2.
104 Franz Hamburger was the director of the *Wiener Universitäts-Kinderklinik* and as such responsible, according to Herwig Czech, for medical experiments conducted with children

due to a congenital disease. It was the consequence of a lesion of the cranial bone that had occurred either in the mother's womb or during birth".[105] The *Dienststelle* felt that it was "almost a duty [for *Lebensborn*] to provide all manner of help to *SS* comrade R. to bring about a potentially achievable consolidation of the child's health".[106] In any case the *Dienststelle* expected *Lebensborn* to lean on the Welfare Authority of the Municipality of Wiener Neustadt to ensure the child's admission to a Viennese clinic.[107]

The distance the *Lebensborn* put between itself and those children born in its homes that did not meet the *SS*'s "selection criteria" is especially visible in the case of Gerhard R. Using this case to make what was presumably for him a point of general significance, Ebner pointed out that the admission of pregnant women to a *Lebensborn*-Heim was a "gesture of goodwill"[108] to single mothers and to parents-in-the-making. From this gesture of goodwill no "welfare obligations incumbent on the *Lebensborn* [can] be deduced, especially no obligation to care for a mentally defective child".[109] It would even be detrimental to the standing of the *Lebensborn* as an "agent of selection" if it were to extend its care activities to such cases.[110] The "discord"[111] between the *Lebensborn* and the *SS-Dienststelle Oberabschnitt Donau* was soon cleared up. For the *Lebensborn*, an invitation of Sollmann to the *SS-Dienststelle Oberabschnitt Donau* on 13 August 1941 "drew the curtain on the affair of R. in the most satisfactory manner".[112]

For the almost two-year-old Gerhard R. the negotiations on who was responsible for him had far-reaching consequences. Whether and to what extent the *Lebensborn* was involved in Gerhard R.'s transfer, initiated a few weeks later, on 25 October 1941, by the Welfare Authority of the district Wiener Neustadt to the *Spiegelgrund* "for observation" is unknown.[113] The "observation" was only of

---

who were patients at the *Spiegelgrund*. It may therefore be presumed that Franz Hamburger was aware of the National Socialist child "euthanasia" program. Czech, "Spiegelgrund-Komplex," 207.

105 *SS-Oberführer* Cassel to Gregor Ebner, Angelegenheit R., 10 July 1941, AA, 4.1.0/8212600, Ref. 82456587, 3.

106 Ibid.

107 Ibid.

108 Letter from Gregor Ebner to the Managing Director of the "Lebensborn e.V". *SS-Standartenführer* Sollmann, 15 July 1941, AA, 4.1.0/8212600, Ref. 82456590, 1.

109 Ibid.

110 Ibid.

111 Letter from *SS-Oberführer* Cassel to the Managing Director of the "Lebensborn e.V.", *SS-Standartenführer* Sollmann, 7 August 1941, AA, 4.1.0/8212600, Ref. 82456592.

112 Letter from *SS-Standartenführer* Sollmann to Gregor Ebner, 13 August 1941, AA, 4.1.0/8212600, Ref. 82456594.

113 Medical expert report, 22 November 1941, WStLA, 1.3.2.209.10, *Wiener Städtische Nervenklinik für Kinder* ("Am Spiegelgrund"), 1940–1945, Medical records of deceased children, Gerhard R., SK 230/41, 1–2. Towards the end, the expert report notes that it was the parents themselves who had their child admitted to the *Spiegelgrund* to "get an accurate assessment

short duration:[114] On 31 October 1941 Gerhard R. was diagnosed with "imbecility, hypertonic tetraparesis with epileptic seizures"[115] and was reported to the *Reichsausschuss*. During Gerhard R.'s stay at the *Spiegelgrund* an encephalography, a painful examination of the brain, was performed on him.[116]

Gerhard R. died on 11 November 1941 in Pavilion 15, reputedly of pneumonia.[117] His mother had visited him several times at the *Spiegelgrund*. It was noted that he did not even recognize her, remaining completely listless. The report also notes that he must be considered "as completely uneducable".[118] In their conclusion, the department doctor, Heinrich Gross,[119] and the director, Erwin Jekelius,[120] noted that, "according to the information provided by the child's parents [...], there are no indications whatever of a hereditary predisposition. Gerhard therefore does not fall under The *Law for the Prevention of Congenitally Diseased Offspring*".[121] Gerhard R.'s brain and his spinal cord were dissected and preserved in formalin.[122]

---

of the child's potential for education and development and to ensure there was a [conclusive] diagnosis".

114 Also noted in medical expert report, 22 November 1941, WStLA, 1.3.2.209.10 *Wiener Städtische Nervenklinik für Kinder* ("Am Spiegelgrund"), 1940–1945, Medical records of deceased children, Gerhard R., SK 230/41, 4.

115 Ibid.

116 Ibid.

117 For the usual sequence, see Dahl, "Tötung," 8. The *Reichsausschuss* was not notified until four to six weeks after admission, after a diagnosis had been made. The *Reichsausschuss* then gave the green light for the "treatment" – for the "treatment", see Klee, "Euthanasie," 339. – Authorisation was usually given six to eight weeks after notification, then death was accelerated by doses of Luminal, a barbiturate, followed by injections. According to Riegele, by 1944 the killing took place as early as four days after notification. In this case, it was even earlier, see Riegele, "Kindereuthanasie," 38. Some children were given a negative assessment on admission, but in isolated cases they continued to be under observation for more than a year, see Dahl, "Tötung," 14. As already mentioned, as opposed to other "special children's wards", the notifications mostly came from the *Spiegelgrund* itself, which points to a high degree of autonomy on the part of the medical staff, see Dahl, "Tötung," 8.

118 Medical expert report, 22 November 1941, WStLA, 1.3.2.209.10, *Wiener Städtische Nervenklinik für Kinder* ("Am Spiegelgrund"), 1940–1945, Medical records of deceased children, Gerhard R., SK 230/41, 5. Crucial diagnoses for the inpatient, frequently terminal admission to the *Spiegelgrund* were "ineducability" and "incapacity for work", see Riegele, "Kindereuthanasie," 31–32, 37. Behind these pseudoscientific criteria, Riegele suspects motives of medical research. For the criteria, see also Klee, "Euthanasie," 333.

119 Heinrich Gross was the department doctor of the pediatrics department at the *Spiegelgrund*. After 1945 he continued his research on children's brains and his career as a psychiatrist and renowned court expert. For more information see e.g. Herwig Czech, Dr. Heinrich Gross – "Die wissenschaftliche Verwertung der NS-Euthanasie in Österreich," in *Jahrbuch 1999*, edited by DÖW (Wien: DÖW, 1999), 53–70.

120 Until the end of 1941, the psychiatrist and expert active in the "*Aktion T4*", Erwin Jekelius, was the director of the *Spiegelgrund*.

121 Medical expert report, 22 November 1941, WStLA, 1.3.2.209.10, *Wiener Städtische Nervenklinik für Kinder* ("Am Spiegelgrund"), 1940–1945, Medical records of deceased children,

The "professional disagreements" and "personal attacks"[123] traded between the *Lebensborn* headquarters and the *SS-Dienststelle Oberabschnitt Donau* in the case of Gerhard R. attest to the dilemma in which those in power found themselves when the child of an SS member and his spouse that was born in a *Lebensborn* home did not meet the SS's "selection criteria". Armed with an expert report, the parents sought to prove that the causes of the child's "symptoms of mental insanity" were to be found either in pregnancy or in faulty care during childbirth and that there was no such thing as a familial predisposition. It is conceivable that this was an attempt to contain the consequences that the birth of a child with physical or mental disabilities might have for his or her parents.

In the death register of the *Spiegelgrund* the official cause cited for Gerhard R.'s death is "imbecility and pneumonia lobularis".[124]

## VI.   Other Cases of Death and Illness

### 6.1   "At this stage, no judgement can be passed on the child's mental faculties"[125]

The case studies of Brigitte Schmidt, Sigune Imma D. and Gerhard R. demonstrate that within the same life stories, the pronatalist measures of National Socialist racial and family policy, such as *Lebensborn*, were linked to one aspect of the National Socialists' antinatalist methods, the National Socialist child "euthanasia" program and what that link looked like. Pneumonia was given as the cause of death for all three. All diagnoses included "imbecility".

According to Ernst Klee, children with mental disabilities who "were classified as *imbeciles* [...] had no chance [to survive]."[126] Brigitte Schmidt, Sigune Imma D., and Gerhard R. were no exceptions: the majority of children who were

---

Gerhard R., SK 230/41, 5. In spite of this statement, Gerhard R. had been reported to the *Reichsausschuss* with the diagnosis "Extreme imbecility (Idiotie) with symptoms of neurological failure". According to Riegele, reports on acquired diseases or diseases with unexplained causes were more frequent than congenital ones, which the directive declared to be notifiable; see Riegele, "Kindereuthanasie," 37.

122 The results of these examinations are noted in the medical report: Medical report, 22 November 1941, WStLA, 1.3.2.209.10 *Wiener Städtische Nervenklinik für Kinder* (Am Spiegelgrund), 1940–1945, Medical records of deceased children, Gerhard R., SK 230/41, 4.

123 Letter from Ebner to Sollmann, 15 July 1941, 2, AA, 4.1.0/8212600, Ref. 82456591.

124 Death Register 1940–1945 of the *Wiener Städtische Nervenklinik für Kinder* ("Am Spiegelgrund"), Gerhard R., WStLA, 1.3.2.209.10.B4.

125 Letter from *SS-Obersturmführer und Heimleiter* Dr. Schwab to the Head of Healthcare at the Lebensborn e.V., *SS-Oberführer* Dr. Ebner, Steinhöring, 30 May 1941, AA, 4.1.0/8213700, Ref. 82460782.

126 Klee, "Euthanasie," 357.

murdered at the *Spiegelgrund* and in other "special children's wards" were given the same diagnosis and assigned the same causes of death.[127] The diagnosis "imbecility/mental deficiency" corresponded to the wording of the directive issued by the *Reichsministerium für Inneres* on 18 August 1939 about notifiable newborns. Vague criteria, such as "ineducability" or "incapacity for work", helped to keep observation periods for the decision between life and death short. The *Spiegelgrund* death registers lump together the admission diagnosis and the cause of death. In light of the systematic obfuscation of the actual cause of death it is therefore impossible to establish how many children were proactively murdered and how many were killed by neglect. Their death in a "special children's ward" made all of them victims of the National Socialist child "euthanasia" program.[128]

Apart from Brigitte Schmidt, Sigune Imma D., and Gerhard R., who were definitively murdered in the context of the National Socialist child "euthanasia" program, it is possible to identify other children from the *Heim Wienerwald* whose life was on the line.

Karin B. was born at the *Heim Wienerwald* in October 1942. *Lebensborn* having assumed guardianship of her, she was referred in May 1943 to paediatrician Erich Gasser at the *DRK-Kinderspital* (Red-Cross Children's Hospital) for exhibiting "oddities [...] in her mental behaviour". Even though the child was due to be taken to Kassel to live with foster parents, home director Schwab wanted to have the child's status assessed. He suspected "that the child was suffering either of a cerebral or an endocrinal malfunction".[129]

It is impossible to tell from the extant correspondence with any certainty whether Schwab was already thinking at that stage of having Karin B. transferred to a "special children's ward" or a comparable institution. The opposite seems to have been the case: He even mentioned the possibility of prolonging her stay at the home should the paediatric assessment take longer than expected. In effect, having "observed" Karin B. in the hospital for several months, Gasser himself proposed letting her stay at the home for another couple of months. According to him, the prospective foster parents could not be expected to put up with a "doubtlessly imbecile" child. She was to remain in the home "until she is a bit older. She should then be transferred to the *Erbbiologische Jugendfürsorge-Klinik*

---

127  Czech, *Erfassung*, 107–08; Dahl, "Tötung," 22: The cause of death assigned to almost two thirds of the children in the Death Register is pneumonia, more than half of the children were diagnosed with "*Idiotie/Schwachsinn*" (imbecility/mental deficiency).

128  Czech, "Der Spiegelgrund-Komplex," 198–99; see also Dahl, Endstation, 77.

129  Letter from *SS-Hauptsturmführer and Heimleiter* Dr. Schwab to the Head of Healthcare at the Lebensborn, *SS-Oberführer* Dr. Ebner, 18 May 1943, AA, 4.1.0/8213700, Ref. 82460842; see also Letter from *SS-Hauptsturmführer and Heimleiter* Dr. Schwab to the *DRK-Kinderspital*, 13 May 1943, AA, 4.1.0/8213700, Ref. 82460843.

of the City of Vienna at the *Spiegelgrund*, where her pathologies would be subjected to further clarification and appropriate measures would be taken if needed".[130] Gasser's diagnosis of "imbecility"[131] led Ebner to plan an examination of Karin B. at the *Heim Wienerwald* in July 1943, to be carried out jointly with a consultant of the *Lebensborn*, the paediatrician Josef Becker. After that examination a decision would be taken on Karin B.s "future".[132] No further details on the life of Karin B. can be gleaned either from the extant files of the *Heim Wienerwald* or of the *Spiegelgrund*. She was at the mercy of the *Lebensborn* doctors.

The situation is different in the case of Uta B. According to the extant files, she was born in the *Heim Wienerwald* in early May 1941. Josef Becker diagnosed her with physical deficiencies and with an impaired capacity for mental development.[133] The *Lebensborn* therefore refused to assume guardianship of her.[134]

Uta B.'s father, Sven L., a flight instructor born in Vienna, acknowledged paternity as early as June 1941.[135] On the evidence of the files, the child was discharged jointly with its mother a few weeks after its birth and shortly after the *Lebensborn*'s refusal to assume guardianship. Karlsbad/Karlovy Vary, the mother's place of birth, is cited as the place of residence for mother and daughter. Whether the assessment that "no judgement can be passed [...] at this stage on the child's mental capacities" saved Uta B. from admission to a "special children's ward" cannot be decided on the basis of the extant files.[136] Perhaps she escaped

---

130 Letter from Schwab to the Head of Healthcare at the Lebensborn, *SS-Oberführer* Dr. Ebner, dated 16 June 1943, AA, 4.1.0/8211200, Ref. 82451650.

131 See also Copy of the report on Ute-Karin B. compiled by the Neonatal Ward of the *DRK-Kinderspital*, 18 June 1943, AA, 4.1.0/8213400, Ref. 82459817.

132 Letter from SS-Oberführer Dr. Ebner to Heimleiter SS-Hauptsturmführer Dr. Schwab, dated 28 June 1943, AA, 4.1.0/8213400, Ref. 82459818.

133 "No judgement can be passed at this stage on the child's mental capacities but one gets the impression that the child will also be feebleminded. The child's development is greatly retarded". See Letter from the *SS-Obersturmführer and Heimleiter* Dr. Schwab to the Head of Healthcare at the Lebensborn e.V., *SS-Oberführer* Dr. Ebner, Steinhöring, 30 May 1941, AA, 4.1.0/8213700, Ref. 82460782.

134 Ibid.; see also Letter from the *Hauptabteilung Vormundschaftsamt* of the Lebensborn e.V. to the Director of the *Heim* Hochland, *SS-Oberführer* Dr. Ebner, Steinhöring, 17 June 1941, AA, 4.1.0/8213700, Ref. 82460783; Letter from *SS-Oberführer* Dr. Ebner to Headquarters – *Hauptabteilung Vormundschaftsamt*, 19 June 1941, AA, 4.1.0/8213300, Ref. 82459622: "Birth of a seriously malformed child. In this case, Lebensborn cannot assume guardianship."

135 Letter from the *Hauptabteilung A* of Lebensborn e.V. to the Registry Office II Pernitz, 13 October 1941, Gemeinde Pernitz, Registry Office Pernitz II, 66/41.

136 Letter from *SS-Obersturmführer und Heimleiter* Dr. Schwab to the Head of Healthcare at the Lebensborn e.V., *SS-Oberführer* Dr. Ebner, Steinhöring, 30 May 1941, AA, 4.1.0/8213700, Ref. 82460782; Uta B., list of *Heim* residents, Gemeinde Pernitz, Registry Office Pernitz II. The family situation of the children could increase their chances of survival. Also, many children who were murdered at the Spiegelgrund were already in public care. Czech, *Erfassung*, 111; Dahl, Tötung, 11; Riegele, "Kindereuthansie," 35–36.

from the grip of the *Lebensborn* because her mother moved to Karlsbad/Karlovy Vary with her. The course her and her parents' lives took is unknown.

## 6.2    "Later his weight gain was more satisfactory"[137]

Doctors made blanket diagnoses of the pathologies and blanket specifications of the causes of deaths to cover up the child murder program. As a result, there is plenty of room for speculation on the number of the murdered children, also outside the "special children's wards". The majority of hospital referrals and illnesses and deaths of children in the *Heim Wienerwald* are documented in 1940 and 1941.[138]

Among the thirty-five deaths in the *Heim Wienerwald* known to date and documented by a variety of sources, there are at least seven stillbirths. For as many as seven other children – those who reputedly died in a "special children's ward" of or with pneumonia are not included in these numbers – pneumonia is the recorded cause of death.[139] At this point, it seems possible, but cannot be proven that some of these children were also victims of National Socialist "euthanasia".

One of these children is Heinrich Günther H., whose mother was admitted to the *Heim Wienerwald* in December 1940. In late February 1941, Schwab had the infant transferred to the *DRK-Kinderspital* because of weight loss and general asthenia.[140] Ebner welcomed this decision. In his view, Heinrich Günther H.

---

137 Letter from Dr. Ebner to the *Reichsführer-SS*, Berlin, 3 May 1941, AA, 4.1.0./8213700, Ref. 82460963 to 82460964, 2.

138 The most common diagnoses were pneumonia, nutritional disorder/dystrophy, diphtheria, and whooping cough. There were frequent referrals – for "dystrophy" and malnutrition or undernourishment – to the *Kinderklinik der Stadt Wien – Glanzing* in the nearby 19th municipal district of Vienna or to the *DRK-Kinderspital*, where Erich Gasser was in charge. Children who had initially been diagnosed with whooping cough or another infectious disease were usually referred to the *Wilhelminenspital*, whereas those diagnosed with "dystrophy" were usually referred to the *DRK-Kinderspital*. The author has compiled a list of certified hospital referrals, illnesses and deaths on the basis of the holdings concerning *Lebensborn*, especially medical topics and general statistics concerning the *Heim Wienerwald*, of the Arolsen Archives and Registry Office Pernitz II.

139 These data are based on files stored at the Registry Office Pernitz II, on correspondence dealing with medical topics and on general statistics in the *Lebensborn* holdings of the Arolsen Archives. More research is needed concerning illnesses and deaths among those children who died at the *Heim Wienerwald*, in hospital or shortly after their discharge. See also Fürstaller, "Lebensbornheime in Österreich", 73. On the evidence of the Arolsen Archives, Fürstaller, too, lists pneumonia as the most frequently cited cause od death.

140 Letter from the Director of the Heim Wienerwald, *SS-Obersturmführer* Dr. Schwab, to the Head of Healthcare at "Lebensborn" e.V., *SS-Oberführer* Dr. Ebner, Steinhöring, 7 March 1941, AA, 4.1.0/8213300, Ref. 82459584.

suffered from a "pronounced nutritional disorder in conjunction with general asthenia". He expressed his hope that the hospital would "see the child through [its difficulties]".[141] Heinrich Günther H. was admitted to the *DRK-Kinderspital* on 5 March 1941.[142] Even though a temporary improvement and a slight weight gain was noted on 26 March 1941,[143] Schwab informed his superior Ebner one week later of the child's poor state of health. "Despite all efforts," he had "not put on a gram". It was to be assumed that "in this case, the cause of the dystrophy is some sort of malformation, be it cerebral or organic in nature". The child was wont to lie "in its cot without showing the least reaction" to its surroundings.[144] Schwab mentioned in his letter that, on account of the child's asthenia, the mother had been given permission to leave the child at the home for six months, while she herself had left the home already.[145]

Roughly two weeks later, Heinrich Günther H. died at the age of three months at the *DRK-Kinderspital*, with pneumonia being cited as the cause of his death. Ebner informed Himmler in the monthly report on deaths in the *Lebensborn* Heimen: weight gain after four weeks at the *DRK-Kinderspital* had been "more satisfactory", but "on 19 April 1941 [...] the child was diagnosed with pneumonia, to which it succumbed on 21 April 1941".[146]

---

141 Letter from *SS-Oberführer* Dr. Ebner to *SS-Obersturmführer* Dr. Schwab, *Lebensbornheim Wienerwald*, 10 March 1941, AA, 4.1.0/8213200, Ref. 82459195.
142 Letter from Dr. Ebner to the Reichsführer-SS, Berlin, 3 May 1941, AA, 4.1.0/8213700, Ref. 82460963 to 82460964, 2.
143 Ibid.: "There [at the *DRK-Kinderspital*] it [the child, Heinrich Günther H.] hardly put on any weight at all during the first four weeks. Later the weight gain was more satisfactory."
144 Letter from the Director of the Heim Wienerwald *SS-Obersturmführer* Dr. Schwab to the Head of Healthcare at Lebensborn e.V., *SS-Oberführer* Dr. Ebner, Steinhöring, dated 4 April 1941, AA, 4.1.0/8213600, Ref. 82460493 to 82460494, 1.
145 Heinrich Günther H.'s sojourn at the home lasted longer than that of his mother, even though she was married. It is conceivable that Schwab chose the wording in the correspondence – that Heinrich Günther H., rather than being a *Lebensborn* child properly speaking, was the child of a married mother who had been given permission to leave the child in the home on account of its asthenia – in light of Heinrich Günther H.'s legitimate birth. As a matter of principle, the distinction between legitimate and illegitimate children was not made. For the wording, see: ibid. That the mother left the home is noted in a letter from Dr. Ebner to the *Reichsführer-SS*, Berlin, 3 May 1941, AA, 4.1.0/8213700, Ref. 82460963 to 82460964, 2.
146 Letter from Dr. Ebner to the *Reichsführer-SS*, Berlin, dated 3 May 1941, AA, 4.1.0/8213700, Ref. 82460963 to 82460964, 2.

## VII.  Conclusion

What these individual life stories of children born in the *Heim Wienerwald* have shown is that, while the *Lebensborn* was not directly involved in the killing of children with physical and mental disabilities or who displayed "behavioural problems", it was part and parcel of the network of the National Socialist child "euthanasia" program.

Up until now, the number of children born in Lebensborn homes who upon admission to a "special children's ward" were almost certainly murdered in the context of the National Socialist child "euthanasia" program has been put at seventeen at a minimum.[147] It is probable that in light of this study and of future research work on the cases of illness and death of Lebensborn children, this minimum number will have to be corrected upwards. "The inhumanity of the National Socialists' racial ideology, which led them to idolize racially 'valuable' individuals and to despise racially 'inferior' individuals and consign them to death was fully revealed in the *Lebensborn*, whenever a malfomed child was born,"[148] wrote Georg Lilienthal, the author of the most comprehensive studies on the *Lebensborn*. The search for information on children who fell victim to the National Socialist child "euthanasia" program and the – albeit fragmentary – reconstruction of their biographies aim at restoring at least a semblance of identity to these victims of the National Socialist regime.

---

147  Lilienthal, "Der 'Lebensborn e.V.' und seine Folgen," 221.
148  Lilienthal, *Der "Lebensborn e.V."*, 102.

# Abstracts

## Lebensborn Maternity Home *Wienerwald*, 1938–1945

*Lukas Schretter / Martin Sauerbrey-Almasy / Barbara Stelzl-Marx*
*National Socialist Population Policy, Racial Hygiene, and* Lebensborn. *Pregnancy and Childbirth in the* Heim Wienerwald, *1938–1945*

The *Heim Wienerwald*, established in Pernitz/Feichtenbach in 1938, served as a maternity home for the *SS Lebensborn* association to increase the birth rate among the "Aryan" population. *Lebensborn*, founded in 1935, had by then become an integral part of National Socialist racial and population policies, whose attempts to control reproduction ranged from anti-natalist measures, such as the forced sterilizations, to pro-natalist measures, such as incentives to marry and have children for the racially and eugenically "fit". This article first situates the history of the *Heim Wienerwald* in the context of National Socialist population policy, racial hygiene, and *Lebensborn*. Drawing on case studies from the *Heim Wienerwald*, it explains the measures taken by *Lebensborn* to keep pregnancy and childbirth secret, the admission of women to *Lebensborn*, and the assessment of the "racial suitability" of mother and child by *Lebensborn*.
Keywords: National Socialism, Racial Hygiene, Population Policy, *Lebensborn*

*Barbara Stelzl-Marx*
Lebensborn *as a Blueprint for the "Nobility of the Future". Daily Life and Ideology in the* Heim Wienerwald

The commingling of sexual and population policies, combined with a hierarchy of blood elevated to an ideology, must be seen as a specific characteristic of National Socialism. In the Third Reich, sexual matters were dealt with dictatorially at the highest level, as they touched on the foundations of the system. For German women in general, and particularly for those in *Lebensborn* homes, the

emphasis was on their importance for procreation and the advancement of the "Aryan" race in general and the "German *Volksgemeinschaft*" in particular. The *Lebensborn* maternity homes were facilities where, according to their charter, children "valuable in mind and body," the "nobility of the future" as envisioned by the SS, were to be born. The article illustrates the extent to which the organisation and daily routines of the *Heim Wienerwald* were imbued with National Socialist ideology: starting with the preferred choice of first names and name consecration ceremonies as Himmler's *Ersatz* baptism through ideological instructions to dietary regulations in the spirit of the true *Volksgemeinschaft*. Everyday life in the *Heim Wienerwald* was corseted in diligence and order.
Keywords: National Socialism, Ideology, *Lebensborn*, Everyday Life

*Nadjeschda Stoffers / Lukas Schretter*
*Student Nurses for* Lebensborn. *Daily Routines in the* Heim Wienerwald, *1940–1945*

The SS association *Lebensborn*, which encouraged "Aryan" women deemed "hereditarily healthy" to have children, set up more than twenty maternity and children's homes between 1936 and 1944. This article provides an insight into the everyday life of the staff in the *Heim Wienerwald*, a *Lebensborn* maternity home established in 1938 in Pernitz/Feichtenbach. It analyses letters written by a (student) nurse of the *Heim Wienerwald* to her mother, and an interview conducted with a former student nurse who worked for *Lebensborn* in Feichtenbach in 1944/1945. The article also draws on *Lebensborn* files that deal with the associaton's staff. Departing from the structure and functions of the employees in the *Heim Wienerwald*, the article discusses the daily routines of the (student) nurses, the festivities in the home, leisure activities of the staff, and how the two nurses experienced the end of the war. It also examines how they evaluated, processed, and described their lived experiences in the home during respectively after the war, thus contributing to the current state of research on nurses in *Lebensborn* and on perceptions and memories of the *Heim Wienerwald*.
Keywords: National Socialism, *Lebensborn*, Nurses in the Third Reich

*Sabine Nachbaur*
*"Undesirables" among the* Lebensborn *children. The* Heim Wienerwald *and the National Socialist child "euthanasia" program*

The *Heim Wienerwald*, established in Pernitz/Feichtenbach in 1938, served as a maternity home for the SS *Lebensborn* association to increase the birth rate among the "Aryan" population. This article focuses on children born in the *Heim*

*Wienerwald* who did not meet the racist standards of a "new elite" that had been set by the *SS*. Moreover it casts light on the question which consequences were drawn by the *Lebensborn* association and the parents. It demonstrates that within the same life stories of three children, the pronatalist measures of National Socialist racial and family policy, such as *Lebensborn*, were linked to one aspect of the National Socialists' antinatalist methods, the child "euthanasia" program. The search for information about these children in documents from various archives and the – albeit fragmentary – reconstruction of the biographies aim at restoring at least a semblance of identity to these victims of the National Socialist regime.

Keywords: National Socialism, *Lebensborn*, child "euthanasia" program, *Spiegelgrund*

# Reviews

„Let them speak – In search of the drowned". Eine hybride Online-Plattform von Gabor Mihaly Toth: https://lts.fortunoff.library.yale.edu.

Seit Jahren ist eine zentrale Frage der Shoah Education, wie mit dem Ableben von Überlebenden der Shoah und der damit verbundenen Unmöglichkeit eines direkten Austausches umgegangen werden kann. Der langjährige Mitarbeiter des Fortunoff Video Archive for Holocaust Testimonies und Historiker mit Schwerpunkt auf Digital Humanities, Gabor Mihaly Toth, will mit dem 2021 veröffentlichten und als „digitale Monografie" titulierten Projekt „Let them speak – In search of the drowned" einen Beitrag zur Bewältigung dieser Herausforderung leisten. Dabei handelt es sich um eine frei zugängliche Online-sammlung von 2666 volltranskribierten, englischsprachigen Interviews mit Shoah-Überlebenden, die mit digitalen Methoden aufbereitet und um Begleit-texte mit Ausführungen des Autors zu seinem auf Emotionen basierenden Konzept einer Beschäftigung mit diesen Interviews ergänzt wurden.[1]

Die Sammlung besteht aus Videos der bekanntesten und größten Datenbanken: Das Yale Fortunoff Archive stellt 176 Interviews zur Verfügung, das USC Shoah Foundation Visual History Archive 976 und das United States Holocaust Memorial Museum 1514. Gegliedert ist die Homepage in zwei Teile: Zunächst bieten die Punkte „Essays" und „Methodology" Begleittexte von Toth, während unter dem Titel „Fragments" die durch einen Algorithmus verschiedenen Emotionen zugeordneten Textfragmente aller Interviews erkundet werden können. Die Interviews können auch im Ganzen und ohne Kontext abgefragt werden, wobei der größte Wert dieser Seite in der Nutzung für die historische Forschung liegt. Dabei bedient sich Toth verschiedener digitaler Maschinen und Analysetools, was die Homepage zu einem beeindruckenden Beispiel für rezente Möglichkeiten des digitalen Datenbankaufbaus macht. Der Zugang zu den Videos ist frei und ohne Anmeldung möglich. Alle Videos, die mit dem Transkript zum Sprechtext verknüpft sind, können im Freitext durchsucht werden. Die Suchmaske ermöglicht es, direkt zu einzelnen Interviewstellen zu gelangen, in denen beispielsweise ein Durchgangslager erwähnt wird. Das ist in den Ursprungsdatenbanken USC, Fortunoff oder USHMM, die nur nach Verschlag-wortung durchsuchbar sind, nicht möglich. Hier bietet das Projekt also eine praktische Ergänzung zu den vorhandenen Datenbanken, ohne diese jedoch ersetzen zu können.

Diese Nutzung der Seite ist allerdings nur ein Nebeneffekt. Toths Hauptan-liegen ist eine Beschäftigung mit den in Interviews zum Ausdruck kommenden Emotionen, wie er im Essay-Bereich der Homepage darlegt. Auf wenigen Seiten argumentiert Toth, dass die Überlebenden-Erzählung für ihn die einzig mögliche

---

1 Siehe URL: https://lts.fortunoff.library.yale.edu/ (abgerufen 5.11.2023).

Form der Annäherung an die Emotionalität der Opfer der Shoah darstellt. Der Holocaust, so Toth, habe zwei Erzählstränge: einerseits die Geschichte der Verfolgung, womit er die wissenschaftliche Beschäftigung im Sinne der Holocaust-Studies meint, und die Geschichte des Leidens der Opfer, wozu er seine Arbeit zählt, die, neben dem Hörbarmachen der Erzählungen, keiner weiteren Erklärung bedürfe.[2] Eine Verortung im aktuellen Forschungsstand oder eine über allgemeine Verweise auf Standardwerke der Shoah-Studies hinausgehende Beschäftigung mit Sekundärliteratur findet sich in dieser digitalen Monografie, die im Bereich des digitalen Gedenkens anzusiedeln ist, nicht. Die Autorität der Zeitzeug:innen ist für Toth unantastbar, weshalb die Erzählungen für sich stehen müssen und nicht durch Interpretationen verfälscht werden sollen. Es geht ihm nicht um eine wissenschaftliche Auseinandersetzung mit Zeitzeug:innenschaft, sondern, wie er schreibt, um das Einlösen einer moralischen Verpflichtung, die Stimmen der Überlebenden zugänglich zu machen.[3] Explizit soll das Projekt den Blick dabei auf Emotionalität, Individualität und Singularität jeder einzelnen Erzählung richten. Dementsprechend lautet auch die Fragestellung des Projekts: „Wie können wir die Emotions-Geschichte des Holocaust bewahren, sodass auch zukünftige Generationen die Stimmen der Stimmlosen hören können?"[4]

Im Bereich „Fragments", dem Herzstück des Projekts, setzt er diesen Ansatz um, indem aus allen Interviews zentrale Emotionen und Erfahrungen der Shoah herausgefiltert werden können. Über eine Gliederung in 27 Hauptkategorien, wie beispielsweise Angst, Schreien, Hoffnung oder Taubheit, können die diesbezügliche Textfragmente aus Interviews gesammelt abgerufen werden, in denen die jeweilige Emotion oder Erfahrung zum Ausdruck kommen. Durch diese Zusammenschau soll, im Sinne der Fragestellung, eine kollektive Erfahrung des Holocaust durch die Aussagen der Überlebenden möglich gemacht werden.

Das Projekt „Let them speak" schafft eine Brücke zwischen digitalem Gedenken und der Beschäftigung mit Überlebenden-Erzählungen der Shoah. Innovativ zeigt Toth, welche Möglichkeiten KI-gestützte Methoden für Gedenkprojekte bestehen, um neue Dimensionen der Shoah zugänglich zu machen. Diese Erkenntnis lässt sich auch innerhalb der Geschichtswissenschaften auf die Durchsuchung eines Quellenkorpus übertragen, was jedoch nicht Ziel des Projekts war. Neben der erwähnten zusätzlichen Recherchemöglichkeit in den über 2000 Interviews bietet Toth mit seiner Sammlung an Textfragmenten zu Ge-

---

2 Vgl. Gabor Mihaly Toth, In Search of the Drowned: Testimonies and Testimonial Fragments of the Holocaust. Epilogue. Yale Fortunoff Archive, 2021, URL: https://lts.fortunoff.library.yale.edu/essays/essay-11 (abgerufen 5. 11. 2023).
3 Vgl. ebd., „The Voice of the Voiceless: How Can We Let Them Speak?"
4 Ebd.

fühlserfahrungen für die Zeitgeschichte auch einen möglichen Ausgangspunkt für Forschungen im Bereich einer „history of emotions" der Shoah.

*Johannes Glack*

**Ina Markova, Otto Koenig (1881–1955). Ein Leben zwischen *Arbeiter-Zeitung* und Volksbildung, Wien/Hamburg: new academic press 2022, 224 Seiten.**

Mit dem Namen Otto Koenig verbinden die meisten Menschen wahrscheinlich die Erinnerung an den 1992 verstorbenen Verhaltensforscher und ehemaligen Leiter der Biologischen Station Wilhelminenberg in Wien. Dessen gleichnamiger Vater Otto Koenig (1881–1955), Redakteur der „Arbeiter-Zeitung" und Volksbildner, ist hingegen nur einschlägig Interessierten noch ein Begriff. Umso verdienstvoller ist es, dass ihn nun Ina Markova, Historikerin am Österreichischen Volkshochschularchiv, mit einer beeindruckenden Biografie der Vergessenheit entrissen hat.

Otto Koenig verbrachte die Kindheitsjahre in Stockerau, wo der aus Deutschland stammende Vater als Beamter der Nordwestbahn stationiert war. 1900 übersiedelte die Familie nach Klosterneuburg, das in der Folge bis zu Koenigs Tod der Lebensmittelpunkt bleiben sollte. Die Herkunft aus einer protestantischen Familie prägte ihn nachhaltig: Koenig war zeitlebens gläubig und in strikter Distanz zum (politischen) Katholizismus. Von diesem Milieu beeinflusst, fand er in jungen Jahren den Weg zu einer deutschnationalen Studentenverbindung, deren Antisemitismus ihn nicht gestört zu haben schien. Er studierte Germanistik, belegte auch Lehrveranstaltungen in Archäologie, klassischer Philologie, Epigrafik, Pädagogik und unterrichtete danach für kurze Zeit als Gymnasiallehrer.

Das leidenschaftliche Bestreben, seine vielseitige Bildung weiterzugeben, wurde zur Berufung und 1905 erregte sein Vortrag im Arbeiterbildungsverein Gumpendorf über „Friedrich Schiller als revolutionärer Dichter" die Aufmerksamkeit von Victor Adler und Friedrich Austerlitz. Der für Reden und Schreiben gleichermaßen talentierte Koenig wurde 1908 für die Mitarbeit in der „Arbeiter-Zeitung" gewonnen, wo er mit Engelbert Pernerstorfer, seinem Vorgesetzten in der Kulturredaktion, die Vorliebe für die deutsche Klassik teilte. Fast fünf Jahrzehnte hindurch – unterbrochen durch die Jahre von Austrofaschismus und Nationalsozialismus – schrieb er hunderte Beiträge: Theater- und Literaturkritiken, Glossen, Berichte über Volksbildung, Radiokritik, Rezensionen über Kinder- und Jugendbücher. Ebenso widmete er sich als Vater einem eher seltenen Genre und ließ die Leserschaft regelmäßig an der Beobachtung des Spielzeugmarktes teilhaben; der Eisenbahnersohn blieb übrigens auch als Erwachsener ein Modellbahnbastler und hatte in der Wohnung eine große Anlage aufgebaut.

Kurz vor und nach dem Ersten Weltkrieg – den Militärdienst leistete er in Graz und am Balkan – war Koenig in der sozialdemokratischen „Dresdner Volkszeitung" tätig und kehrte 1919 nach Österreich zurück, wo eine Fülle von Aufgaben auf ihn wartete. Dem von Josef Luitpold Stern geleiteten Reichsbildungsamt der republikanischen Volkswehr diente er als Vortragender und Verfasser von Lehrinstruktionen. Diesem Engagement wurde nach dem Zerfall der Koalitionsregierung und der vom Christlichsozialen Vaugoin vorangetriebenen „Umpolitisierung" des Heeres ein baldiges Ende gesetzt. Danach nahm er das Engagement in der sozialdemokratischen Zentralstelle für das Bildungswesen auf; die junge Republik und das „Rote Wien" verschafften der Arbeiterbildung großen Aufschwung. Koenig war in der Pädagogischen Kommission der Bildungszentrale aktiv, betätigte sich als Autor der Zeitschrift „Bildungsarbeit", in der Ausbildung der Arbeiterbibliothekare und als Rhetoriklehrer in der Parteischule. Mit sozialistischer Theorie setzte sich Koenig kaum auseinander. Er begnügte sich mit der Einbettung seiner Praxis in einen auf scheinbar naturwissenschaftlicher Gesetzmäßigkeit basierenden Fortschrittsglauben. Ob die Aneignung klassischer Bildung dem Emanzipationskampf der Arbeiterklasse dienlich war oder an deren Interessen vorbeiging, blieb hingegen als Frage offen und wurde bereits von Zeitgenossen kontrovers diskutiert. Otto Koenig stand dabei in einer kulturkonservativen Traditionslinie, die von den aus bürgerlich-liberalen Verhältnissen stammenden und von humanistischen Bildungsidealen erfüllten Pionieren der Arbeiterbewegung vorgegeben wurde. Dennoch bleibt eine gewisse Breitenwirkung dieses Konzepts bis heute beeindruckend und verdankt sich zweifelsohne auch dem Charisma von Menschen wie Otto Koenig.

In der Redaktion der „Arbeiter-Zeitung" übernahm nach dem Tod Pernerstorfers David Josef Bach die Leitung der Feuilletonredaktion und wurde, was die Heranführung der Arbeiter an die Hochkultur betrifft, für Koenig zu einem kongenialen Partner. Chefredakteur Austerlitz, dessen cholerische Ausbrüche gefürchtet waren, stand dem Feuilleton ambivalent gegenüber und war in einem ständigen Spannungsverhältnis zu Koenig, dem er vorwarf, am Zielpublikum vorbei zu hochgestochen zu schreiben. Tatsächlich gab es diesbezüglich auch aus der Hörerschaft von Koenigs Kursen immer wieder Beschwerden: Bei aller Verehrung für seine Persönlichkeit, sein Ethos und die lautere Gesinnung fühlten sich einige Schüler von ihrem Lehrer und dessen Frontalunterricht überfordert.

War die Arbeiterbildung organisatorisch und inhaltlich eng mit der Sozialdemokratischen Arbeiterpartei verbunden, so klammerte die „neutrale" Volksbildung die Tagespolitik aus. Hier war Koenig in seinem Element und vor allem die Volkshochschule „Volksheim" Ottakring bot ihm eine Wirkungsstätte innerhalb der literarischen Fachgruppe. Aufgabe einer wissenschaftsbasierten

Volksbildung war für ihn die Schaffung kritisch denkender und logisch orientierter Menschen. Während der Zwischenkriegszeit sah sich die Volksbildung mit Kritik der aus der Weimarer Republik kommenden „Neuen Richtung" konfrontiert. Der aufklärerische Anspruch wurde in Frage, und individualisierende Konzepte in den Vordergrund gestellt, gleichzeitig aber Volksbildung als „Volkbildung" verstanden, was in späterer Folge einige Exponenten für völkische Ideologien anfälliger machte: Ina Markova gelingt eine inhaltlich äußerst instruktive Darstellung dieser Diskussionen. Obwohl oder gerade weil zu Koenigs Lehrinhalten auch Runenkunde, „Gotische Übungen" und „Altnordische Übungen" zählten, grenzte er sich gegen „Nationale Irrlichterei" (so der Titel seines Manuskriptes) besonders deutlich ab.

1934 verlor Koenig schlagartig alle Arbeiten und bezog in den nächsten elf Jahren kein Einkommen. Während der Ära von Austrofaschismus und Nationalsozialismus blieb er standhaft. In Klosterneuburg zurückgezogen und in „innerer Emigration" lebend, war er Anlaufstelle und Gesprächspartner für Gesinnungsgenossen.

Nach der Befreiung 1945 versuchte er dort weiterzumachen, wo er 1934 aufgehört hatte. Da in Koenigs Fortschrittsideologie seinerzeit die mörderische Barbarei als Möglichkeit nicht vorgesehen war, fiel es ihm jetzt ebenso schwer, als ein von der historischen Entwicklung „Überrumpelter" den Nationalsozialismus und seine Konsequenzen umfassend zu verstehen – der Zivilisationsbruch wirkte wahrscheinlich auch auf relativ „unversehrt" Gebliebene zu traumatisch. Als früherer Deutschnationaler distanzierte er sich nun – durchaus im damaligen österreichischen Mainstream stehend – von „Deutschem". Nicht mehrheitlichen Gefühlen der Bevölkerung folgte Koenig allerdings in der Frage der Entnazifizierung, in die er eingebunden war: Hier vertrat er eine konsequente Linie und plädierte auch noch nach der Minderbelastetenamnestie dafür, „Ehemalige" nicht in den Verband demokratischer Schriftsteller und Journalisten Österreichs aufzunehmen.

Stets von eher bescheidenen Einkünften lebend, war er in fortgeschrittenem Alter noch zur Lohnarbeit gezwungen und trat wieder in die Redaktion der „Arbeiter-Zeitung" als Ressortleiter für Kunst und Kultur ein. Von Chefredakteur Oscar Pollak als Vertreter einer Generation hoch geschätzt, die bereits unter Victor Adler zur Arbeiterbewegung gestoßen war, musst er sich dennoch abermals die Kritik anhören, „zu hoch" zu schreiben. Mehrmals wurde er von Pollak ermahnt, an die Leserschaft der Zeitung zu denken. Umgekehrt ließ der streitbare Koenig Pollak nicht ungeschoren und nannte ihn einen „Banausen".

Unmittelbar nach der Befreiung hielt Koenig in der Volkshochschule „Volksheim" Ottakring wieder gut besuchte Literaturkurse und einen Lateinkurs ab und übernahm ebendort die Funktion eines Vizeobmanns. Er polemisierte gegen das Vordringen pseudowissenschaftlicher und esoterischer Inhalte in der

Volksbildung ebenso wie gegen die Lektüre von Karl May und sprach sich klar gegen die Berufsbildung durch Volkshochschulen aus. In neuen Konzepten einer „Erziehung zur Demokratie" sah er die hehren Prinzipien der „neutralen" Volksbildung verletzt. In vielem wirkte er jetzt aus der Zeit gefallen, wenn er die alten Ideale einforderte. Es war kein Zufall, dass ihn nun eine starke freundschaftliche Achse mit dem aus dem amerikanischen Exil zurückgekehrten Josef Luitpold Stern verband. Auch Stern, der als Leiter eines gewerkschaftlichen Bildungsheimes ins Mühlviertel abgeschoben wurde, war die österreichische Realität nach 1945 fremd geworden und die beiden Männer tauschten einander öfters ihre Enttäuschungen – nicht zuletzt über die Nachkriegsentwicklung der Sozialdemokratie – aus. Bei zwei 1948 abgehaltenen Fortbildungswochen der Wiener Städtischen Büchereien in Sterns Bildungshaus Schloss Weinberg unterstützte Koenig seinen Freund mit der Übernahme einiger Programmteile.

Es fällt auf, dass Koenig nach 1945 mit etlichen nicht zurückgekehrten Vertriebenen, mit denen er die Trauer über das Verlorene aus der Welt vor 1934 teilen konnte, in vertrauter brieflicher Verbindung war und auf der anderen Seite parteiübergreifende Freundschaften mit einigen Konservativen – darunter der frühere RAVAG-Direktor und Funktionär der Vaterländischen Front Rudolf Henz – schloss. Während der letzten Lebensjahre wurden ihm noch Ehrungen zuteil. Aber auch die Enttäuschungen wären ohne seine große und tiefe Verbundenheit mit der Volksbildung nicht zu verstehen. Koenig selbst fasste das in die Worte: „Kann man denn unpersönlich sein, wenn man was lieb hat, wenn einem die Sache am Herzen liegt und man sich um sie sorgt und für sie hofft?" (S. 202). In der Volkshochschule Ottakring erinnert eine Gedenktafel und in der Thaliastraße ein Wohnhaus an Otto Koenig.

Ina Markova ist für diese Arbeit zu danken, die auf der gründlichen Auswertung aller verfügbaren Quellen – darunter auch das Privatarchiv der Familie Koenig – basiert. Sie gibt nicht nur – lebendig geschrieben – Einblick in eine beeindruckende, konfliktträchtige und leidenschaftliche Persönlichkeit, sondern vermittelt ebenso exemplarisch Geschichte und Stellenwert von Arbeiter- und Volksbildung.

*Heimo Gruber*

Katja Hoyer, Diesseits der Mauer. Eine neue Geschichte der DDR 1949–1990, Hamburg: Hoffmann und Campe 2023, 576 Seiten.

Ein Politikum: Zwei persönlich gehaltene Bücher zur DDR – von Dirk Oschmann[1] und Katja Hoyers – kletterten schnell auf die Bestsellerlisten des „Spiegel" und erlebten innerhalb kürzester Zeit gleich mehrere Auflagen. Die Werke fallen ähnlich und doch höchst unterschiedlich aus. Ähnlich deshalb, weil der Tenor jeweils um Verständnis für die Menschen im Osten des vereinigten Landes wirbt. Unterschiedlich deshalb, weil Hoyer ihre Sicht auf den damaligen Alltag richtet, während Oschmann die Zeit nach der Einheit in den kritischen Blick nimmt.

Hier wird Katja Hoyers Buch in den kritischen Blick genommen. Geboren 1985 in Brandenburg und schon länger in London Geschichte lehrend, schildert die Autorin in neun, chronologisch gegliederten Kapiteln die Geschichte der DDR – allerdings ist es, anders als der Untertitel suggeriert, keine „neue Geschichte der DDR". Die Stärke des Werkes: das Verknüpfen der Alltagsgeschichte einzelner bekannter und weniger bekannter Personen mit der „großen Politik". Ausgesprochen lebendig und bildhaft geschrieben, zeichnet die Arbeit Schicksale bekannter und unbekannter Personen nach, zum Teil in Interviews. Gewiss, über die Auswahl der Sachverhalte lässt sich immer streiten – so irritiert die unterproportionale Gewichtung der Bürgerrechtler, die den „Realsozialismus" herausforderten. Deren Sichtweise dürfte nicht die der Autorin widerspiegeln. Hoyer wollte offenkundig keineswegs erneut das Bild vom „Stasi-Staat" revitalisieren, dominierte doch im ersten Dezennium nach dem Ende der DDR das Bild vom „Stasi-Staat" als eine Reaktion auf die Vernachlässigung der repressiven Elemente in den 1979er- und 1980er-Jahren, jedenfalls bei vielen Wissenschaftern und Publizisten, die zur DDR gearbeitet haben.

Eine Apologie der ostdeutschen Diktatur ist gleichwohl nicht entstanden, wiewohl die Begründung für das Buch irritiert: „Jetzt ist es endlich an der Zeit, einen neuen Blick auf die DDR zu wagen. Wer dies mit offenen Augen tut, wird eine bunte Welt entdecken, keine schwarz-weiße. Es gab Unterdrückung und Brutalität, ja, aber auch Chancen und Zugehörigkeit. [...] Die Bürger der DDR lebten, liebten, arbeiteten und wurden alt" (S. 23). Was ist an derartigen Befindlichkeiten der Menschen erwähnenswert oder gar neu? Und wenn der LDPD-Politiker Carl Klußmann 1957 in der DDR-Presse erklärte, es sei die Pflicht „für jeden Menschen in der Deutschen Demokratischen Republik, sich zu diesem Staat zu bekennen" (S 149), folgert Hoyer daraus, es sei „also für einen liberalen Politiker möglich [gewesen], innerhalb der SED-Diktatur einen sinnstiftenden Platz zu finden" (S. 149). Aber war Klußmann ein Liberaler – und überhaupt überzeugt von den Floskeln?

---

1 Vgl. Dirk Oschmann, Der Osten: eine westdeutsche Erfindung, Berlin 2023.

Manche Einschätzung, etwa zum Neutralitätsangebot Stalins von 1952, das sich entgegen der Annahme Hoyers nicht an Konrad Adenauer richtete, fällt einigermaßen kühn aus. Die Deutschen in Ost und West hätten damals die Wiedervereinigung unterlaufen, wobei es doch sonst heißt, sie seien „Teil eines weltpolitischen Machtspiels [gewesen], in dem sie zunächst Figuren waren, die von den Sowjets und den Amerikanern nach Bedarf eingesetzt oder geopfert wurden" (S. 220). Hoyer hält an der Legende fest, die Stalin-Note sei kein Propaganda-Trick gewesen.[2]

Eine Schwäche: Die Autorin wirft der DDR-Führung in der zweiten Hälfte der 1980er-Jahre mangelnde Reformbereitschaft vor. Aber eben diese Abwehrhaltung war aus Sicht der Herrschenden notwendig, um einem Systemzerfall vorzubeugen. Honecker dachte weitsichtiger als Gorbatschow. Insofern ist Hoyers Kernthese nicht haltbar: „Mitte der 1980er-Jahre war das System verkalkt, unflexibel und brüchig geworden und bedurfte dringend einer Überholung. Als Reformen ausblieben, ergriff das ostdeutsche Volk selbst die Initiative, um einen Wandel herbeiführen" (S. 22). Die Geschichte der Sowjetunion unter Gorbatschow ist ein schlagkräftiges Beispiel dafür, wohin Reformen führen mussten. Der Kommunismus war nicht reformfähig.

In den letzten Passagen des Werkes finden sich manche Faktenfehler und Ungereimtheiten. Woher weiß Hoyer, dass „die Mehrheit der Ostdeutschen 1988 weder die Abschaffung des Staates wünschte noch von einer baldigen Wiedervereinigung mit den Westen träumte" (S. 488) und 1989 die „meisten Ostdeutschen [...] nicht [auf] den Zusammenbruch des Staates" (S. 501) hofften? Wurden erst durch die verhärtete Haltung der Obrigkeit auch Personen, die „nicht offen politisch waren, zunehmend unzufrieden" (S. 506)?

Der Erfolg des Werkes vor allem beim ostdeutschen Lesepublikum ist kein Indiz für seine Wissenschaftlichkeit, aber eines für das Rumoren in Teilen Ostdeutschlands, mehr als eine Generation nach dem Ende der DDR. Die gut komponierte, weil mit eingängigen Beispielen anschaulich ausgestattete Publikation Hoyers kommt einem „Stich ins Wespennest" gleich. Sie zielt auf eine Aufwertung des Lebens in der DDR. Offenbar fühlt sich mancher „Ossi" noch immer (oder wieder) fremd im eigenen Land – die politische Kultur in Ost und West weicht bekanntlich nach wie vor voneinander ab. Wenn Menschen 40 Jahre lang in zwei politisch und gesellschaftlich unterschiedlichen Systemen gelebt haben, kann dies vielleicht nicht anders sein. Gleichwohl sehnt sich so gut wie niemand nach dem „realen Sozialismus" der DDR zurück. Bei aller Kritik an

---

2 Vgl. dagegen überzeugend Peter Ruggenthaler (Hg.), Stalins großer Bluff. Die Geschichte der Stalin-Note vom 10. März 1952, München 2007; Gerhard Wettig, Die Stalin-Note. Historische Kontroverse im Spiegel der Quellen, Berlin 2015; anderer Aufassung: Wilfried Loth, Stalins ungeliebtes Kind. Warum Moskau die DDR nicht wollte, München 1996.

Versäumnissen und Verletzungen, die die Autorin zur Sprache bringt: Ein einheitliches Deutschland in Freiheit ist nach den Verheerungen durch den Nationalsozialismus ein Glücksfall der Geschichte. Die DDR, eine Satrapie der Sowjetunion, konnte niemals auf eigenen Beinen stehen. Und die Frage, ob jemand demokratische Positionen akzeptiert oder nicht, ist allemal wichtiger als die Haltung im (tatsächlichen oder vermeintlichen) Ost-West-Konflikt, der mit zunehmender Zeit immer weniger Emotionen hervorrufen dürfte. Gleiches gilt für die DDR-Geschichte.

Dass Hoyers Werk, und das von Oschmann, zu einem solchen Erfolg avancierte, muss zunächst einmal verwundern. Neues wird im Kern nicht geboten. Die lebendige Art der Präsentation gefällt, auch wenn sie in ihrem Schwarz-Weiß-Denken mitunter reichlich plakativ anmutet und dadurch Stereotypen bestätigt, etwa durch die folgende Aussage: „Und Geschichte wird von Siegern geschrieben – auch die der DDR" (S. 20). Vielleicht erklärt sich das große Interesse des (Ost-) Publikums mit dem Eindruck, hier werde westlicher Deutungshoheit der Marsch geblasen.

*Eckhard Jesse*

# Authors

Johannes Glack, BA MA
Researcher (prae doc), ERC research group GLORE – "Global Resettlement Regimes: Ambivalent Lessons learned from the Postwar (1945–1951)", Department of Contemporary History, University of Vienna, johannes.glack@univie.ac.at

Heimo Gruber
Former librarian of the Vienna City Libraries, heigru@aon.at

Univ.-Prof. Dr. Eckhard Jesse
Institute of Political Science, TU Chemnitz, eckhard.jesse@phil.tu-chemnitz.de

MMag.ª Sabine Nachbaur
Researcher at the Ludwig Boltzmann Institute for Research on Consequences of War, Graz – Vienna – Raabs, contemporary historian at the University of Graz, sabine.nachbaur@bik.ac.at

Mag. Martin Sauerbrey-Almasy
Researcher at the Ludwig Boltzmann Institute for Research on Consequences of War, Graz – Vienna – Raabs, contemporary historian at the University of Graz, martin.sauerbrey@bik.lbg.at.at

Mag. Dr. Lukas Schretter, MA
Research Group Leader at the Ludwig Boltzmann Institute for Research on Consequences of War, Graz – Vienna – Raabs, lukas.schretter@bik.lbg.ac.at

Univ.-Prof.in Dr.in Barbara Stelzl-Marx
Head of the Ludwig Boltzmann Institute for Research on Consequences of War, Graz – Vienna – Raabs, contemporary historian at the University of Graz, barbara.stelzl-marx@bik.ac.at

Nadjeschda Stoffers, MA
Researcher at the Ludwig Boltzmann Institute for Research on Consequences of
War, Graz – Vienna – Raabs, nadjeschda.stoffers@bik.lbg.ac.at

# Zitierregeln

Bei der Einreichung von Manuskripten, über deren Veröffentlichung im Laufe eines doppelt anonymisierten Peer Review Verfahrens entschieden wird, sind unbedingt die Zitierregeln einzuhalten. Unverbindliche Zusendungen von Manuskripten als word-Datei an: verein.zeitgeschichte@univie.ac.at

## I. Allgemeines

**Abgabe:** elektronisch in Microsoft Word DOC oder DOCX.

**Textlänge:** 60.000 Zeichen (inklusive Leerzeichen und Fußnoten), Times New Roman, 12 Punkt, 1 ½-zeilig. Zeichenzahl für Rezensionen 6.000–8.200 Zeichen (inklusive Leerzeichen).

**Rechtschreibung:** Grundsätzlich gilt die Verwendung der neuen Rechtschreibung mit Ausnahme von Zitaten.

## II. Format und Gliederung

**Kapitelüberschriften** und – falls gewünscht – Unterkapiteltitel deutlich hervorheben mittels Nummerierung. Kapitel mit römischen Ziffern [I. Literatur], Unterkapitel mit arabischen Ziffern [1.1 Dissertationen] nummerieren, maximal bis in die dritte Ebene untergliedern [1.1.1 Philologische Dissertationen]. Keine Interpunktion am Ende der Gliederungstitel.

Keine Silbentrennung, linksbündig, Flattersatz, keine Leerzeilen zwischen Absätzen, keine Einrückungen; direkte Zitate, die länger als vier Zeilen sind, in einem eigenen Absatz (ohne Einrückung, mit Gänsefüßchen am Beginn und Ende).

**Zahlen** von null bis zwölf ausschreiben, ab 13 in Ziffern. Tausender mit Interpunktion: 1.000. Wenn runde Zahlen wie zwanzig, hundert oder dreitausend nicht in unmittelbarer Nähe zu anderen Zahlenangaben in einer Textpassage aufscheinen, können diese ausgeschrieben werden.

**Daten** ausschreiben: „1930er" oder „1960er-Jahre" statt „30er" oder „60er Jahre".

**Datumsangaben:** In den Fußnoten: 4.3.2011 [keine Leerzeichen nach den Punkten, auch nicht 04.03.2011 oder 4. März 2011]; im Text das Monat ausschreiben [4. März 2011].

**Personennamen** im Fließtext bei der Erstnennung immer mit Vor- und Nachnamen.

**Namen von Organisationen** im Fließtext: Wenn eindeutig erkennbar ist, dass eine Organisation, Vereinigung o. Ä. vorliegt, können die Anführungszeichen weggelassen werden: „Die Gründung des Öesterreichischen Alpenvereins erfolgte 1862." „Als Mitglied im Womens Alpine Club war ihr die Teilnahme gestattet." **Namen von Zeitungen/Zeitschriften** etc. siehe unter „Anführungszeichen".

**Anführungszeichen** im Fall von Zitaten, Hervorhebungen und bei Erwähnung von Zeitungen/Zeitschriften, Werken und Veranstaltungstiteln im Fließtext immer doppelt: „"

**Einfache Anführungszeichen** nur im Fall eines Zitats im Zitat: „Er sagte zu mir: ‚....'"

**Klammern:** Gebrauchen Sie bitte generell runde Klammern, außer in Zitaten für Auslassungen: [...] und Anmerkungen: [Anm. d. A.].

Formulieren Sie **bitte geschlechtsneutral bzw. geschlechtergerecht.** Verwenden Sie im ersteren Fall bei Substantiven das Binnen-I („ZeitzeugInnen"), nicht jedoch in Komposita („Bürgerversammlung" statt „BürgerInnenversammlung").

**Darstellungen und Fotos** als eigene Datei im jpg-Format (mind. 300 dpi) einsenden. Bilder werden schwarz-weiß abgedruckt; die Rechte an den abgedruckten Bildern sind vom Autor/von der Autorin einzuholen. Bildunterschriften bitte kenntlich machen: Abb.: Spanische Reiter auf der Ringstraße (Quelle: Bildarchiv, ÖNB).

**Abkürzungen:** Bitte Leerzeichen einfügen: vor % oder €/zum Beispiel z. B./unter anderem u. a.

Im Text sind möglichst wenige allgemeine Abkürzungen zu verwenden.


III.    Zitation

**Generell keine Zitation im Fließtext, auch keine Kurzverweise. Fußnoten immer mit einem Punkt abschließen.**

Die nachfolgenden Hinweise beziehen sich auf das Erstzitat von Publikationen.
Bei weiteren Erwähnungen sind Kurzzitate zu verwenden.
- Wird hintereinander aus demselben Werk zitiert, bitte den Verweis **Ebd./ebd.** bzw. mit anderer Seitenangabe **Ebd., 12./ebd., 12.** gebrauchen (kein Ders./Dies.), analog: Vgl. ebd.; vgl. ebd., 12.
- Zwei Belege in einer Fußnote mit einem **Strichpunkt;** trennen: Gehmacher, Jugend, 311; Dreidemy, Kanzlerschaft, 29.
- Bei Übernahme von direkten Zitaten aus der Fachliteratur **Zit. n./zit. n.** verwenden.
- Indirekte Zitate werden durch **Vgl./vgl.** gekennzeichnet.

**Monografien:** Vorname und Nachname, Titel, Ort und Jahr, Seitenangabe [ohne „S."].

Beispiel Erstzitat: Johanna Gehmacher, Jugend ohne Zukunft. Hitler-Jugend und Bund Deutscher Mädel in Österreich vor 1938, Wien 1994, 311.

Beispiel Kurzzitat: Gehmacher, Jugend, 311.
Bei mehreren AutorInnen/HerausgeberInnen: Dachs/Gerlich/Müller (Hg.), Politiker, 14.

**Reihentitel:** Claudia Hoerschelmann, Exilland Schweiz. Lebensbedingungen und Schicksale österreichischer Flüchtlinge 1938 bis 1945 (Veröffentlichungen des Ludwig-Boltzmann-Institutes für Geschichte und Gesellschaft 27), Innsbruck/Wien [bei mehreren Ortsangaben Schrägstrich ohne Leerzeichen] 1997, 45.

**Dissertation:** Thomas Angerer, Frankreich und die Österreichfrage. Historische Grundlagen und Leitlinien 1945–1955, phil. Diss., Universität Wien 1996, 18–21 [keine ff. und f. für Seitenangaben, von–bis mit Gedankenstich ohne Leerzeichen].

**Diplomarbeit:** Lucile Dreidemy, Die Kanzlerschaft Engelbert Dollfuß' 1932–1934, Dipl. Arb., Université de Strasbourg 2007, 29.

**Ohne AutorIn, nur HerausgeberIn:** Beiträge zur Geschichte und Vorgeschichte der Julirevolte, hg. im Selbstverlag des Bundeskommissariates für Heimatdienst, Wien 1934, 13.

**Unveröffentlichtes Manuskript:** Günter Bischof, Lost Momentum. The Militarization of the Cold War and the Demise of Austrian Treaty Negotiations, 1950–1952 (unveröffentlichtes Manuskript), 54–55. Kopie im Besitz des Verfassers.

**Quellenbände:** Foreign Relations of the United States, 1941, vol. II, hg.v. United States Department of States, Washington 1958.
[nach Erstzitation mit der gängigen Abkürzung: FRUS fortfahren].

**Sammelwerke:** Herbert Dachs/Peter Gerlich/Wolfgang C. Müller (Hg.), Die Politiker. Karrieren und Wirken bedeutender Repräsentanten der Zweiten Republik, Wien 1995.

**Beitrag in Sammelwerken:** Michael Gehler, Die österreichische Außenpolitik unter der Alleinregierung Josef Klaus 1966–1970, in: Robert Kriechbaumer/Franz Schausberger/Hubert Weinberger (Hg.), Die Transformation der österreichischen Gesellschaft und die Alleinregierung Klaus (Veröffentlichung der Dr.-Wilfried Haslauer-Bibliothek, Forschungsinstitut für politisch-historische Studien 1), Salzburg 1995, 251–271, 255–257.
[bei Beiträgen grundsätzlich immer die Gesamtseitenangabe zuerst, dann die spezifisch zitierten Seiten].

**Beiträge in Zeitschriften:** Florian Weiß, Die schwierige Balance. Österreich und die Anfänge der westeuropäischen Integration 1947–1957, in: Vierteljahreshefte für Zeitgeschichte 42 (1994) 1, 71–94.
[Zeitschrift Jahrgang/Bandangabe ohne Beistrichtrennung und die Angabe der Heftnummer oder der Folge hinter die Klammer ohne Komma].

**Presseartikel:** Titel des Artikels, Zeitung, Datum, Seite.
Der Ständestaat in Diskussion, Wiener Zeitung, 5.9.1946, 2.

**Archivalien:** Bericht der Österr. Delegation bei der Hohen Behörde der EGKS, Zl. 2/pol/57, Fritz Kolb an Leopold Figl, 19.2.1957. Österreichisches Staatsarchiv (ÖStA), Archiv der Republik (AdR), Bundeskanzleramt (BKA)/AA, II-pol, International 2 c, Zl. 217.301-pol/57 (GZl. 215.155-pol/57); Major General Coleman an Kirkpatrick, 27.6.1953. The National Archives (TNA), Public Record Office (PRO), Foreign Office (FO) 371/103845, CS 1016/205
[prinzipiell zuerst das Dokument mit möglichst genauer Bezeichnung, dann das Archiv, mit Unterarchiven, -verzeichnissen und Beständen; bei weiterer Nennung der Archive bzw. Unterarchive können die Abkürzungen verwendet werden].

**Internetquellen:** Autor so vorhanden, Titel des Beitrags, Institution, URL: (abgerufen Datum). Bitte mit rechter Maustaste den Hyperlink entfernen, so dass der Link nicht mehr blau unterstrichen ist.
Yehuda Bauer, How vast was the crime, Yad Vashem, URL: http://www1.yadvashem.org/yv/en/holocaust/about/index.asp (abgerufen 28.2.2011).

**Film:** Vorname und Nachname des Regisseurs, Vollständiger Titel, Format [z.B. 8 mm, VHS, DVD], Spieldauer [Film ohne Extras in Minuten], Produktionsort/-land Jahr, Zeit [Minutenangabe der zitierten Passage].
Luis Buñuel, Belle de jour, DVD, 96 min., Barcelona 2001, 26:00–26:10 min.

**Interview:** InterviewpartnerIn, InterviewerIn, Datum des Interviews, Provenienz der Aufzeichnung.
Interview mit Paul Broda, geführt von Maria Wirth, 26.10.2014, Aufnahme bei der Autorin.

Die englischsprachigen Zitierregeln sind online verfügbar unter: https://www.verein-zeitge schichte.univie.ac.at/fileadmin/user_upload/p_verein_zeitgeschichte/zg_Zitierregeln_en gl_2018.pdf

**Es können nur jene eingesandten Aufsätze Berücksichtigung finden, die sich an die Zitierregeln halten!**